William Cobbett

William Cobbett

A BIBLIOGRAPHICAL ACCOUNT
OF HIS LIFE AND TIMES

BY

M. L. PEARL

WITH A FOREWORD BY G. D. H. COLE

GREENWOOD PRESS, PUBLISHERS
WESTPORT, CONNECTICUT

Originally published in 1953
by Geoffrey Cumberlege, Oxford University Press, London

Reprinted with the permission
of Nuffield College

Reprinted from an original copy in the collections
of the Brooklyn Public Library

First Greenwood Reprinting 1971

Library of Congress Catalogue Card Number 78-136079

SBN 8371-5229-1

Printed in the United States of America

FOREWORD

I HAVE to thank Nuffield College for making possible the publication of this bibliography and Mr. M. L. Pearl, of that College, for his work in making it. It was conceived as the first of a series to be based on my own collections, now in the possession of the College— the garnering of more than forty years perambulation of bookshops and modest buying from catalogues, reinforced by a few very valuable private gifts. It was in the autumn of 1904, while I was lying in bed at the age of fifteen, that the feeling came over me that I had somehow to possess a library of my own; and from that time on I haunted the bookshops and spent most of my spare money on books, resolved never to pay a long price but to go on hunting till I found what I wanted, not necessarily dirt-cheap, but at a price I could afford without feeling grossly self-indulgent. When I began, mainly with poetry and novels with a social interest, there was plenty to be picked up both easily and cheaply. Within a very few years I was deeply interested in social history and in Radical and working-class movements, and began the collection of which the Cobbett volumes are part. At the age of seventeen I became a Socialist—mainly through reading William Morris—and my Socialism made me a student of Radical and working-class history and therewith of social and economic history in a much wider sense.

Mr. Pearl shares my tastes in these matters; but he lives in harder times. I doubt if anyone could now get together a complete set of Cobbett's *Political Register*, as I did, by adding volume to volume over a number of years; and Cobbett's books and pamphlets, except a few of the most popular in his own day, are a great deal more difficult to find than they were when I began hunting for them, or even than when I was writing his life soon after the first war. Not that, even now, Cobbett is a particularly difficult writer to collect, or expensive as such things go. But the rarities have almost disappeared. With all my assiduity I never succeeded in getting near completeness, even to the extent of having all he published in *some* edition—much less in gathering a complete set of first editions. I never even tried to get his American writings in their first editions; and after all these years I still occasionally get wind of an unknown pamphlet—usually a

v

reprint from the *Political Register* or a locally reported speech—and I fully expect that, despite Mr. Pearl's further searches, a few more such items have yet to come to light. But I think Mr. Pearl has got as near completeness as anyone could expect to get at present; and I am sure he has done his work with an ability equal to his diligence.

My own collection included, besides the printed writings, a considerable number of manuscript letters; and this part of it has been greatly reinforced by Lt.-Colonel W. O. Cobbett's gift of a large further collection to Nuffield College. But many of the letters and manuscripts that were in the possession of the family not so long ago cannot now be traced, though they may still be rediscovered. Another important find, now deposited in Nuffield College on loan, has recently come to light in the offices of Messrs. Faithfull of Winchester, who were Cobbett's solicitors for a number of years; and there are, of course, other important manuscripts in the British Museum and other libraries. But there remain certain obscure points in Cobbett's private life, which cannot be cleared up until more of the letters are found or recovered; and I very much hope that anyone who reads this Foreword and knows where any unrecorded material is will be good enough to let me know.

G. D. H. COLE

OXFORD
November 1952

CONTENTS

INTRODUCTION

THE need has often been expressed for a bibliography of the writings of William Cobbett, and this is not the first time such a compilation has been attempted. Most of the leading biographers have, in fact, added something to the list, although none has completed it, and the present work, which does not claim to be the last word on the subject, may be regarded as taking the process a stage farther. The task of compiling a final and definitive bibliography is, however, formidable. Cobbett wrote or published a tremendous number of works in many different forms in both England and America, and should the unfortunate compiler also attempt to describe the vast quantity of writings about Cobbett—chiefly, but not entirely, the angry answers to pricks from the spines of a young, middle-aged, or elderly 'Porcupine'—he may well find himself lost in a general bibliography of the social history of the period.

The present work, then, does not claim to be all-embracing. Nevertheless it is much fuller than earlier compilations; it includes a selection of the writings about Cobbett; and its annotations introduce a new feature into Cobbett bibliography. These latter are intended not only to supply the minimum data demanded in a bibliography by book-lovers, but also to provide a more generally required guide to the student of his life and times. Cobbett's very great influence was achieved mainly by the written word (although he was also no mean 'performer', in a double sense, on the platform), and it is fitting that an account of his writings should serve to illustrate his own vivid personality as well as the great economic and social changes which took place during his lifetime.

In the main, the present work is based on the very large collection of Cobbett books and pamphlets assembled by Professor G. D. H. Cole—itself only a section of the remarkable library now acquired by Nuffield College and known as the 'Cole Collection'. I am very much indebted to the Warden and Fellows of the College for giving me the opportunity of working in this library and for the generous spirit in which they have given me every facility to complete the work and have it published. By the kindness of other libraries concerned, a description is included of important Cobbett works not in the Cole Collection. I am especially indebted also to Mr. Arnold Muirhead for much information and for allowing me to examine his fine private collection.

Cobbett lends himself well to the fun of writing what is beginning to be called 'bio-bibliography'. He is the most autobiographical of writers; his memory is amazingly retentive, and is usually reliable; and there is a great deal of information about his writings (and other people's writings) to be found in his works. I owe a great deal in this present study to Cobbett himself. But much is also owed to the leading writers on the subject whose works are used and discussed elsewhere in this book. Above all, I am deeply grateful to Cobbett's greatest interpreter, Professor Cole, but for whose encouragement and advice this work would never have been written.

The problem of the biographer begins when he is confronted with the sheer mass of Cobbett's writings. Nearly 200 different titles are known, published in at least treble that number of separate editions and issues—and there are numerous reprints of articles, reports of popular speeches and debates (often republished locally), and variant issues yet to be discovered. Even the 'bloody old *Times*', as Cobbett first called it, paid a tribute on his death to one 'who was by far the most voluminous writer that has lived for centuries'. On the score of journalism alone, Cobbett's output seemed to justify the description.

His *Political Register*, begun in 1800, had run to eighty-eight volumes when he died in 1835, and during his active period as a writer at least fourteen different periodicals of one sort or another were started by him. Nearing his end, an old man in his seventies, he was planning to issue an evening paper among other ventures, and had turned to writing short plays as a new form of political propaganda. The list of his 'introductions' to an extraordinarily varied collection of books by others is an amazing one. Translations and compilations of many kinds seemed to flow from his pen. It is true that in most of these, as in the *French & English Dictionary* and in the *Parliamentary Debates* (with the *History* it became the later *Hansard*), the labour had been done by others, and Cobbett could claim no more than the energy and enterprise which marked their organization. Nevertheless, apart from these two classes of publication, it can be confidently said that the major part of the vast

2

output that appeared under Cobbett's name was written by him. Indeed, one of his most indignant retorts was made to a 'monster' who had said that Cobbett's children had 'written all his books'.

The many different forms of publication in which Cobbett's works were issued impose additional burdens on the bibliographer. His writings were frequently issued on both sides of the Atlantic by himself and also by a succession of different firms, for Cobbett quarrelled with his publishers as often as he did with his political allies. Finally, he took to publishing for himself, but by no means consistently, and both types of publication sometimes carry misleading dates on the title-page. Some works, moreover, before being sold bound together in one volume would appear in parts of varied edition and issue and would then be put together regardless of proper sequence. Cobbett's main periodical, the *Political Register*, appeared for several years both in a stamped and an unstamped form, and many of the most popular articles were often reprinted, sometimes, to his dismay, without his permission. Whole issues of the *Register* would, he alleged, appear in pirated editions. The most popular works reached a bewildering number of issues and editions, and of these there were many authorized and unauthorized translations. Friend and foe added to the bibliographical confusion—the former often published his local lectures and debates; the latter tendentiously selected extracts from his earlier writings in order to discredit him.

It is worth while to recount the circumstances in which Cobbett began to write, for his amazing career was not begun in substance until he was already past thirty and settled in America. It is true that about two years earlier than this, in the midst of his brush with the War Office, young ex-sergeant major Cobbett, recently discharged at his own request from the army, may have written a part of *The Soldier's Friend*, a bitter account of the private soldier's grievances and an exposure of army corruption. There is nothing earlier than this pamphlet to show his skill, for we possess no Cobbett juvenilia, although there is evidence that some existed. A recently discovered manuscript 'Memoir' (now in Nuffield College), written by one of his sons, tells how, when aged eighteen or nineteen, he had 'composed a little book entitled *A History of the Kings and Queens of England*', the manuscript of which was subsequently lost. Shortly afterwards, according to the same source, during his unhappy clerkship with an attorney, he was busily translating Voltaire's *Candide*, apparently for his own and for his friends' amusement.

At this stage Cobbett joined the army. We know very little of his early studies or of his strivings and hopes. He tells us in his auto-biography[1] that while on garrison duty at Chatham he joined a small circulating library and read the 'greatest part' of its contents 'more than once over'. In this way, with 'nearly equal avidity' and without 'any degree of taste or choice', he read 'novels, plays, history, (and) poetry'. But Dean Swift was his first love. As a boy he had been thrilled by the discovery of *A Tale of a Tub*, purchased with his last threepence, and as a young soldier he had been disconsolate when this selfsame copy, till then carefully preserved, had been swept overboard in a storm at sea.[2] Perhaps he already dreamed of following in the footsteps of one whose style was intended 'to vex the world rather than divert it'. Edwin Paxton Hood, a sympathetic editor of Cobbett's writings, recorded the observation of an officer who had joined his regiment 'shortly after Cobbett had left it', and had found 'Written out in some of the regimental books, *Directions for a Sergeant-Major, or an Orderly*, in the manner of Swift's *Advice to Servants*, which were full of admirable humour and grave irony'.[3] The life of a soldier stationed abroad left little time for such fancies, and even one such as Cobbett, who memorized Bishop Lowth's *Grammar* on sentry-go, must have found it difficult to combine soldiering with authorship. Nevertheless he managed to compile for his superiors, who took the credit, an official report on the state of Nova Scotia and New Brunswick. For himself and his fellow soldiers there were military plans and exercises, mentioned in his son's manuscript 'Memoir', and the documented exposure of a corrupt group of officers carefully prepared for a future court-martial.

At length, on his discharge, Cobbett obtained this court-martial, one far more dangerous for the accuser than the accused—but by then, in March 1792, he and his young wife were in flight for France, his departure hastened also by the appearance of *The Soldier's Friend*, and, characteristically, by a vague intention to perfect his French as he had done his English and become a teacher.

---

[1] *The Life and Adventures of Peter Porcupine*, 1796.

[2] *Political Register*, 19 February 1820.

[3] *Tait's Edinburgh Magazine*, 1835; also E. P. Hood, *The Last of the Saxons . . .*, 1854.

4

But with war threatening, revolutionary France was no refuge for an Englishman and his wife; and in August 1792 the young couple left Le Havre for the United States. There Cobbett maintained himself at first by teaching English to French *émigrés*, and although he had claimed 'a few useful literary talents' in a letter to Jefferson soon after his arrival, he was as yet content to remain a teacher. It was, in fact, not until about six months after his arrival in America that his literary career can be said to have begun.

From this date his remarkable progress as a writer and politician can be studied in five more or less distinct stages. First, the ultra-Tory period of his first literary and political activity in America from 1793 to 1800; secondly, from 1800 to 1806, the years of his homecoming and growing uncertainty; thirdly, from 1806 to late in 1816, a time of new beginnings which started with Cobbett's revulsion against the Ministry of all the Talents, and ended with his *Addresses to the Journeymen and Labourers*; fourthly, from 1817 to around 1830, the period of maturity and of his greatest literary achievement, merging finally from 1830 to his death in 1835 into the last years of fame and intense political activity.

The first period, his apprenticeship in both journalism and politics, embraces a short but vivid period in America. It begins mildly enough in February 1793 with a translation of a French pamphlet on the impeachment of Lafayette, prefaced and annotated by Cobbett with what he described as the 'most scrupulous impartiality'. The tone was soon to change. In August 1794 the violent *Observations on the Emigration of Dr. Joseph Priestley* marked the appearance of a passionate defender of the old order, of monarchy, of England, and of all that stood opposed to the French Revolution and republicanism. It was said to have been provoked by the enthusiasm with which the Americans and also one of Cobbett's scholars greeted the Birmingham exile, but from then until 1800 a flood of pamphlets and periodicals, most of them brutal and blackguarding, and nicely calculated to strengthen the Federal Party against the Democrats, poured from his pen. The *Observations* reached a third edition in February 1795 and were reprinted in England. In the rest of that year four more long pamphlets appeared, two parts of *A Bone to Gnaw for the Democrats*—a savage attack on the British exiles and their American sympathizers; *A Kick for a Bite*—a pitiless reply to a female critic; and *A Little Plain English*

5

addressed to the People of the United States—a bitter and effective assault on the opponents of a British treaty. Two more works in 1795—*Le Tuteur Anglais*, an enormously successful guide for teaching English to Frenchmen, and a translation from the French of Martens's *Law of Nations*—formed a contrast to this aggressive writing and may have helped Cobbett in his profession as a teacher, for so far, despite his notoriety, he earned little by his pen.

Near the close of 1795 an important change occurred. Thomas Bradford, a Philadelphia bookseller and publisher, engaged him to report the proceedings of the United States Congress meeting in the same town, then the capital, and Cobbett produced the successful pamphlet *A Prospect from the Congress Gallery*. Dissatisfied with the terms he had obtained, however, he decided, after fruitless negotiations with other publishers, to break with Bradford, to set up in business for himself and to continue the *Prospect* as *The Political Censor*, a monthly periodical. The *Censor*, the first of his many periodicals, lasted till March 1797, when it was replaced by a daily paper, *Porcupine's Gazette*. In a short while Cobbett had reached the front rank of American journalism. His own shop stood in the centre of Philadelphia, its windows provocatively filled with royalist prints. His publications were well calculated to infuriate 'the prejudices and caprice of the democratical mob' and showed a shrewd appreciation of American politics. Cobbett had arrived, and tutoring—at least, private tutoring—was laid aside for ever.

Meanwhile the stream of invective showed no signs of drying up. 1796 opened with *A New Year's Gift to the Democrats*, another British broadside in favour of the Treaty, written, Cobbett claimed, in five days, and followed, among other pamphlets, by *The Bloody Buoy*, a very popular atrocity-mongering account of revolutionary excesses in France. In August, turning from national affairs to more personal matters, a new Cobbett suddenly appeared. Defending himself against Bradford, he decided to write his autobiography, and adopting the abusive name bestowed on him, he called it *The Life and Adventures of Peter Porcupine*. Gone was the one-sided vilification, the bitter abuse, the political bludgeon wielded in defence of the kings and courts of Europe. In its place, for a moment, was a simple, intimate, heart-warming tale of the progress of an English plough-boy. But only for a moment. The kindly human spirit which shines from *The Life and Adventures* and gives it such great power was out of place in the sort of struggle Cobbett was waging in America, and it was not to be discovered again until he had served his apprentice-ship as a writer and had seen for himself, in an England strangely different from the land he had known in his youth, the plight of the English labourer. Before the end of 1796 Cobbett had returned to his old style. In the September number of the *Political Censor* he published his scurrilous *Life of Thomas Paine*, and in October, in the *Gros Mousqueton Diplomatique*, Adet, the French envoy, was held up to ridicule. The year closed with more attacks on Paine and more pamphleteering.

In 1797 Cobbett turned his full attention to his new daily news-paper *Porcupine's Gazette*, and at last the stream of pamphlets diminished. It was this intense newspaper activity, libellous and harsh, but useful in its training for the future, which ultimately drove Cobbett out of America. He had been fortunate so far in avoiding serious entanglement with the law, and his first trial for libel early in 1797 ended in a triumphant acquittal which Cobbett celebrated in a pamphlet, *The Democratic Judge*. In it, in character-istic fashion, Chief Justice McKean was made to look criminal and foolish. A second trial for libel based on selections from his writings was a little more successful, and he was bound over in a large sum to be of good behaviour. But the Porcupine had little intention of behaving himself. When yellow fever raged in Phila-delphia, he incurred the enmity of the powerfully placed Dr. Rush, a believer in the effectiveness of low diets, purgings, and frequent bleedings. Cobbett dubbed him Sangrado, after the doctor in *Gil Blas* who thought it was 'a gross error to suppose that blood is necessary to the conservation of life'.[1] The circulation of his paper soared, but he found himself defending yet another suit for libel. For the next two years the action was continually postponed until finally there could be no more delay. Near the end of 1799 Cobbett suspended publication of his *Gazette* and moved to New York, hoping to start a new bookselling business there, but his days in America were now drawing to a close. The Rush case was decided against him and he was heavily fined; his assets in Philadelphia were

---

[1] I have found in the Bodleian Library *An Eulogium intended to Perpetuate the Memory of David Rittenhouse* . . . by Rush (Godwin Pamph. 314), published in Philadelphia (1796–7?), which contains some characteristically abusive marginalia in, what I believe to be, Cobbett's hand (see footnote to p. 40 of the present work).

seized. Instead of a New York *Porcupine's Gazette* he issued five numbers of the *Rush-Light*, a monthly tirade of denunciation against his persecutors. It was plain that the whole of America was now becoming too hot for him, and in June 1800, having disposed of his property as best he could, he set sail for England, not without a characteristic parting shot in his 'Farewell Address'.

The second period opened in London in October 1800 with Cobbett seemingly well established. The protégé of Windham and, on one rare occasion, even the dinner-companion of Pitt, he now had a house in Pall Mall and a newspaper office near the Strand. Many of his American works had been published in England and he had been the agent in America for many anti-revolutionary publications. Well known already, he seemed to be rapidly ascending the ladder to respectability and riches.

The period began with a short-lived ultra-Tory daily newspaper, *The Porcupine*, soon to be replaced by the *Political Register*. The *Register*'s early years are marked by the appearance of such compositions as the *Important Considerations* of 1803, a truculent anti-revolutionary proclamation circulated by the Government when war was renewed with France. But although Cobbett moved in a world of ministerial writers where 'gifts' and favours were the accepted custom, he refused to sell his own independence. 'I could do none of those mean and infamous things by which the daily press for the far greater part was supported', he wrote later, describing such attempts. In 1805 he decided to purchase a farm at Botley. To this stage belong the days of large, old-fashioned hospitality, the promotion of 'manly' sports, and the attempt to combine the editing of the *Register* with farming and woodland improvements. But the pleasant dream of becoming a yeoman farmer of the old school was soon shattered. Gradually Cobbett grew disillusioned with the classes whom he had so long respected. The stock-jobbing, money-making society which seemed to be absorbing the old England appalled him, and reluctantly he turned to the Radicals. Apart from the *Political Register*, which now ran almost unbroken from week to week until his death, this period was not one of great literary activity. His farm, his family, the promotion and progress of the *Register* left him at first little time to write anything else. Above all, it was for Cobbett a time of doubt and dismay when the high hopes he had entertained, not only for himself, but for the country

8

at large, were cruelly disappointed. Painfully and slowly, in his own blundering way, despising 'theories', this Radical John Bull needed time for a new reorientation.

The appointment of the Ministry of all the Talents in 1806, among whom was his old patron, Windham, marked a turning-point in his career. Disappointed with their cold reception of his attack on political corruption, he slowly adopted the whole of the Radical programme. Even so, the early part of this third period was one of constant misgivings and uncertainties. The farm and his family were close to his heart, and in 1810, at one critical moment in his life, when threatened with imprisonment, he was almost ready to forsake politics for them. It was this imprisonment, and a fine of a thousand pounds for an attack on the flogging of British militiamen under the guard of German mercenaries, which set the seal on his conversion to Radical politics. Confined in Newgate from 1810 to 1812, he wrote *Paper Against Gold*, a financial treatise and an offering to the memory of the Thomas Paine he had vilified.

In 1815 the ending of the war with France gave new life to the Reform agitation. Cobbett, in his financial writings, had given warning of an impending catastrophe, and, from the spring of 1816, the tale of riots and repression seemed to justify his prophecies. He was beginning to despair of the 'respectable' classes and his *Addresses to the Journeymen and Labourers* of 1816 and the issue of the cheap *Register* marked another major development in his career. Cobbett had decided to make his appeal to the labourers, and his 'twopenny trash' penetrated into every working-class club and meeting-place. In some districts magistrates might harry and even flog the hawkers who sold it from town to town. Nevertheless, its circulation rose to unprecedented heights. From now on there was no turning back. In an age fearful of revolution, this appeal to the poor by one of Cobbett's ability terrified and infuriated many of his opponents, and although such a cautious observer as Samuel Bamford later testified to the moderating influence of his pen, few among the governing classes saw this aspect at the time.

At the end of March 1817 Cobbett was once more in flight, this time *to* America as a Radical. For the next two years he conducted his *Register* from across the Atlantic, utilizing this unusual leisure to produce such works as the *Grammar of the English Language* and *A Year's Residence in the United States*, both brilliant forerunners of a remarkable series of books of many kinds of instruction, admirably adapted to his audience, and sparkling with political advice. This period of his literary career from his return to England in 1819 until the tumultuous year 1830, when he threw all his energies into the struggle for parliamentary reform, gives us at last a Cobbett in maturity. Although he was in 1819 only about three years short of sixty, he was beginning the greatest literary period of his life. Convinced now of the need to address himself mainly to the working class, despairing more and more of the benevolent intervention of the aristocracy, and supremely confident of his own powers, he wrote with more fire than ever, producing volume upon volume of what he lovingly and proudly called 'The Cobbett Library'. The wide variety of his work in this period is astonishing.

Even whilst the *Register* was being regularly issued every week, with Cobbett writing most of it and from 1822 publishing it as well, he was busily experimenting with new journalistic ventures. In January 1820 he began with a shortlived daily newspaper, *Cobbett's Evening Post*, and undismayed by its failure, produced his only slightly more successful *Parliamentary Register*. In December of the same year he was toying with the idea of reviving the *Evening Post* under the title of *The Gridiron*, but the project never matured and instead, in March of the following year, he began a very popular series of monthly political *Sermons*. In 1822 he bought a large share in *The Statesman*, a daily newspaper, and contributed numerous articles to its columns. Some of these giving a report of proceedings in Parliament were reissued in a volume called *Cobbett's Collective Commentaries*, intended to be the first of an annual series, but in 1823 he separated from his fellow proprietor and the venture came to an end. Unperturbed, he tried to start yet another weekly in 1823, the *Norfolk Yeoman's Gazette*. It, too, was a failure, lasting only a few weeks, but of more significance than this reverse was the great movement he was trying to build up at the time among the smaller landowners, farmers, and farm labourers.

His 'rustic harangues', as he called his lectures, the frequent tours, the crowded county meetings and dinners were all aided by a remarkable number of books addressed to the countryman or to those who looked back nostalgically to the countryside. The *Year's Residence in the United States* had set the tone, and in 1821 Cobbett published *The American Gardener*. In the following year he issued 'a new and improved edition' of Jethro Tull's *Horse Hoeing Husbandry* and reprinted from the *Register* such special articles as *The Farmer's Friend*. But more popular than all these was *Cottage Economy*, first issued in threepenny parts during 1821 and 1822, and then as a half-crown volume in 1822. Into such homely things as recipes for brewing beer and baking bread Cobbett poured all his hatred of the Industrial Revolution and all his love for the independent English cottager. For those with greater means he began *The Woodlands*, a manual for planters, published at first in parts in 1825, but not completed till 1828. In that year he issued a *Treatise on Cobbett's Corn*, one of many attempts to popularize the growing of Indian corn. In 1829 came *The English Gardener*, an adaptation of his earlier American work, and finally in 1830 the incomparable *Rural Rides*.

These, the day-to-day account of his travels through the country since 1821, had already appeared in the *Register*, and now Cobbett decided to incorporate most of them into a book. It is a work without a plan—the journal of a traveller in love with the countryside—sometimes written at sunrise, sometimes at the tag-end of a hard day's riding or after a 'rustic harangue'. Yet it remains a model of its kind, a work of astonishing vitality full to the brim with marvellous powers of description and observation.

In this period also Cobbett issued many works in cheap numbers, developing the practice he had begun with *Paper Against Gold* and continued with *Cottage Economy*, the *Sermons*, and *The Woodlands*. In this way in 1824 and 1825 he published *The History of the Protestant Reformation*, a brilliant, if unhistorical polemic, inspired by his support of Catholic Emancipation and his hazy veneration for the glories of medieval England. The work achieved an immediate success. It was succeeded by a second part in 1827 and translated into various languages all over the world. In the following years still more works were issued in numbers. Between 1826 and 1827 there were five parts of *Cobbett's Poor Man's Friend*, intended in the first place for every working-class family in Preston during his election campaign there, and described as 'the most learned work that I ever wrote'. To this succeeded in 1829 the fourteen parts of the *Advice to Young Men and (incidentally) to Young Women*, a famous series offering good counsel addressed, this time, to the 'Middle and Higher Ranks of Life'. In the following year he started to issue and continued till 1834—also in parts—*The History of the Regency and Reign of George IV*. Finally, from 1830 to 1832, in a class difficult to differentiate from that of a periodical, appeared the monthly *Twopenny Trash*, issued to overcome the prohibitions of the 'Six Acts' and consisting partly of articles reprinted from the *Register*.

The next and last period of his career from around 1830 to 1835 included the most vigorous years of his life. He was now one of the central figures in the struggle for Parliamentary Reform, and apparently still at the peak of his powers. In these last years, when nearing seventy, Cobbett scored a redoubtable success against the Whig Government when he was acquitted of a charge of inciting the labourers to rise in their bloodless, but brutally repressed, 'Rural War', and he crowned his triumph by being elected to sit for Oldham in the reformed Parliament. Even now the energy that had made him write at such a furious pace was little dimmed. He began fresh 'rural rides' and lecture tours ranging as far afield as Scotland and Ireland. The products of some of these he printed in the *Register*, which appeared as regularly as ever; some such as the *Tour in Scotland* he also issued separately, and others—the reports of speeches published only by his local admirers, as at Halifax in 1830—still provide a fascinating bibliographical quest. In this period, too, Cobbett was busily turning out various reference books and similar compilations. Moreover, some of the works issued in parts in the previous period ran on in this, and a new series of small volumes, the *Legacies*, made its appearance. Shortly before his death in these last days we leave him planning to publish, among other works, a book on 'The Sufferings of Ireland', an evening newspaper, an autobiography, a *Poor Man's Bible*, a *Legacy to Lords*, which, in name at least, was actually issued by his eldest son after his death, and even another play to be called *Bastards in High Life*.

It will not be amiss here to say a little about the quality of Cobbett's writing. He himself claimed to disdain 'style', much as he disdained anything that seemed abstract, given to theorizing, or pretentious. 'My mode of estimating a writing' he wrote to some admiring female reformers, 'is by the *effect* which it produces. I listen to nothing about *style* as it is called, or anything else. As the man, who soonest and best weaves a yard of cloth is the best weaver, so the man, who soonest and best accomplishes an object with his pen, is the best writer.' Similarly as a protest against fashionable cults he also claimed to disdain Shakespeare and Milton, although there are many passages in his works which show his appreciation of them. The truth is, of course, that although Cobbett was so strongly opposed to theoretical abstractions, and usually abhorred his fellow journalist and the littérateur, 'the race that write', as he called them, he himself had become a master of his own particular style, one based on a natural talent which he had cultivated and improved by a lifetime of devoted industry.

Hardly altering a line, he frequently wrote his articles and books very rapidly in his own hand under difficult conditions or, amid the burden of many other affairs, dictated them, when he could, to one of his children or a secretary. It is not surprising that out of this vast output some of his writing should lack polish or that much of it should be uneven. At its best, however, his direct clear idiomatic English with its genius for the apt nickname is great in its own right. 'The only critics I look to are the public', he wrote; but one whose first tutor had been Swift, even though the pupil had none of the master's detachment or elegance, was not unmindful of the need to write well. 'He who writes badly, thinks badly', he cautioned his son in his *English Grammar*, and not a little proud that he, the self-taught ploughboy turned journalist and politician, could instruct 'your college and university bred men', he added, to a later edition, *Six Lessons, intended to prevent Statesmen from using false grammar, and from writing in an awkward manner.*

Cobbett was fond of pointing out that his success had been achieved by rules of sobriety, application to hard work, orderliness, and early rising, although he was utterly opposed to the common corollary of this advocacy of the 'triumph of knowledge over difficulties'—the arguments that it was a way of escape for the victims of the expanding industrial system or that it was an alternative to political action. He constantly referred to his preference for early morning work, especially in a room with a 'stone floor', and on one occasion he even claimed that 'a full half of all that I have written has been written before ten o'clock in the day'. His daughter Anne in a manuscript account (now in Nuffield College) gives some backing to this claim. She says that in the winter of 1821 her father resumed 'the practice of rising two hours before daylight, lighting a fire in his study and writing till breakfast time. When on a visit to friends in the country, he has been known to be getting up when his host would be going to bed.' Describing his sincerity as a writer, she adds: 'He *felt* as he wrote; would look pale with earnestness in the subject, folding his hands which would seem to get thinner and thinner, colder and colder, and his voice would falter.'

Anne hastens to explain that, despite all her father's emotion and energy, he was 'a great respecter of persons'. Only if he was in a 'great rage' did he forget the honour due to 'a person of any title or one of any rank above himself'. It is a strangely mixed conclusion, for Cobbett was often in a 'great rage'. It is true that despite all his violent talk he did all he could to bring about a peaceful reform within the system he knew as a boy, and he died believing in the rank and order of society. As is widely known, he failed to comprehend the new industrial forces, and it is an easy task today to enumerate his many stupid foibles. But no apology needs to be made for his anger. It was inspired by a deep love of the common people whom he saw helpless before an advancing financial and industrial power. Much of Cobbett's explosiveness misfired. His bitter words directed towards the restoration of an old, half-imagined relationship between master and man came to be adopted as the battle cry of many factory workers struggling and organizing for different things. His plea for a return to the harmonious lives of peasant, yeoman, aristocrat, and priest served to expose the conditions of the wage labourer. But it was this 'great rage' of his, this eloquent peasant protest, giving, paradoxically enough, courage and cohesion to an emerging working class which is in many ways his greatest memorial.

An account of the far-reaching effects of the new temper he created in British politics would take the reader too far afield. The student of his life and times, for whom this work will be only an introduction, may perhaps be tempted to seek the echoes of Cobbett's voice for himself and to search out alone the signs of his influence in the years which saw the victory of the machine. If this account of his writings serves as a rough but ready signpost along that road, the writer will be content.

NOTE

THE items are arranged chronologically and, with a few exceptions, appear in their order of publication. This usually corresponds with the order in which they were written, but, in a few cases, works published some time after they were written appear also under the earlier date. Such insertions are plainly indicated in the text. Part I, in the main, consists of writings by or about Cobbett, written or published during his lifetime; Part II of writings published after his death; Part III is mainly MSS. and Portraits in the Cole Collection.

Those items which form part of the Cole Collection in Nuffield College are indicated by an asterisk (*) and, if they are in Part I and are original editions and not part of a collected edition (e.g. *Porcupine's Works*), by the provision of bibliographical details and by the fact that the titles of their earliest editions in the Collection are printed to correspond roughly with the originals, including the use of a dash (/) to denote end-of-line spacing. Hence those titles (or editions) which are not in the Cole Collection are indicated by the absence of these features. Editions and locations for this class are given where they are considered important or where they are known. Abbreviations for library locations are confined to the minimum— B.M. for British Museum, Bodl. for Bodleian Library, Oxford, and L. of C. for Library of Congress. Names of other libraries are not abbreviated. The British Museum location is given when copies of a work are also to be found elsewhere.

The Index of Titles includes the variants and short titles of Cobbett's books together with cross-references to their main titles (e.g. *English Grammar*, 1818, see *Grammar of the English Language, A*, 1818). Index references under main titles begin with a main number reference inside square brackets ([ ]) followed by page references. Main number references inside square brackets are also given throughout the book. The Index of Titles also includes the Cole Collection MSS. and all the works annotated or cited in the text. The Index of Persons with their dates give page references only. It includes the printers and publishers mentioned in Part I and in the earlier section of Part II.

PART I
WRITINGS BY, OR RELATING TO,
WILLIAM COBBETT
WRITTEN OR PUBLISHED
BETWEEN 1792 AND 1835

THE/SOLDIER'S FRIEND;/OR,/CONSIDERATIONS/
ON THE/LATE PRETENDED AUGMENTATION/OF
THE/SUBSISTENCE/OF THE/PRIVATE SOLDIERS./

ANONYMOUS

Authorship dubious, probably written with Cobbett's assistance.

[1792, London, 1st edition (B.M.); 1793, London,* another edition (B.M.).]

* Typescript copy of 1st edition.

* 1793, 'Written by a Subaltern', 15 pp. (Price 2*d*.), 8vo.

This pamphlet first appeared early in 1792, shortly after the Government had proposed the raising of soldiers' allowances to three shillings a week. It quotes the admission by the Secretary at War in his speech in the Commons (15 February 1792) that this sum was laid down in 'former years' by a regulation (actually enacted annually), but that 'it has of late years so happened that he [the soldier] had not . . . above eighteenpence or two shillings'. The pamphlet contains a merciless attack on the corruption that hid behind the admission and refers, bitterly and contemptuously, to those officers who 'delight in extorting the poor wretches' pay'. Cobbett had just withdrawn from such a battle as this with the military authorities (see *Proceedings of a General Court Martial*, 1809 [69]), but it is not quite certain that he was the author. Before the work was published (it was reviewed in June 1792 in the *Monthly Review* and elsewhere) he had left for France, perhaps to save himself from arrest. There are certain similarities with the style of his later work, even to the italics, but Cobbett himself denied writing it in 1805 (*Political Register*, 5 October 1805) after it was known that it had circulated amongst the sailors in the mutinies of 1797, affirmed it in 1832 (ibid., 23 June 1832), and more ambiguously in 1833 (ibid., 28 December 1833). It is significant that the second, cheaper and very popular edition ('by a subaltern') bore no imprint, and Cobbett would have been prudent to deny its authorship. Probably, however, he was not the sole author, and he may have written the pamphlet, his first attempt at political writing, in conjunction with other enemies of corruption, whom he joined at this time in the struggle for the rights of soldiers.

Cobbett's military experience was part of his earliest political development. The third son of a small farmer and one-time inn-keeper of Farnham in Surrey, disgusted with a brief spell as a London attorney's clerk, he enlisted in the army in 1784 at the age of 21. Soon promoted to the rank of corporal, he remained in Chatham, his regimental depot, for thirteen months, and then sailed with his regiment, the West Norfolk 54th Foot, for Nova Scotia. In the army, he read, learned,[1] and taught with a passion that lasted all his life; he was made a sergeant-major, and much of the administrative work of the regiment passed into his hands. It was this 'book-keeping' which brought him his first shock of disillusion-ment with Authority. Some of his officers, Cobbett discovered, were drunken and illiterate scoundrels who were helping themselves to the regimental funds. He decided to preserve the evidence with a view to exposing them. When the regiment returned to England (November 1791), he hastily procured his discharge (19 December 1791), accused his late officers of corruption, and petitioned for a court martial, which was finally called to take place in London on 24 March 1792. Cobbett now began to realize the danger of his position. A friend brought him news of a plot to ensnare him; the incriminating books remained unsecured; his most vital witness was refused his discharge; and, face to face with a hostile, silent War Office, he realized that he had no chance of success in this almost single-handed encounter with a vast, corrupt machine. As gracefully as he could he withdrew by absenting himself from the court martial, left for France and, possibly, hid his part in writing this pamphlet, *The Soldier's Friend*, reputedly his first publication. Later, in 1809, he was bitterly attacked by his enemies for this 'French leave' (see *Proceedings of a General Court Martial* 1809 [69]).

---

[1] [2]
A Short Introduction to English Grammar: with critical notes, by Robert Lowth (1710–87, scholar and divine) 1762, 1st edition.
    *1764, 'a new edition, corrected', xv, 192 pp. Printed for A. Millar, in the Strand; and R. and J. Dodsley in Pall Mall, London. 12mo.
This was the book used by Cobbett when, as a young soldier, he studied night and day in an effort to master the rules of grammar. In his *Life and Adventures of Peter Porcupine*, 1796 (see in *Porcupine's Works*, 1801, and Cole's 1927 edition) he described how he wrote the 'whole Grammar out two or three times . . . got it by heart, . . . repeated it every morning and every evening', and when on guard, imposed on himself the task of saying it all over to himself once more.

IMPEACHMENT OF MR. LAFAYETTE: CONTAIN-
ING HIS ACCUSATION, (STATED IN THE REPORT
OF THE EXTRAORDINARY COMMISSION TO THE
NATIONAL ASSEMBLY, ON THE 8TH OF AUGUST,
1792.) SUPPORTED BY MR. BRISSOT OF WARVILLE;
AND HIS DEFENCE BY MR. VAUBLANC; WITH A
SUPPLEMENT, CONTAINING THE LETTERS, AND
OTHER AUTHENTIC PIECES RELATIVE THERETO.
TRANSLATED FROM THE FRENCH BY WILLIAM
COBBETT . . .

Translated by WILLIAM COBBETT

[1793, Philadelphia (New York Public Libr.); 1794 Hagerstown, Md.
(Historical Society of Pennsylvania).]

Cobbett and his young wife came to America from Le Havre in
October 1792. They had left France in the turbulent days of
August when the Tuileries had fallen, and for over a year they
lived in Wilmington on the Delaware, where Cobbett made his
living by giving private lessons in English to French *émigrés* and
other expatriates. There he translated this work on the trial of
Lafayette, and added a signed preface, dated Wilmington, 19
February 1793. It was a cautious introduction to his American
career, for in it Cobbett spoke of having 'everywhere observed the
most scrupulous impartiality', in order 'to do justice to Lafayette as
well as to those who have persecuted him' (cited in *Peter Porcupine
in America*, 1939, Philadelphia, by E. M. Clark [254]). The
translation was published in 1793 by John Parker of Philadelphia,
and at the end of January 1794 Cobbett and his family moved to the
same town.

OBSERVATIONS ON THE EMIGRATION OF DR.
JOSEPH PRIESTLEY, AND ON THE SEVERAL
ADDRESSES DELIVERED TO HIM ON HIS ARRIVAL
AT NEW YORK.

By PETER PORCUPINE

[1794 (August), Philadelphia, 1st edition, published anonymously; 1794,
New York, reprint (Harvard Libr.); 1794, London (Stockdale) reprint

(B.M.); 1794, London (Stockdale 'new edition'), reprint (Birmingham Reference Libr.); 1794, London (Richardson) reprint (Birmingham Reference Libr.); 1794, Birmingham (Bodl.); 1794 (?Liverpool); 1795 (February) Philadelphia, 3rd edition, naming Bradford as publisher and with additional *Story of a Farmer's Bull*, &c. (Bodl.); 1795, Philadelphia (Folwell), another edition (University of Pennsylvania Libr.); 1796, Philadelphia, 4th edition, now first described as by 'Peter Porcupine' (B.M.); 1798, London, 4th edition (Bodl.).]

Reissued in vol. i, *Porcupine's Works . . .*, 1801.

Cobbett's first open assault in pamphleteering. It is a violent attack on Dr. Joseph Priestley (1733–1804), the famous chemist, Unitarian and Radical, who had arrived in America in June 1794, a refugee from the Birmingham mob and government repression. The pamphlet was brought out with some trepidation on the part of the booksellers, Priestley being very popular in Philadelphia. Cobbett, rejected by the Irish publisher, Mathew Carey (1760–1839), had to omit the original title, 'The Tartuffe Detected', and content himself with the sub-title (his only concession), before he found an amenable, and, at first, anonymous publisher, Thomas Bradford (1745–1838). This early pamphlet (August 1794), his first acknowledged publication, already shows the power of Cobbett's style. It helped to make him famous as a defender of the old order in Europe, and in America to establish him as an ally of the Federalists. In it, Priestley's claim for the damage done to his house and laboratory are ridiculed, his revolutionary ideas are said to have aroused the very violence he had suffered, he comes as a defender of the 'dreadful calamities' of the French Revolution, and the American addresses of welcome, together with Priestley's replies, are ironically examined. *The Observations* . . . were quickly reprinted in New York and London and shortly afterwards in Birmingham and, possibly, in Liverpool. In America a third edition appeared in February 1795 with an 'introductory address to the Gazetteers of the City of Philadelphia' and much additional matter including *A Story of a Farmer's Bull*. In 1796, a year in which he and Cobbett quarrelled publicly, Bradford issued a fourth edition, now described as by 'Peter Porcupine': it was reprinted in London in 1798 and in 1801 it was included in Cobbett's collected American writings, published in this country as *Porcupine's Works* . . . .

A / BONE TO GNAW / FOR THE / DEMOCRATS. /
By PETER PORCUPINE; / . . . TO WHICH IS PRE-
FIXED / A ROD, / FOR THE / BACKS OF THE
CRITICS; / Containing an HISTORICAL SKETCH of The/
Pre- / sent State of POLITICAL CRITICISM in Great /
Britain; as exemplified in the Conduct of the / MONTHLY,
CRITICAL, and ANALYTICAL RE- / VIEWS, &c. &c.
Interspersed with Anecdotes. / By HUMPHREY HEDGE-
HOG. /

By PETER PORCUPINE and HUMPHREY HEDGEHOG

[1795, Philadelphia, Part I, 1st edition (L. of C.); 1795, Philadelphia,
Part I, 2nd edition (Bodl.); 1795, Philadelphia, Part I, 3rd edition (Bodl.);
1796, Philadelphia, Part I, 4th edition, by 'Peter Porcupine' (B.M.); 1797,
Philadelphia, Part I, '3rd edition', published by Cobbett (Library Com-
pany, Philadelphia); 1795, Philadelphia, Part II, 1st edition (Bodl.); 1795,
Philadelphia, Part II, 2nd edition (B.M.); 1797, Philadelphia, Part II,
another edition published by Cobbett (New York Public Libr.); *1797,
London, Parts I and II, with *A Rod for the Backs* . . .]

Part of Part II of *A Bone to Gnaw*, published separately as part of *Democratic Principles Illustrated by Example*, 1795.

*1797, [Parts I and II] xcv, v, 175 pp. [+ 1 p. publishers' advts.]. Printed
for J. Wright, opposite Old Bond Street, Piccadilly, London. 12mo.

Part I of *A Bone to Gnaw* . . . was written by Cobbett as a rejoinder
to an anonymous pamphlet by James Thomson Callender, *The
Political Progress of Britain* . . . (first published, autumn 1792,
Edinburgh, London; American edition, November 1794, Philadelphia). Callender (1758–1803), a Scottish writer who had escaped
from an English prison, aroused Cobbett's fury by this attack on the
British Government and, even more decisively than Dr. Priestley,
served to launch Cobbett into his important intervention in
American politics. Cobbett's pamphlet, its preface dated 10 January
1795, appeared at first anonymously without even the name of the
publisher, Thomas Bradford. A successful second edition (preface,
19 February) and a third (preface, 10 March) followed; in these
Bradford was named and in 1796 an edition by 'Peter Porcupine'
appeared. In 1797, after his quarrel with Bradford, Cobbett published his own 'Third Edition, Revised', dated it 'Philadelphia,
February 19, 1795', used the 'second edition' preface, and had it

reprinted in London—see above. A mildly critical review of *A Bone to Gnaw* . . . in the *American Monthly Review*, No. 2, February 1795, probably by its founder Samuel Harrison Smith (1772–1845), drew from Cobbett the savage *A Kick for a Bite* (preface, 6 March 1795), the first pamphlet in which he described himself as 'Peter Porcupine', a nickname evidently borrowed from another hostile reviewer. Part I of *A Bone to Gnaw* . . . had concerned itself with rebutting Callender's pamphlet and had provided a convenient spring-board for an attack on the Democratic support for the French Revolution. In March 1795 Cobbett produced in Part II a spirited attack on a pamphlet issued by the Society of United Irishmen in Dublin, some horrifying accounts of the atrocities committed by the Convention at Lyons, and a violent assault on those 'Frenchified citizens of the United States of America' who toasted British 'convicts' and French 'sans-culottes'. Part II was republished in London with a preface dated 28 May 1795, together with Part I, to which Cobbett's publisher in London, John Wright, prefixed a long preface entitled *A Rod for the Backs of the Critics* . . .—see above—by 'Humphrey Hedgehog', the pseudonym of John Gifford (1758–1818), a government pamphleteer, earlier known as John Richards Green. Gifford's preface is for the most part a laboured attack on the British reformers and the hostile reviewers of Cobbett's *Observations* . . . (for Gifford see note on *The Porcupine*, a periodical he acquired from Cobbett in 1801 [48]). Part of Part II of *A Bone to Gnaw* . . . was incorporated into another work and published separately by Cobbett under its sub-title *Democratic Principles illustrated by Example* (see [38]) and Parts I and II were reprinted in *Porcupine's Works*, vol. ii, 1801.

[6] # 1795

A KICK FOR A BITE; OR REVIEW UPON REVIEW, WITH A CRITICAL ESSAY ON THE WORKS OF MRS. S. ROWSON, IN A LETTER TO THE EDITOR, OR EDITORS, OF THE AMERICAN MONTHLY REVIEW.

By PETER PORCUPINE

[1795, Philadelphia, 1st edition (Bodl.); 1796, Philadelphia, 2nd edition (L. of C.).]

Reissued in vol. ii of *Porcupine's Works* . . ., 1801.

In this pamphlet dated 6 March 1795 Cobbett first called himself 'Peter Porcupine'. Its savage style was evoked by a fairly temperate review of *A Bone to Gnaw . . . in the American Monthly Review ascribed to its founder and publisher, Samuel Harrison Smith (1772–1845). Cobbett used the occasion to belabour also Mrs. Susannah Rowson, to the great indignation of the lady's Democratic friends. Mrs. Rowson (1762?–1824) was a very popular writer and a leading actress of the American stage whose 'advanced' opinions, plays, and style of writing he found as bad as 'her sudden conversion to republicanism'.

[7]   1795

LE TUTEUR ANGLAIS, OU GRAMMAIRE REGU-
LIÈRE DE LA LANGUE ANGLAISE EN DEUX
PARTIES. PREMIÈRE PARTIE, CONTENANT UNE
ANALYSE DES PARTIES DE L'ORAISON. SECONDE
PARTIE, CONTENANT LA SYNTAXE COMPLETTE
DE LA LANGUE ANGLAISE, AVEC DES THÈMES,
ANALOGUES AUX DIFFÉRENS SUJETS QU'ON Y A
TRAITÉS.

Par WILLIAM COBBETT

[1795, Philadelphia, 1st edition (B.M.); 1801, Le Maître d'Anglais . . . . Paris, '2nd edition' (B.M.); 1805, Philadelphia, '2nd edition' (L. of C.); 1861, Paris, 35th edition (B.M.); numerous other editions.]

* 1803, 'LE / MAÎTRE D'ANGLAIS, / OU / GRAMMAIRE RAISONÉE, / POUR FACILITER AUX FRANÇAIS / L'ÉTUDE DE LA LANGUE ANGLAISE, / . . .,' 3rd edition, xiv, 458 pp. [p. 459 missing] Chez Fayolle, . . . Warée l'aîné, . . . Bossange, Masson et Besson. Paris. 8vo.

A famous work for 'teaching French people English' written by Cobbett at Wilmington and published at Philadelphia in March 1795, over a year after he had moved there. A draft of it may have been used in the interval before publication to aid his pupils in memorizing their lessons, a favourite method of his in teaching. Cobbett later recalled that the son of Bradford, the publisher, had 'fetched the manuscript from me by piecemeal', and with more modesty than he usually displayed, he called it 'a work of haste'. But this was perhaps meant to rebut a French plagiarist (*Political Register*, 21 February 1818), for the work enjoyed an enormous success and was frequently reprinted and revised. Cobbett claimed it had reached a sixtieth edition in 1833 (*Political Register*, 5 October 1833), and although this seems to be an exaggeration, there is no doubt of its great popularity.

[8]   1795

A LITTLE PLAIN ENGLISH ADDRESSED TO THE PEOPLE OF THE UNITED STATES, ON THE TREATY NEGOTIATED WITH HIS BRITANNIC MAJESTY, AND ON THE CONDUCT OF THE PRESIDENT RELATIVE THERETO; IN ANSWER TO 'THE LETTERS OF FRANKLIN.' WITH A SUPPLEMENT CONTAINING AN ACCOUNT OF THE TURBULENT AND FACTIOUS PROCEEDINGS OF THE OPPOSERS OF THE TREATY.

By PETER PORCUPINE

[1795, Philadelphia, London, 1st editions (B.M.); New York, Boston; 1796, Philadelphia (Library Company, Philadelphia.]

Reissued without *Supplement* in vol. ii of *Porcupine's Works . . ., 1801.

The *Letters of Franklin* were a series of articles in the Philadelphia *Aurora* attributed to Alexander James Dallas (1759–1819), an active Democratic lawyer and politician of Scottish extraction. The author's violent opposition to a British Treaty was enough to make Cobbett undertake the task of replying to him, but, in addition, an abstract of the proposed Treaty was made public in the *Aurora* in June 1795; rowdy meetings followed in a number of places including Philadelphia, and Cobbett hastily added a *Supplement* to his pamphlet, which was published in August.

[9]   1795

A / COMPENDIUM / OF THE / LAW OF NATIONS, / FOUNDED ON THE / TREATIES AND CUSTOMS / OF THE / MODERN NATIONS OF EUROPE: / TO WHICH IS ADDED, / A COMPLETE LIST / OF ALL THE / TREATIES, CONVENTIONS, COMPACTS, DECLARATIONS, &c. / FROM / THE YEAR 1731 TO 1788, INCLUSIVE, INDICATING THE / SEVERAL WORKS IN WHICH THEY ARE TO BE FOUND. /

By G. F. VON MARTENS; translated by WILLIAM COBBETT

[1795, *Summary of The Law of Nations* . . ., Philadelphia, 1st edition (B.M.); *1802, London; 1829, London, 4th edition (B.M.).]

*1802, '. . . the list of treaties, &c. brought down to June 1802 . . . ', xxxii, 454 pp. [+2 pp. publisher's advts.]. Published by Cobbett and Morgan, Pall Mall, London. 8vo.

In 1795, whilst Cobbett was still teaching English to French *émigrés* in Philadelphia, he began some translating from the French for Bradford. Before the end of the year he had completed a *Summary of the Law of Nations* . . ., an English version of an internationally renowned authority on treaties and on international law, the *Prècis du Droit* . . ., Göttingen (1789), by G. F. von Martens (1756–1821), a German jurist and professor. Cobbett later described how he had translated it for 'a quarter of a dollar . . . a page' and how the work was done before breakfast or at night 'writing in the same room where my wife and child were in bed and asleep' (*Political Register*, 22 August 1829). The book had an immediate success in America, where the 1795 edition bore a dedicatory address to Washington, dated December 1795 and signed by the publisher, Thomas Bradford—although written by Cobbett. It was reissued in London in June 1802 as *A Compendium of the Law of Nations* . . .—see above—(also in later editions) with up-to-date additions and a dedication to John Penn (1760–1834), a descendant of the famous William Penn. This copy has an advertisement of *Cobbett's Weekly Political Register* at the end.

[10]   1795

THE WORKS OF PETER PORCUPINE, D.D. [*sic*], A NEW EDITION.

[1795, Philadelphia, 'new edition' (Bodl.); 1796, Philadelphia, '4th edition' (B.M.); 1796, Philadelphia, *Porcupine's Works* (on spine), another edition (Arnold Muirhead Collection).]

Several issues of this one-volume collection issued by Bradford in 1795 and 1796 are known. The first ('a new edition') contained: *A Bone to Gnaw, Pt. I*, 3rd edition; *A Bone to Gnaw, Pt. II*, 1st edition; *A Little Plain English*, 1st edition; *Observations on the Emigration of Dr. Joseph Priestley*, 3rd edition; *A Kick for a Bite*, 1st edition. The 'fourth edition' (1796) of the *Works* (from the title of which the 'D.D.' had been removed) contained: *Observations on the Emigration of Dr. Joseph Priestley*, 4th edition; *A Bone* to *Gnaw, Pt. I*, 4th edition; *A Bone to Gnaw, Pt. II*, 2nd edition; *A Little Plain English*, 1st edition; *A New Year's Gift*, 2nd edition. A variant collected edition of 1796 added *A Kick for a Bite* (Arnold Muirhead Collection) and several other issues of a two-volume collected edition, *Porcupine's Works*, also appeared in 1796–7 (see [26]).

[11]   1796

A TOPOGRAPHICAL AND POLITICAL DESCRIP-
TION OF THE SPANISH PART OF SAINT-DOMINGO,
CONTAINING GENERAL OBSERVATIONS ON THE
CLIMATE, POPULATION, AND PRODUCTIONS;
ON THE CHARACTER AND MANNERS OF THE
INHABITANTS; WITH AN ACCOUNT OF THE
SEVERAL BRANCHES OF THE GOVERNMENT: TO
WHICH IS PREFIXED, A NEW, CORRECT, AND
ELEGANT MAP OF THE WHOLE ISLAND. BY
M. L. E. MOREAU DE SAINT-MÉRY, MEMBER OF
THE PHILOSOPHICAL SOCIETY OF PHILA-
DELPHIA, &C. TRANSLATED FROM THE FRENCH
BY WILLIAM COBBETT.

*By M. L. E. MOREAU DE SAINT-MÉRY; translated by
WILLIAM COBBETT*

[1796, Philadelphia, 2 vols. (B.M.).]

This two-volume work by M. L. E. Moreau de Saint-Méry (1750–1819), a French *émigré*, was translated by Cobbett and published by him early in 1796, together with an imposing list of subscribers, which included the Vice-President of the United States, and also the French Minister. Moreau de Saint-Méry later issued from his bookshop some of the most virulent anti-Porcupine publications, and perhaps for this reason Cobbett made no further reference to his efficient translation.

[12]   1796

A NEW YEAR'S GIFT TO THE DEMOCRATS; OR,
OBSERVATIONS ON A PAMPHLET ENTITLED 'A
VINDICATION OF MR. RANDOLPH'S RESIGNA-
TION.'

By PETER PORCUPINE

[1796, Philadelphia, 1st–2nd editions (B.M.); 1798, Philadelphia, 3rd edition (American Antiquarian Soc.).]
Reissued in *Porcupine's Works, vol. ii, 1801.

This pamphlet was part of Cobbett's contribution to the great controversy in the United States over a British Treaty. Edmund Randolph (1753–1813), the Secretary of State, had recently been forced out of office on an unproved charge of having demanded a French bribe as the price of his opposition to the Treaty. He resigned in August 1795 and wrote his *Vindication* . . ., a dignified defence, published on 18 December 1795 by S. H. Smith (of *A Bone to Gnaw* . . ., q.v.), in which he offered to submit his papers to public investigation. Cobbett seems to have had little inclination to pursue Randolph's offer. He wrote this slashing attack on him in five days (*A Prospect from the Congress Gallery*, preface, cited by Clark, 53, op. cit.) and, with great effect, it was published early in January by Bradford.

[13] 1796

A PROSPECT FROM THE CONGRESS GALLERY, DURING THE SESSION, BEGUN DECEMBER 1795, CONTAINING THE PRESIDENT'S SPEECH, THE ADDRESSES OF BOTH HOUSES, SOME OF THE DEBATES IN THE SENATE, AND ALL THE PRINCIPAL DEBATES IN THE HOUSE OF REPRESENTATIVES; EACH DEBATE BEING BROUGHT UNDER ONE HEAD, AND SO DIGESTED AND SIMPLIFIED AS TO GIVE THE READER THE COMPLETE VIEW OF THE PROCEEDINGS WITH THE LEAST POSSIBLE FATIGUE.

By PETER PORCUPINE

Continued as the *Political Censor, 1796–7.

[1796, Philadelphia, 1st–2nd editions (B.M.).]
Reissued in vol. iii of *Porcupine's Works . . ., 1801.

During the winter of 1795–6 Cobbett was engaged to report the proceedings of Congress for Bradford, who published his commentary under this title in January. It was a great success, but difficulties arose between author and publisher. Cobbett transferred the publication of the second number, with the title changed to the *Political Censor* (q.v.), to Davies and then decided to continue it for himself.

THE / BLOODY BUOY, / THROWN OUT AS A /
Warning to the Political Pilots of all Nations. / OR, A / FAITH-
FUL RELATION / Of a Multitude of / ACTS OF HORRID
BARBARITY, / Such as the EYE never witnessed, the TON-
GUE expressed, or / the IMAGINATION conceived, until the
commencement of / THE FRENCH REVOLUTION. / TO
WHICH IS ADDED, / AN INSTRUCTIVE ESSAY, /
Tracing these dreadful Effects to their real Causes. /

By PETER PORCUPINE

Part of the additional *Essay* republished as *Democratic Principles . . .*, Part II,
1798, q.v.

> [1796, Philadelphia, 1st edition (B.M.); 1796, Philadelphia, another edition
> (L. of. C.); 1797, Reading, Pa. (German ed.) (Bodl.); 1796(?)–8, London,
> (Owen, n.d.; Wright), '11th edition' (Harvard Libr.); 1797, another edition,
> *Annals of Blood*, Cambridge (B.M.); 1823, Philadelphia (Davis), '3rd edition'
> (L. of C.); 1823, Paradise, Pa. (Witmer), '2nd edition' (L. of C.).]

> *1798, 4th edition, xvi, 259 pp. Printed for J. Wright, No. 169, opposite
> Old Bond Street, Piccadilly, London. 12mo. [This copy is bound with
> another work by Cobbett—*The Life of Thomas Paine*.]

Reissued in vol. iii, *Porcupine's Works . . .*, 1801.

A lurid account of atrocities alleged to have been committed by the
revolutionaries in France: it repeats the most grisly stories of the
French *émigrés*.[1] The first edition, embellished by four gruesome
engravings (omitted from the English editions), was published in
Philadelphia in February 1796 by Benjamin Davies. (Cobbett had
separated from Bradford, his previous publisher, in January, and he
opened his own shop in Philadelphia in July.) Davies, a Philadelphia
bookseller and a friend of Cobbett's, published the *Political Censor*
and other writings for him, and was himself the author of *John
Clothier and Sylvanus Planter*, a pamphlet favouring the claims of
British subjects against American debtors, published in 1799 in
Porcupine's Gazette over the signature of 'Querist'. *The Bloody
Buoy* was one of the most successful of Cobbett's publications. He
issued it in a second edition from his shop; it was translated into
German and published in Reading, Pennsylvania, as *Die Blut-*

---

[1] Cobbett's acknowledged sources were the Abbé Barruel's, *L'Histoire du Clergé . . .*
and several anonymous works, *La Relation Cruautés . . . Lyonnois*, *Procès Criminel
. . . Nantes*, &c.

Fahne, and it appeared in this country in numerous editions, one of them published at Cambridge in 1797 under the title, '*Annals of Blood*, by an American'.

[15]   1796

THE POLITICAL CENSOR OR MONTHLY REVIEW OF THE MOST INTERESTING POLITICAL OCCUR- RENCES, RELATIVE TO THE UNITED STATES OF AMERICA.

[1796-7, Nos. 1-9, Philadelphia (B.M., Bodl., L. of C.).]

Nos. 1-9, slightly abridged and reissued in vols. iii, iv, and v of *Porcupine's Works*, 1801.

Having changed *A Prospect from the Congress Gallery* (q.v.) into the first number of the *Political Censor*, Cobbett now turned it into a monthly periodical of a general character from which he could effectively snipe at all his opponents. He produced eight more very popular numbers from March 1796 to March 1797, when the *Political Censor* was replaced by a more ambitious daily paper, *Porcupine's Gazette* . . . (see [28]). Some of these were reprinted at the same time, as pamphlets, and they were all included in a slightly abridged form in Cobbett's edition of *Porcupine's Works*, published in 1801. (No. 9, the last number of the *Political Censor*, March 1797, appears there as 'Gazette Selections'.)

[16]   1796

THE SCARE-CROW; BEING AN INFAMOUS LETTER SENT TO MR. JOHN OLDDEN, THREATENING DESTRUCTION TO HIS HOUSE, AND VIOLENCE TO THE PERSON OF HIS TENANT, WILLIAM COB- BETT; WITH REMARKS ON THE SAME.

By PETER PORCUPINE

[1796, Philadelphia, 1st edition (B.M.); 1796, Philadelphia, 2nd edition (L. of C.).]

Reprinted from the *Political Censor*, 1796.

Reissued in vol. iv of *Porcupine's Works* . . ., 1801, and in Cole's edition of *Life and Adventures of Peter Porcupine* . . ., 1927.

This was Cobbett's reply to an anonymous letter-writer's attempt to have him evicted from his Philadelphia shop by threats against his Quaker landlord, John Oldden (d. 1799). Cobbett had provocatively filled his windows with as many royalist and anti-revolutionary prints as he could find. His windows remained unbroken; his landlord was not intimidated; it was even said that Peter Porcupine had himself written the letter, but Cobbett turned the incident to good account in his pamphlet which he dated 'From the Free Press of William Cobbett, July 22, 1796'.

[17]   1796

THE LIFE AND ADVENTURES OF PETER PORCU-
PINE, WITH A FULL AND FAIR ACCOUNT OF ALL
HIS AUTHORING TRANSACTIONS; BEING A SURE
AND INFALLIBLE GUIDE FOR ALL ENTERPRISING
YOUNG MEN WHO WISH TO MAKE A FORTUNE
BY WRITING PAMPHLETS.

By PETER PORCUPINE

[1796, Philadelphia, 1st edition (B.M.); Philadelphia, 2nd edition (L. of C.); 1797, London (B.M.); 1798, Glasgow (Mitchell Libr., Glasgow).]

Reissued in vol. iv of *Porcupine's Works . . .*, 1801, and in:
   Life and Adventures of Peter Porcupine with other Records of His Early Career in England and America, viz.—Life & Adventures, The Scare-crow, Remarks of the Pamphlets, Talleyrand: a Spy, Farewell to America, A Court Martial, A Retrospect. Introduction and Notes by G. D. H. Cole, 1927, 164 pp. [illus.]. Printed by T. A. Constable, Edinburgh, published by the Nonesuch Press, London.

Slightly abridged versions in:
THE / LIFE / OF / WILLIAM COBBETT, / BY HIMSELF. / INTENDED AS AN ENCOURAGING EXAMPLE / TO / ALL YOUNG MEN OF HUMBLE FORTUNE; / BEING A PROOF OF WHAT CAN BE EFFECTED / BY STEADY APPLICATION AND HONEST EFFORTS. /

By WILLIAM COBBETT; edited anonymously

*1809, 2nd edition, 61 pp. [+1 p. publisher's advts.]. Printed by B. M'Millan, Bow Street, Covent Garden, for T. Purday & Son, No. 1, Paternoster Row, London. 'Price Two Shillings and Sixpence'. 8vo.

* 1816, '9th edition . . . THE / LIFE / OF / WILLIAM COBBETT / AUTHOR OF THE / *Political Register* / WRITTEN BY HIMSELF.' / 16 pp., printed by Macdonald and Son, 46, Cloth Fair, for W. Hone, 55, Fleet Street, and 67, Old Bailey, London. 'Price Four-pence.' 8vo.

By the middle of 1796 Cobbett had made himself one of the most talked-of men in American politics. He was widely thought (at least among the Democrats) to be an agent in the pay of the British Government (a charge which has been finally disproved by Cole's *Letters from William Cobbett to Edward Thornton*, 1937, q.v.), and his quarrel with Bradford, his publisher, was held to show his general lack of integrity. To answer these and similar attacks Peter Porcupine decided to write this autobiography. For the first time a wonderfully sympathetic figure, risen from a ploughboy to a great journalist, appeared before his readers. Cobbett cleared himself sensationally, but he also showed, if only momentarily at this stage, that he could write with great human dignity and kindliness. The *Life*, first published in August 1796, is the chief source for details of his early career, and tendentiously selected extracts from it were often used to confound his Radical supporters in later years. Most notably, in 1809, Gillray chose texts from the *Life* to illustrate a series of caricatures in this way. (For reproductions see *Advice to Young Men*, 1930 edition, and Cole's 1927 edition of the *Life and Adventures* ....) There were many other garbled editions, but both the 1809 and 1816 versions (above) faithfully reproduced the original text, apart from some minor cuts at the beginning and the end. The 1816 edition is of special interest in that it was published by the Radical William Hone, and was sold at fourpence as against the half-crown of the 1809 edition.

[18]   1796

CHRISTIANITY CONTRASTED WITH DEISM: OR
THE PRESENT RELIGION OF FRANCE.

By PETER PORCUPINE

Wrongly attributed to Cobbett in order to discredit him.

[1796, New York ?; 1796, Philadelphia, 2nd edition (L. of C.).]

The authorship of this pamphlet was strenuously repudiated by Cobbett. He said it 'abounded with the most daring impiety' (*Republican Judge*, 1798) and claimed that it had first been published in the summer of 1796 'by one Stephens', who, 'by a masterpiece of baseness, inserted the name of Peter Porcupine in the titlepage' (ibid., and *Porcupine's Gazette*, 7 March 1797).

[19] **1796**

AN ANSWER TO PAINE'S RIGHTS OF MAN. BY H. MAKENZIE [*sic*] ESQ., OF EDINBOROUGH. TO WHICH IS ADDED A LETTER FROM P. PORCUPINE TO CITIZEN JOHN SWANWICK, AN ENGLISHMAN, THE SON OF A BRITISH WAGGON-MASTER, AND MEMBER OF CONGRESS FOR THE CITY OF PHILA-DELPHIA.

By H. MACKENZIE and PETER PORCUPINE

[1796, Philadelphia (Bodl.).]

Cobbett republished this reply to Paine by Henry Mackenzie (1745–1831), the 'man of feeling', in October 1795. He added an abusive letter to John Swanwick (1760?–98), a Democratic politician and a poet who advocated the 'Rights of Women' and defended the French. Swanwick was for a long time one of Cobbett's favourite victims.

[20] **1796**

THE / LIFE / OF / THOMAS PAINE, / INTERSPERSED WITH / REMARKS AND REFLECTIONS/

By PETER PORCUPINE; taken from H. MACKENZIE'S abridgement of 'The Life of Thomas Pain' by George CHALMERS ('Francis Oldys').

First published in the *Political Censor*, No. 5, September 1796, Philadelphia. [1797, reprinted London, n.d. (B.M.); another edition (L. of C.); 1819, Sunderland?, Durham (B.M.); 1796? *Cobbett's Review of the Life* . . . London (L. of C.).]

*1797, 60 pp., Philadelphia printed, reprinted for J. Wright, opposite Old Bond Street, Piccadilly, London. 12mo. [This copy is bound with Cobbett's *The Bloody Buoy* . . . 1798, which it precedes.]

Reissued in vol. iv, *Porcupine's Works* . . ., 1801.

Cobbett's *Life of Thomas Paine* appeared originally in his *Political Censor*, No. 5, September 1796, Philadelphia. It was mainly a copy of an abstract by Henry Mackenzie, *The Life of Thomas Paine* (B.M.) which, in turn, had been taken from a scurrilous biography by George Chalmers ('Francis Oldys', see Paine, Cole Collection);[1]

[1] [21]

THE / LIFE / OF / THOMAS PAIN, / [*sic*] THE / Author of the Seditious Writings, it was followed, in the December number, by an equally savage *Letter to the Infamous Tom Paine*, ([24]) and both were speedily reprinted in London. In Cobbett's later years these slanders were to be a bitter memory, deeply regretted, and, strangely expiated, by his journey home in 1819, amid much derision, with Paine's bones (see *Paper Against Gold*, Letter XXV, 1810, and *Political Register*, 27 January 1820).

[22]   1796

THE GROS MOUSQUETON DIPLOMATIQUE; OR DIPLOMATIC BLUNDERBUSS. CONTAINING CITIZEN ADET'S NOTES TO THE SECRETARY OF STATE. AS ALSO HIS COCKADE PROCLAMATION, WITH A PREFACE.

By P. A. ADET, *translated and edited by WILLIAM COBBETT*

[1796, Philadelphia (Bodl.).]

Reissued in vol. iv of *Porcupine's Works . . .*, 1801.

The *Diplomatic Blunderbuss* was Cobbett's rejoinder to the French envoy to the United States, P. A. Adet (1763–1832), who had published some indiscreet documents in the *Aurora*. Cobbett reprinted these in November 1796 together with his own short preface and the official reproof of Adet by Timothy Pickering

----

ENTITLED / RIGHTS OF MAN.

*1793, 10th edition, iii, 171 pp. [illus.] + 5 pp. [publisher's advts.]. Printed for John Stockdale, Piccadilly, London. 4to.

George Chalmers (1742–1825), a Scottish antiquary, historian, and government clerk, who wrote this work in 1791 under the pseudonym of 'Francis Oldys', was never at the University of Philadelphia as his title-page had claimed, although he had practised as a lawyer at Baltimore before the American Revolution. The *Life . . .* is a clever, ably written work, and it established the reputation of the author, then a clerk in the Board of Trade and the Plantations under Lord Hawkesbury (1727–1808: Charles Jenkinson, later the 1st Earl of Liverpool), who was said to have paid him £500 for his work (see W. T. Sherwin's *Memoirs of the Life of Thomas Paine . . .*, 1819, Cole Collection). Chalmer's book is a compendium of fact and fiction which manages to infer, by a careful selection of half-truths and slanders, that Paine is an utter scoundrel. He is held to be an unbaptized and ungrateful son, a brutal unfaithful husband, a swindling excise-man, and a venal, ignorant, ungrammatical demagogue. It is significant that Chalmers only gradually felt his way to this out-and-out attack on Paine. In the first edition, probably to attract readers, he entitled his work a 'Defence . . .' of Paine's writings; in the third this had become 'a Review . . .', and in later editions—as in the above—the title-page bore a vignette of a ragged Paine bringing the 'seditious' *Rights of Man* to an assembly of apes.

(1745–1829), the Secretary of State who had replaced Randolph (see *A New Year's Gift 1796 [12]).

[23] **1796**

THE HISTORY OF JACOBINISM, ITS CRIMES, CRUELTIES AND PERFIDIES: COMPRISING AN INQUIRY INTO THE MANNER OF DISSEMINATING, UNDER THE APPEARANCE OF PHILOSOPHY AND VIRTUE, PRINCIPLES WHICH ARE EQUALLY SUBVERSIVE OF ORDER, VIRTUE, RELIGION, LIBERTY AND HAPPINESS. BY WILLIAM PLAYFAIR. WITH AN APPENDIX BY PETER PORCUPINE CONTAINING A HISTORY OF THE AMERICAN JACOBINS, COMMONLY DENOMINATED DEMOCRATS.

By WILLIAM PLAYFAIR; edited, with an Appendix by PETER PORCUPINE

[1796, Philadelphia, 2 vols. (with *Appendix*) (L. of C.); 1796, Philadelphia, *History of The American Jacobins* (New York Public Libr.); 1797, *History of the American Jacobins* . . ., Edinburgh (Codrington Libr., All Souls Coll., Oxford); 1798, London, 2 vols. (with *Appendix*) (B.M.).]

In November 1796 Cobbett published this American edition of a popular work by William Playfair (1759–1823), an erstwhile revolutionary who had become violently opposed to the Revolution. It had originally been published in one volume in London during the previous year (see a copy in the Cole Collection). Cobbett issued a two-volume edition from his shop in Philadelphia and added a *History of the American Jacobins* in which he likened the Democratic societies to the clubs of the Jacobins. This appendix was also separately issued in Philadelphia and reprinted the following year in Edinburgh with a preface dated Philadelphia, 10 December 1796.

[24] **1796**

A LETTER TO THE INFAMOUS TOM PAINE, IN ANSWER TO HIS LETTER TO GENERAL WASHINGTON.

By PETER PORCUPINE

First published in *Political Censor*, No. VII, Philadelphia.

[1796, Philadelphia, 1st edition (L. of C.); 1797, London (B.M.); Glasgow (Mitchell Libr., Glasgow); Edinburgh (Univ. of Pennsylvania Libr.); 1798, n.p. (New York Public Libr.).]
Reissued in vol. iv of *Porcupine's Works . . .*, 1801.

Paine's famous *Letter addressed to George Washington* (q.v. PAINE, Cole Collection), first published in August 1796 in Philadelphia and republished in the Democratic newspapers, reproached the President for his apparent failure to intervene when Paine lay in danger of his life in the *Luxembourg* in Paris. This was enlarged into an arraignment of the President's whole policy and career, and Paine was especially indignant about the recently concluded British Treaty. Cobbett, in the December *Political Censor*, wrote this powerful reply—a skilful piece of writing which delighted the Federalists. Washington himself called it 'not a bad thing' and made 'allowances for the asperity of an Englishman for some of his strong and coarse expressions and a want of official information of many facts' (*The Writings of George Washington*, ed. Worthington Chauncey Ford, New York, 1889–93, vol. xiii, p. 361). The *Letter to . . . Paine* was promptly reprinted in London by David Ogilvy, the Holborn bookseller; in Glasgow by James Gillies and in Edinburgh by J. G. Henderson. Cobbett's activity in America was now becoming appreciated in influential circles at home, and his writings were constantly being reissued, chiefly by John Wright (1770?–1844), the Tory bookseller and editor with a bookshop in Piccadilly.

[25]

1796

A LETTER FROM THE RIGHT HONOURABLE EDMUND BURKE TO A NOBLE LORD ON THE ATTACKS MADE UPON HIM AND HIS PENSION IN THE HOUSE OF LORDS, BY THE DUKE OF BEDFORD, AND THE EARL OF LAUDERDALE, EARLY IN THE PRESENT SESSION OF PARLIAMENT.

By EDMUND BURKE; preface by PETER PORCUPINE

[1796, Philadelphia, 1st American edition (B.M.).]

This was the first American edition of Burke's *Letter to a Noble Lord*. It was published by Davies, and Cobbett added a preface in which he warned the 'wealthy sansculottes' of America that they would 'be the first to fall a sacrifice' to revolutionary principles.

[26]   1797

PORCUPINE'S WORKS.

[1796-7, Philadelphia, 2 vols. (New York Public Libr.); 1797, London, 2 vols. and 1 vol. collected editions (Arnold Muirhead Collection).]

There were several issues of this two-volume collected edition of *Porcupine's Works*. One American edition contained (vol. i): *Observations on the Emigration* ... (Folwell's edition, 1795); *A Bone to Gnaw* (3rd ed. 1797); *A Kick for a Bite* (Bradford's 2nd ed. 1796); *A Bone to Gnaw, Pt. II* (Cobbett's ed. 1797); *A Little Plain English* (Bradford's ed. 1796); *A New Year's Gift* (Bradford's 2nd ed. 1796); *A Prospect* . . . (Bradford's 2nd ed. 1796). Vol. ii: *Political Censor*, March, April, May, 1796 (Cobbett's 3rd eds. 1796); *The Scare-Crow* (Cobbett's 2nd ed. 1796); *Life and Adventures* ... (Cobbett's 2nd ed. 1796); *Political Censor*, September, November, December 1796 (Cobbett's 2nd eds. 1796–7). Other collected editions were also issued in London in 1797.

[27]   1797

OBSERVATIONS ON THE DEBATES OF THE AMERICAN CONGRESS, ON THE ADDRESSES PRESENTED TO GENERAL WASHINGTON, ON HIS RESIGNATION: WITH REMARKS ON THE TIMIDITY OF THE LANGUAGE HELD TOWARDS FRANCE; THE SEIZURES OF AMERICAN VESSELS BY GREAT BRITAIN AND FRANCE; AND ON THE RELATIVE SITUATIONS OF THOSE COUNTRIES WITH AMERICA. BY PETER PORCUPINE TO WHICH IS PREFIXED GENERAL WASHINGTON'S ADDRESS TO CONGRESS; AND THE ANSWERS OF THE SENATE AND HOUSE OF REPRESENTATIVES.

By PETER PORCUPINE

[1796, reprinted London (Bodl.).]

First published in *Political Censor*, No. VII, December 1796. Reissued in *Porcupine's Works . . .,* 1801, vol. iv.

This was a London reprint, published by Ogilvy, of No. VII of the *Political Censor* (December 1796). It began with Washington's retiring Address to Congress (7 December 1796) and concluded with Cobbett's report and comments on the stormy debates which followed. Cobbett was particularly incensed with the 'poor, piping, pusillanimous language' towards France, and compared it with 'the daring and insulting tone formerly assumed towards Britain'.

[28] # 1797

PORCUPINE'S GAZETTE AND UNITED STATES DAILY ADVERTISER.

Edited by WILLIAM COBBETT

[Daily periodical: (title shortened to *Porcupine's Gazette* with issue of 24 April 1797) Philadelphia, 4 March 1797, vol. 1, No. 1—28 August 1799, vol. 4, No. 770; weekly periodical: Bustleton, 6 September 1799, vol. 5, No. 771—11 October 1799, vol. 5, No. 776; 19–26 October 1799, vol. 5, No. 777—No. 778: New York, 13 January 1800, 'farewell number' (L. of C.).]

Selections reprinted in vols. v, vi, vii, viii, ix, x, xi of *Porcupine's Works . . .,* 1801.

Porcupine's Gazette, a daily newspaper, was begun on 4 March 1797 in Philadelphia at about the same time as the last *Political Censor* appeared. Cobbett may have intended to continue his monthly journal as well, for he promised annual subscribers a free copy of the *Censor* (December *Political Censor,* cited by Clark, 94, op. cit.). Perhaps it was the immediate success of the paper which induced him to drop this plan, and he now turned his whole attention to the *Gazette.* From the beginning it seems to have sold well. In the first issue Cobbett claimed that the 'subscribers already amount to more than a thousand, not including some hundreds whose names have not reached me'; three weeks later (*Porcupine's Gazette,* 25 March 1797) he spoke of 150 subscribers in New York; and in August (ibid. 12 August 1797) he compared his circulation of between 2,500 and 2,600 with that of the Democratic *Philadelphia Gazette,* which, he asserted, had declined from 1,900 to 1,500. This progress continued until 3,000 copies a day were being printed in November (Clark, 94, op. cit.) despite some obstruction by the Post Office in the previous month. (*Porcupine's Gazette*, 3 October 1797.) Cobbett's experiment in journalism came at an opportune moment. A bitter struggle was being waged around Washington, the departing President; the British commissioners who had come to negotiate under the terms of the Treaty found themselves sharply at variance with their American counterparts; and the Embassy itself was unofficially involved with an American senator, William Blount, in an unsavoury project for the seizure of Florida, then a Spanish possession. Moreover, there were many other points of friction between the two countries, some of them going back to the War of Independence, others dating from the beginning of the war with revolutionary France. Cobbett joyously participated to the full in all these controversies, and it was not long before his writing in the *Gazette* led to a series of libel suits. The first two of these— one leading to a binding-over for 'good behaviour', and the other defeated by one vote—were on charges of libelling the King of Spain and the Spanish Ambassador, and drew from him in March 1798 an even more libellous pamphlet, *The Democratic Judge* (published in England as *The Republican Judge*, q.v.), in which the character of Thomas McKean (1734–1817), then Chief Justice of Pennsylvania, was torn to shreds. Meanwhile, in the late summer of 1797 Philadelphia was visited by one of its periodical epidemics of yellow fever, and Cobbett saw another chance to hit at his enemies and boost his paper. This time he selected Dr. Benjamin Rush (1745–1813), an eminent public figure in medicine and politics,[1] whom he dubbed 'Sangrado' after the medico in *Gil Blas* who was given to copious blood-lettings and purges as a cure for all ills. In

---

[1] The Bodleian Library has *An Eulogium Intended to Perpetuate the Memory of David Rittenhouse* . . . [1796], Philadelphia, by Rush, with abusive MS. marginalia by Cobbett. Rittenhouse (1732–96) was an American astronomer of Democratic sympathies, and Rush's lawyers, at Cobbett's trial in 1799, brought evidence to suggest that it was the *Eulogium* and not the yellow fever which had first given rise to Cobbett's venom. They produced a family doctor who had seen the pamphlet at Cobbett's house and had heard him determine to 'damn' Rush 'for it'. (See *The Rush-Light*, 1800, and *A Report of an Action for a Libel brought by Dr. Benjamin Rush against William Cobbett . . .*, Philadelphia, 1800—Oldham Public Library). This Bodleian copy may have been sent by Cobbett to Jonathan Boucher (1738–1804), a loyalist divine who left America in 1775; he was one of the subscribers to Cobbett's *Porcupine's Works* (q.v.) in 1801, and this pamphlet formed part of a set of volumes bought from his library in 1836.

October 1797 Rush took out an action for damages for libel which, according to McKean's decision, was to be tried at Philadelphia before McKean himself. For the next two years Cobbett complained that this action was kept hanging over his head, although there is hardly any evidence that his writing was in any way modified. Indeed, from the beginning of 1798 he was in touch with the large German community in Pennsylvania concerning a *Gazette*-inspired weekly *Deutsche Porcupein*,[1] and on 3 March 1798 he began another edition of his paper which he published three times a week, called *The Country Porcupine*.[2] It ran for nearly eighteen months until 28 August 1799, around which time Cobbett moved to Bustleton, just outside Philadelphia. But now the end of the *Gazette* was near. It seems to have been losing readers, and it became a weekly paper. The Rush case could now not be postponed much longer, Cobbett was thinking of returning to England, and from 6 September to 26 October 1799 only eight numbers of the *Gazette* were issued (see above, and C. S. Brigham, *History and Bibliography of American Newspapers, 1690–1820*, Worcester, Mass., 1947; **Porcupine's Works* . . ., 1801, however, gives selections from the 'November' and 'December' issues, although 26 October 1799 is referred to as the 'last number'). Finally, in December Cobbett moved to New York; in the same month the Rush action was heard, and heavy damages were awarded against him (see *The Rush-Light*, 1800, which soon provided a new vehicle for his talent). In January 1800 he produced a farewell number of *Porcupine's Gazette*, in which he spoke of his pleasure in laying down what was now 'a most troublesome and weighty burden'.

[29]   1797

A VIEW OF THE CAUSES AND CONSEQUENCES OF THE PRESENT WAR WITH FRANCE, IN ANSWER TO MR. BURKE'S REGICIDE PEACE. BY THE HONOURABLE THOMAS ERSKINE. WITH A DEDICATION TO THE AUTHOR, BY P. PORCUPINE; AND

---

[1] *Der Deutsche Porcupein und Lancaster Anzeigs Nachrichten*, 3 January 1798, No. 1— 25 December 1799, No. 104; it became *Der Americanische Staatsbothe* (L. of C.).

[2] Begun as a tri-weekly edition of *Porcupine's Gazette*, Philadelphia, 3–5 March 1798 (title changed to *Country Porcupine* with issue of 30 April 1798). Last issue, 28 August 1799, vol. 3, No. 232 (L. of C. and Massachusetts Historical Society).

AN APPENDIX CONTAINING THE CORRESPON-
DENCE BETWEEN MILES AND THE INFAMOUS LE
BRUN, MINISTER OF WAR, AT THE TIME WHEN
WAR WAS DECLARED AGAINST GREAT BRITAIN;
WHICH DEVELOPS THE REAL CAUSES OF THAT
DECLARATION, ALL THE SECRET STEPS WHICH
THE FRENCH TOOK PREVIOUS TO IT, AND
CLEARLY UNRAVELS THE THREAD OF THEIR
AMBITIOUS PROJECTS.

*By THOMAS ERSKINE and &c.; edited with a 'dedication' by
WILLIAM COBBETT*

[1797, Philadelphia (Bodl.).]

Cobbett republished this very popular pamphlet (see 18th and 32nd
London editions, 1797, ERSKINE, Cole Collection) by Thomas
Erskine (1750–1823: Baron Erskine and Lord Chancellor, 1806)
in order to strike a blow in America at the supporters of the French
Republic. He prefaced it with an ironical 'dedication' (dated,
Philadelphia, 16 May 1797) to Erskine, who was told that his
allegation 'that the refusal to receive the republican minister was
the cause of war' came 'too late' to deceive 'us' (the Americans),
although it might have succeeded 'three years ago'. Cobbett seems
to have had a half-hearted respect for the author, and although he
condemned his 'dirty work . . . from Lord George Gordon down
to the infamous Tom Paine and Hardy the Cobler', he added a
rider to the effect that Erskine came 'of honest stock, at least', unlike his 'leader' [Charles James Fox], 'begotten in corruption and
brought up, as it were, to pluck the nation'. Cobbett added an
appendix to this edition composed of extracts from the *Authentic
Correspondence with M. Le Brun* (London, 1796) by William
August Miles (1753?–1817), a government pensioner who had
been one of Pitt's confidential agents, but sometimes followed his
own star (see MILES, Cole Collection). *The Gentleman's Magazine*
(1796, Pt. II, 676) described the *Observations* he attached to his
Authentic Correspondence as a 'rant of Jacobinism', but Cobbett
reprinted this extract in order to refute Erskine out of the mouth of
one who had been 'a friend to the French Revolution' and had
'attacked Mr. Burke with more violence than any of his numerous
antagonists'.

1797

Letters from / WILLIAM COBBETT / to / EDWARD THORNTON / written in the years / 1797 to 1800. / EDITED WITH / AN INTRODUCTION AND NOTES / BY G. D. H. COLE. /

By WILLIAM COBBETT; edited by G. D. H. COLE

*1937, xlvi, 127 pp. [incl. Index]. Published by Humphrey Milford, Oxford University Press, London. 8vo.

A collection of letters from Cobbett to Edward Thornton (1766–1852, knighted 1822) written between 1797 and 1800 when Thornton was Secretary to the British Embassy in the United States. The letters, with Professor Cole's Introduction and Notes, bring to light much fresh material regarding personalities and politics during part of Cobbett's first sojourn in America. The originals are now in Nuffield College (see [269]).

[31] **1798**

THE DEMOCRATIC JUDGE; OR THE EQUAL LIBERTY OF THE PRESS, AS EXHIBITED, EXPLAINED, AND EXPOSED, IN THE PROSECUTION OF WILLIAM COBBETT, FOR A PRETENDED LIBEL AGAINST THE KING OF SPAIN AND HIS AMBASSADOR, BEFORE THOMAS MCKEAN, CHIEF JUSTICE OF THE STATE OF PENNSYLVANIA.

By PETER PORCUPINE

[1798, Philadelphia (Bodl.).]

Published in England as:

[32]

THE REPUBLICAN JUDGE; OR THE AMERICAN LIBERTY OF THE PRESS, AS EXHIBITED, EXPLAINED, AND EXPOSED, IN THE BASE AND PARTIAL PROSECUTION FOR A PRETENDED LIBEL AGAINST THE KING OF SPAIN AND HIS AMBASSADOR, BEFORE THE SUPREME COURT OF PENN-

SYLVANIA. WITH AN ADDRESS TO THE PEOPLE OF ENGLAND.

By PETER PORCUPINE

[1798, London (Bodl.); London, 2nd edition; London, 3rd edition (John Carter Brown Libr., Providence, R.I.).]

Reissued in vol. vii, *Porcupine's Works . . .*, 1801.

Cobbett's account of his first series of libel trials for his attacks on the Spanish ambassador, the Chevalier de Yrujo (1763–1824), in *Porcupine's Gazette* (q.v.), was published in March 1798 at Philadelphia as *The Democratic Judge*. It was reprinted by Wright in London under the title of *The Republican Judge* with a preface dated 10 April 1798, addressed to 'the people of England' (dated, 'Philadelphia, November 30th, 1797' in *Porcupine's Works*). Cobbett had emerged fairly successfully from his first bout with American justice, but nothing could be less conciliatory or more tactless than the savage style of this pamphlet in which Thomas McKean (1734–1817), the Chief Justice of Pennsylvania and a powerful Democrat, was described as 'the Fouquier-Tinville of America', and called 'wife-beater', 'drunkard', 'judicial murderer', and much else.

[33]   **1798**

OBSERVATIONS ON THE DISPUTE BETWEEN THE UNITED STATES AND FRANCE...

By ROBERT GOODLOE HARPER and others; edited by WILLIAM COBBETT

[1797, Philadelphia, 1st–2nd editions; 1798, numerous editions, London, Philadelphia, Boston, Dublin, &c. (L. of C.).]

According to an advertisement in *Porcupine's Gazette* of 11 May 1798 (cited by Clark, op. cit.) Cobbett had just published this new edition of an anti-French pamphlet by Robert Goodloe Harper (1765–1825), a busy lawyer and politician, whose *Observations . . .*, issued in 1797, had been warmly greeted in the British Parliament. Cobbett's edition included some of the speeches made in Congress together with his own preface and notes. In 1799 Harper was one of Cobbett's counsel in the successful libel suit brought by Dr. Rush (see [28], note to *Porcupine's Gazette*). Cobbett contended that

44

he had deliberately weakened his case, and now claimed to have written most of Harper's speeches in Congress. As to the *Observations . . .*: 'I furnished the materials, gave the hints, drew the plan, and if my name had been put to the work, I should not have been so much of a plagiarist as he was.' Even the subsidizing of the pamphlet, Cobbett claimed, had been his responsibility; but, he did 'not repine', for the 'pamphlet did great good to both countries, and great injury to France, which far outweighed . . . all the dollars in the world' (see *Porcupine's Works*, vol. ix, and Cole's *Letters from William Cobbett to Edward Thornton*).

[34] 1798

DETECTION OF A CONSPIRACY FORMED BY THE UNITED IRISHMEN WITH THE WIDEST INTENTION OF AIDING THE TYRANTS OF FRANCE IN SUBVERTING THE GOVERNMENT OF THE UNITED STATES OF AMERICA.

[1798, Philadelphia; 1799, Dublin (Bodl.); 1799, London (Arnold Muirhead Collection).]

Reissued in vol. viii, *Porcupine's Works . . .*, 1801.

Cobbett had discovered in the existence of a Philadelphia Society of United Irishmen led by Dr. James Reynolds (d. 1807) a vast French plot to suborn the United States from within as a preparation to invading her. For this reason, in this pamphlet of May 1798 he welcomed the Alien Laws soon to be enacted. A year or so later his own activities were to be in danger from this same legislation.

[35] 1798

FRENCH ARROGANCE; OR, 'THE CAT LET OUT OF THE BAG': A POETICAL DIALOGUE BETWEEN THE ENVOYS OF AMERICA, X. Y. Z. AND THE LADY.

By PETER PORCUPINE

[1798, Philadelphia (L. of C.); 1915 reprint, New York (Bodl.).]

A satirical poem published in May 1798 in which Cobbett in hudibrastic style dealt with the difficult negotiations then going on with the French.

[36] 1798

[THE ANTIDOTE] REMARKS ON THE INSIDIOUS
LETTER OF THE GALLIC DESPOTS.

By PETER PORCUPINE

[1798, Philadelphia (American Antiquarian Society Libr.).]
First published in *Porcupine's Gazette*, 1798; reissued in vol. viii, *Porcupine's Works . . .*, 1801.

In June 1798 Benjamin Franklin Bache (1769–1798), the editor of the *Aurora*, had published a letter from Talleyrand to the American envoys in Paris claiming that France, in contrast to Britain, desired peace. Cobbett immediately replied in the columns of his *Gazette* with this *Antidote*, which he reprinted and sold separately (see Clark, op. cit. 130).

[37] 1798

THE DETECTION OF BACHE; OR FRENCH DIPLO-
MATIC SKILL DEVELOPED.

By WILLIAM COBBETT

[1798, Philadelphia (Historical Society of Pennsylvania Libr.).]
First published in *Porcupine's Gazette*, 20 June 1798.

Cobbett accompanied his attack on Bache in the *Antidote* (see [36]) with this broadsheet exposure reprinted from *Porcupine's Gazette*, alleging that Bache was in treasonable communication with Talleyrand (see Clark, op. cit. 132, and *Porcupine's Works . . .*, viii. 245).

[38] 1798

DEMOCRATIC PRINCIPLES / ILLUSTRATED / BY
EXAMPLE. / PART THE FIRST. / DEMOCRATIC
PRINCIPLES / ILLUSTRATED. / PART THE SECOND. /
CONTAINING / AN / INSTRUCTIVE ESSAY, /
TRACING / ALL THE HORRORS / OF / THE FRENCH
REVOLUTION / TO THEIR REAL CAUSES; / the

46

LICENTIOUS POLITICS and INFIDEL / PHILOSOPHY
OF the Present Age. /

By PETER PORCUPINE

['1797' ?–8, Dublin (University of Illinois Libr.); 1798, London, 1st to 11th
editions; Aberdeen, 7th edition (B.M.); Edinburgh, 7th edition and another
edition (New York Public Libr.); Birmingham, another edition, . . . *A
Faint Picture of the Horrors and Calamities* . . . (Birmingham Reference
Libr.).]

Part the First published previously as a part of Part II of **A Bone to Gnaw for the
Democrats*, 1795, q.v.

* 1798, Part I, 8th edition, 24 pp. Printed for J. Wright, opposite Old
Bond Street, Piccadilly, London, price 3*d*, and sold by Mundell and Son,
Edinburgh, and I. Mundell, Glasgow. 12mo.

Part the Second published previously as part of *The Bloody Buoy, 1796, q.v.

* 1798, Part II, 7th edition, 52 pp. Printed for J. Wright, opposite Old
Bond Street, Piccadilly, price 4*d*, 12mo.

This pamphlet in two parts consisted of sections taken from Part
II of *A Bone to Gnaw . . . and *The Bloody Buoy . . . (q.v.), suitably
amended for the English public. Thus in the first part all the atrocity
stories of the French Revolution were left intact, whilst the names
of Thelwall, Hardy, and Tooke were substituted for those of
Butler, Bond, and Rowan; and the 'Whig Club, and Corresponding
Societies' for the 'United Irishmen' and 'American self-created
societies'. It does not appear to have been issued in this form in the
United States, but it was widely distributed and reprinted in
Britain, with a separate edition in Aberdeen and also in Birmingham. In the latter place it expressed the contemporary fear of a
French invasion, and a slightly shortened version of Part I appeared
as a penny pamphlet entitled *Read and Reflect! . . . A Faint Picture
of the Horrors and Calamities, which have proceeded from The
French Revolution* . . . (Birmingham Reference Library).

[39] 1798

THE CANNIBAL'S PROGRESS: OR, THE DREADFUL
HORRORS OF FRENCH INVASION, AS DISPLAYED
BY THE REPUBLICAN OFFICERS AND SOLDIERS,
IN THEIR PERFIDY, RAPACITY, FEROCIOUS-
NESS, AND BRUTALITY, EXERCISED TOWARDS

·47·

THE INNOCENT INHABITANTS OF GERMANY.
ABRIDGED FROM THE TRANSLATION OF AN-
THONY AUFRERE, ESQ.

Edited by WILLIAM COBBETT from a translation by ANTHONY AUFRERE (or AUFRER).

[1798, London, Philadelphia, &c., numerous editions (B.M., L. of C.)]
Reissued in vol. viii, *Porcupine's Works . . .*, 1801.

An edition by Cobbett in June 1798 of a translation by Anthony
Aufrere (1756–1833), first published in London, of one of the
most harrowing accounts of the atrocities supposed to have been
committed by the French Army in Germany and Austria in 1796.
It was sold for only six cents with great success. Cobbett sent a copy
to Edward Thornton (1766–1852), the secretary to the British
Legation on 27 August 1798, and wrote: 'I have published 25
thousand of this work, and about as many more have been issued, by
my permission, from the German and other presses in the States. It
has been, and long will be, a mighty engine' (Cole's *Letters from
William Cobbett to Edward Thornton*; see also Evan's *American
Bibliography*, vol. xii, for details of widespread American editions
in 1798, including a contemporary account of its large sale in
Philadelphia). Three years later, when he was back in England, he
included it in his *Works* (vol. viii) and added a footnote claiming
that over a hundred thousand copies had been sold in America
besides a large edition in German (the latter was entitled *Der
Fortgang der Menschenfresser*; see Evans, op. cit.).

[40]   1798

REMARKS ON THE EXPLANATION, LATELY
PUBLISHED BY DR. PRIESTLEY, RESPECTING THE
INTERCEPTED LETTERS OF HIS FRIEND AND
DISCIPLE, JOHN H. STONE. TO WHICH IS ADDED A
CERTIFICATE OF CIVISM FOR JOSEPH PRIESTLEY,
JUN.

By PETER PORCUPINE

[1798, Philadelphia; 1799, reprinted London (B.M.).]

First published in Cobbett's *Porcupine's Gazette*, September 1798, Philadelphia;
reprinted London, 1799.

Reissued in vol. ix, *Porcupine's Works . . .*, 1801.

The 'intercepted letters', favouring a French invasion of England, were alleged to have been seized in 1798 on board a neutral ship. They may have been forgeries, but their 'discovery' created a great deal of excitement at the time and they were reprinted by Wright[1] in London as well as in Philadelphia in Cobbett's *Porcupine's Gazette*, and in newspapers in both countries. These *Remarks* by Cobbett were also reprinted by Wright early in the following year. John H[urford] Stone (1763–1818), the reputed author of the letters, was an English Unitarian who had fled to France and there joined a group of British exiles. His brother William had been acquitted in London on a charge of high treason (29 January 1796), a point of little consequence to Cobbett, who violently attacks Priestley and many others who had left England for political reasons. Among those named in the pamphlet are the 'United Irishmen', James Reynolds, who is mentioned in the *Detection of a Conspiracy*, and Archibald Hamilton Rowan (1751–1834), who had organized a rowdy meeting in Philadelphia in 1795 (see *A Little Plain English*); D. I. Eaton, who is accused of living with an Indian squaw; 'Poor Merry' (Robert Merry, 1755–98), the romantic poet who gave his pseudonym to the Della Cruscans; Benjamin Vaughan (1751–1835), an ex-M.P. to whom Priestley was to deliver one of the 'intercepted letters'; 'the virtuous Citoyenne Williams' (Helen Maria Williams, 1762–1827, Stone's companion in Paris); and Priestley's second son, Joseph (1768–1833), who in an extract reprinted from *Porcupine's Gazette* (15 January 1799) is granted an ironical 'certificate of civism' for his return to England.

[42]   1799
THE TRIAL OF REPUBLICANISM: OR, A SERIES OF POLITICAL PAPERS, PROVING THE INJURIOUS AND DEBASING CONSEQUENCES OF REPUBLICAN GOVERNMENT AND WRITTEN CONSTITUTIONS.

---

[1] [41]
Copies of Original Letters recently written by Persons in Paris to Dr. Priestley in America. Taken on board of a neutral vessel. 1798, 2nd edition, x, 36 pp. Printed in London for J. Wright, Piccadilly. 8vo. The publisher advertised the forthcoming publication of 'An Interesting Pamphlet, addressed to the People of Great Britain, by Peter Porcupine'.

WITH AN INTRODUCTORY ADDRESS TO THE HON. THOMAS ERSKINE, ESQ.

By WILLIAM COBBETT

[1799, Philadelphia; 1801, London (Bodl.).]
Reissued in vol. x, *Porcupine's Works . . .*, 1801.

Cobbett wrote this pamphlet in June 1799 when he was beginning to doubt whether anything good could be expected to come from the American Republic. The Federalists, under the Presidency of Adams from whom he had hoped for better things, were adopting a firmer attitude about the British debt negotiations, and relations with France were becoming friendlier. Cobbett skilfully cast his pamphlet into the form of a political cross-examination at a 'trial' in which Dr. Joseph Priestley and William Griffith (1766–1826), an American lawyer who had called for a new Constitution, were severely examined by Peter Porcupine. He prefaced his work with an 'introductory address' to Thomas Erskine (1750–1823), whom he presented as 'the advocate of republicanism', and wisely allowed no further part in the 'proceedings'. The *Trial of Republicanism* was reprinted in London in April 1801, and Cobbett included it in his **Works* (vol. x), where he added a *Postscript* describing the refusal of *The Morning Chronicle* to insert an advertisement for the pamphlet.

[43]   1799

PROPOSALS FOR PUBLISHING BY SUBSCRIPTION A NEW ENTIRE, AND NEAT EDITION OF PORCU-PINE'S WORKS.

By WILLIAM COBBETT

[1799, Philadelphia (B.M.).]

Cobbett's plan to republish his American writings came to naught at the close of 1799. His effects were seized on behalf of his creditors aiter he had lost the Rush case, and among them were the unbound sheets of this intended edition. They were sold as waste paper, and Cobbett had to postpone his 'proposals' until he returned to England (see **Porcupine's Works . . .*, 1801).

[44]

THE RUSH-LIGHT

[1800, Nos. 1-5, New York; London, No. 6 (B.M.); London, No. 7 is spurious (L. of C.).]

By WILLIAM COBBETT

[45]

Republished in London as:

THE AMERICAN RUSH-LIGHT; BY THE HELP OF WHICH WAYWARD AND DISAFFECTED BRITONS MAY SEE A COMPLETE SPECIMEN OF THE BASE-NESS, DISHONESTY, INGRATITUDE, AND PERFIDY, OF REPUBLICANS AND OF THE PROFLIGACY, INJUSTICE, AND TYRANNY, OF REPUBLICAN GOVERNMENTS.

[1800, Nos. 1-4, London. (Bodl.).]
Nos. 1-5 reissued in vol. xi, *Porcupine's Works . . .*, 1801.

Mulcted of 5,000 dollars damages in the Rush action (see [28], note to *Porcupine's Gazette*), and with legal costs and a further fine for his breach of good behaviour coming to as much again, Cobbett decided to strike another blow at his enemies, and if possible recoup some of his lost fortune. On 15 February 1800 he began a new fortnightly paper, *The Rush-Light*, of which five numbers now appeared in New York (15, 28 February, 15, 31 March, and 30 April 1800) and a sixth, dated 30 August 1800, in London[1] (the first four of these were republished in London as *The American Rush-Light*—a seventh number, *The Republican Rush-Light*, undated, appears to be a forgery). *The Rush-Light* was chiefly made up of an even more vehement repetition of the attacks on McKean and Rush. No. 5, the last New York issue, composed of a letter to Dr. Priestley, to whose reception in 1794 Cobbett owed his introduction to American politics, was leavened with a little sympathy for a personal tragedy that had befallen the doctor, but in the main this was a bitter, abusive, libellous journal almost entirely occupied with his personal grievances. Yet Cobbett was

---

[1] This sixth number was republished in America as *An Address to the People of England* (1800?, n.p. and 1812, Philadelphia,—the latter by John Binns.—L. of C.).

making it pay, and he even claimed that '*The Rush-Light* has surpassed in circulation any publication ever before issuing from my press' (Cole, *Letters . . .*, op. cit. 74). By now, however, he had lost his interest in the American scene, his words were mainly intended for British ears, and having cleared up a large part of his debts, he thankfully took his departure from England via loyal Nova Scotia. Characteristically, he advertised a 'Farewell Address' which ended, 'With this I depart for my native land, where neither the moth of *Democracy* nor the rust of *Federation* doth corrupt, and where thieves do not, with impunity, break through and steal five thousand dollars at a time.'

[46]   1800

COBBETT'S ADVICE. /

By WILLIAM COBBETT

*[1800] S. sh. Printed by J. F. Dove, 178, Piccadilly, opposite Burlington House, London. 4to.

Cobbett, embittered and nearly ruined by his intervention in American politics, returned to England (4 July 1800) still a Tory. Moving in a political world notorious for its venal journalism, he resolved to maintain his own integrity by starting an independent daily paper, *The Porcupine* (q.v.), in support of the Government. On 9 September 1800, before he launched his paper, he issued this violently anti-Reform broadsheet. The *Advice* eulogized Pitt, but Cobbett was soon to break with the ministerial party over the Peace, and in November 1801 he published the critical *Collection of Facts and Observations Relative to the Peace with Bonaparte . . .* (q.v.).

[47]   1800

PROSPECTUS OF A NEW DAILY PAPER TO BE ENTITLED THE PORCUPINE. [begins:] BY WILLIAM COBBETT.

By WILLIAM COBBETT

[1800, London (Bodl.).]

This eight-page 'prospectus', advertising *The Porcupine* (q.v.), dated 'Pall Mall, 29th Sept., 1800', is almost identical with *Cobbett's Advice*, 1800 (see [46]), issued at about the same time.

[48]   1800

THE PORCUPINE. /

Edited by WILLIAM COBBETT

[Daily periodical, London, Nos. 1–365, 30 October 1800–31 December 1800, latterly styled *The Porcupine and anti-Gallican Monitor*; absorbed by *True Briton*, 1802 (B.M.).]

*1800–1 [incomplete], No. 2, 31 October 1800–No. 130, 30 March 1801 (No. 18, 19 November 1800, No. 101, 24 February, No. 103, 26 February, No. 107, 3 March 1801, missing). Printed and published for William Cobbett at No. 3, Southampton Street, Strand, 'Price 6d.' Folio.

The first number of *The Porcupine*, a daily sixpenny newspaper, owned and edited by Cobbett, appeared on 30 October 1800 (see note to *Cobbett's Advice*, 1800). Staunchly anti-Republican, although proudly 'independent', it bore the motto, 'Fear God, Honour the King', and appealed, in Cobbett's words, not to 'the numerous pot-houses of this metropolis', but to the 'persons of property, rank, and respectability' (9 December 1800). Apparently it began with some success in this sphere. Despite the short notice of its commencement, 700 orders were said to have been received (ibid.), and among its distinguished correspondents were Lord Grenville ('Sulpicius') and Jeremy Bentham ('Censor'; see *Porcupine*, 1 December 1800, also Bentham's* *Works* . . ., vol. x). After three weeks Cobbett announced that he was reprinting the earlier numbers in a second edition (giving the curious reason of a publication date 'twenty-five days earlier than was first proposed'), and a few weeks later he was claiming a circulation of 1,500 a day (21 November, 9 December 1800). A host of difficulties were soon to appear, however, and these were to bring *The Porcupine* down. The real circulation figure may not have been so high as was claimed, and heavy Post Office charges hindered his transatlantic sales and brought him into conflict with the authorities. So also did the withdrawal of Post Office advertisements and the malicious substitution of other papers for his by corrupt government clerks then sometimes responsible for country orders (see Cobbett's correspondence on the question in B.M. Add. MSS. 34455, ff. 393–417, *Political Register*, 27 November 1802 and *Letter to Lord Auckland*, 1802). Moreover, with the opening of peace *pourparlers* with France, Cobbett found himself opposed both to Pitt and to popular feeling (see **A Collection of Facts and Observations Relative to the Peace* 1801 [50]), although William Windham (1750–1810) and he drew much closer together. The net effect, however, was a rapid decline of *The Porcupine*, and on 23 November 1801 (B.M. Add. MSS. 37853, f. 17) Cobbett sold it to Henry Redhead Yorke (1772–1813) and 'a Mr. Bateman', of whom he said he knew 'nothing, except that . . . Yorke has an allowance from the Ministry'. Before this transfer Cobbett seems to have disposed of a share in the paper to John Gifford (1758–1818, originally John Richards Green), the editor of the *Anti-Jacobin Review and Magazine*, an old colleague of Cobbett's who was later rewarded for his political services by being made a metropolitan police magistrate. *The Porcupine* was no more fortunate under its new owners than it had been under Cobbett, and in less than two months it was absorbed (January 1802) by the *True Briton* (see a copy of **The True Briton and Porcupine*, 11 January 1802, Cole Collection), a Government daily newspaper owned by John Heriot (1760–1833) and edited, for a short time, by Yorke. Cobbett later declared that before starting *The Porcupine* he had been offered a partnership in the *True Briton* as a gift from the Government, and later still he claimed that he had been offered its outright control, as well as a choice between this paper and the *Sun* (*Political Register*, 20 August 1802, 4 January 1817, 10 April 1830). Undoubtedly some such offers were made to him at this time. They were indignantly rejected, and indeed, in a letter to Windham on 24 November 1801, a day after he had transferred the paper to Yorke, Cobbett complained that 'Mr. Gifford has lost about £300, and I about £450' (B.M. Add. MSS. 37853, f. 17). Four years later Cobbett claimed that he had lost £750 of his own money on *The Porcupine* (*Political Register*, 12 October 1805). Perhaps he had to pay Gifford's share, but even if Cobbett was exaggerating his loss, it is plain that he did manage to preserve his independence. Nevertheless, not long after his death the charge was made that Windham had brought him £3,000 from the Government for the paper (see *Westminster Review*, October 1835).

PORCUPINE'S / WORKS; / CONTAINING VARIOUS / WRITINGS AND SELECTIONS, / EXHIBITING A FAITHFUL PICTURE / OF THE / UNITED STATES OF AMERICA; / OF THEIR / GOVERNMENTS, LAWS, POLITICS, AND RESOURCES; / OF THE CHARACTER OF THEIR / PRESIDENTS, GOVERNORS, LEGIS-LATORS, MAGIS- / TRATES AND MILITARY MEN; / AND OF THE / CUSTOMS, MANNERS, MORALS, RELIGION, VIRTUES / AND VICES / OF THE PEOPLE: / COMPRISING ALSO / A COMPLETE SERIES OF HISTORICAL DOCUMENTS / AND RE-MARKS, / FROM THE END OF THE WAR, IN 1783, / TO THE / ELECTION OF THE PRESIDENT, IN MARCH, 1801. /

By WILLIAM COBBETT

* 1801, (May) 12 vols.; [for Contents, see below], 400 pp., 472 pp., 440 pp., 444 pp., 432 pp., 432 pp., 430 pp., 480 pp., 412 pp., 449 pp. [+ 3 pp.], 434 pp., 252 pp. [+ 82 pp., unnumbered, Index]. Printed for Cobbett and Morgan, at the Crown and Mitre, Pall Mall, London. 8vo.

GENERAL CONTENTS

Vol. I

1. A Summary View of the Politics of the United States from the Close of the War to the Year 1794.
2. Addresses to Dr. Priestley.
3. Observations on Priestley's Emigration.
4. The Story of a Farmer's Bull.
5. Account of the Insurrection in the Western Counties of Pennsylvania, in 1794.
6. Dispute between America and Great Britain.

Vol. II.

1. A Bone to Gnaw for the Democrats, Part I.
2. A Kick for a Bite.
3. A Bone to Gnaw for the Democrats, Part II.
4. A Summary of the Proceedings of Congress, during the Session which commenced on the 4th of November, 1794.
5. Popular Proceedings relative to the British Treaty, previous to its Ratification.
6. The British Treaty.
7. Popular Proceedings relative to the British Treaty, after the Ratification.

8. A little Plain English, addressed to the People of the United States, on the Treaty, and on the Conduct of the President relative thereto, in Answer to the 'Letters of Franklin'.
9. An Analysis of Randolph's Vindication.
10. A New Year's Gift for the Democrats; or Observations on a Pamphlet, entitled, 'A Vindication of Randolph's Resignation'.

Vol. III

1. The Political Censor, No. I; or a Review of Political Occurrences relative to the United States of America.
2. The Bloody Buoy, thrown out as a Warning to the political Pilots of all Nations; or, a faithful Relation of a Multitude of Acts of Barbarity, such as the Eye never witnessed, the Tongue expressed, or the Imagination conceived, until the Commencement of the French Revolution. To which is added, an instructive Essay, tracing these dreadful Effects to their real Causes.
3. Political Censor, No. II.
4. Political Censor, No. III.
5. Political Censor, No. IV.

Vol. IV

1. The Scare-Crow:—Being an Infamous Letter, sent to Mr. John Oldden, threatening Destruction to his House, and Violence to the Person of his Tenant, William Cobbett; with Remarks on the same.
2. The Life and Adventures of Peter Porcupine, with a full and fair Account of all his authoring Transactions; Being a sure and infallible Guide for all enterprising young Men who wish to make a Fortune by writing Pamphlets.
3. Political Censor, No. V.
4. The Diplomatic Blunderbuss, containing Adet's Notes to the Secretary of State; as also his Cockade Proclamation.
5. Political Censor, No. VI.
6. Political Censor, No. VII.
7. Political Censor, No. VIII.
8. A Brief Statement of the Injuries and Insults received from France.
9. Washington's retiring from the Presidency.

Vol. V

Selections from Porcupine's Gazette, from the Beginning of March, to the End of May, 1797:

Vol. VI

Selections from Porcupine's Gazette, from the Beginning of June, to the 15th of August, 1797.

Vol. VII

1. Selections from Porcupine's Gazette, from the 16th of August, to the End of November, 1797.
2. The Republican Judge: or, The American Liberty of the Press, as exhibited, explained, and exposed, in the base and partial Prosecution

of William Cobbett, for a pretended Libel against the King of Spain and his Ambassador, before the Supreme Court of Pennsylvania. With an Address to the People of England.

3. Selections from Porcupine's Gazette, for the Month of December, 1797.

Vol. VIII

1. Selections from Porcupine's Gazette, from the Beginning of January, to the End of May, 1798.
2. Detection of a Conspiracy, formed by the United Irishmen, with an evident Intention of aiding the Tyrants of France in subverting the Government of the United States of America.
3. Selections from Porcupine's Gazette, for the Month of June, 1798.
4. The Cannibal's Progress: or the dreadful Horrors of French Invasion, as displayed by the republican Officers and Soldiers, in their Perfidy, Rapacity, Ferociousness, and Brutality, exercised towards the innocent Inhabitants of Germany.   [the United States.
5. Authentic History of the Depredations committed on the Commerce of
6. Selections from Porcupine's Gazette, for the Month of June, 1798.

Vol. IX

1. Selections from Porcupine's Gazette, for the Month of July, 1798.
2. The Impeachment of Senator Blount.
3. Selections from Porcupine's Gazette, for August and September, 1798.
4. J. H. Stone's Letters to Dr. Priestley.   [Stone.
5. Remarks on Dr. Priestley's Explanation respecting the Letters of
6. Selections from Porcupine's Gazette, for October, 1798.
7. Miscellaneous Anecdotes of various Dates.
8. Priestley's Poor Emigrants.
9. Postscript, containing an Address of the Welsh People residing in Cambria, in the State of Pennsylvania, to their Brethren in Wales.

Vol. X

1. Selections from Porcupine's Gazette, from November, 1798, to June, 1799, inclusive.
2. Dr. Morse's Exposure of French Intrigue in the United States.
3. Galloway's Exposure of Howe.
4. The Trial of Republicanism.

Vol. XI

1. Selections from Porcupine's Gazette, July, 1799, to January, 1800.
2. A concise and comprehensive History of Prince Suwarrow's [sic] Campaign in Italy, in the Year 1799.[1]
3. The American Rush-Light (No. I), by the help of which wayward and disaffected Britons may see a complete Specimen of the Baseness, Dishonesty, Ingratitude, and Perfidy of Republicans, and of the Profligacy, Injustice, and Tyranny of republican Governments.

---

[1] [Included in *History of the Campaigns of . . . Suworow*, New York, 1800, a translation from the German of J. F. Anthing, published by Cobbett.]

4. The American Rush-Light, No. II.
5. The American Rush-Light, No. III.
6. The American Rush-Light, No. IV.
7. The American Rush-Light, No. V.

Vol. XII

Cobbett, in partnership in London with his friend, John Morgan, whom he had known in Philadelphia, collected many of his American writings in this twelve-volume edition (dated 29 May 1801) which he dedicated to John Reeves (1752–1829) of the 'Loyal Association'. The list of subscribers (see vol. i) was headed by the Royal Princes, and among the 750 names drawn from both sides of the Atlantic were leading members of the British Government. An earlier American edition had been less fortunate. Whilst awaiting binding it had been seized in sheets by Cobbett's creditors and political enemies, sold as waste paper, and destroyed (see Cole, *Letters from William Cobbett to Edward Thornton . . .*, 1937).

[50]   1801

A / COLLECTION / OF / FACTS AND OBSERVA-TIONS, / RELATIVE TO THE / PEACE WITH BONA-PARTE, / CHIEFLY EXTRACTED FROM / THE

PORCUPINE, / AND INCLUDING / MR. COBBETT'S LETTERS / TO / LORD HAWKESBURY. / TO WHICH IS ADDED / AN APPENDIX, / Containing the divers Conventions, / Treaties, State Papers, and Dispatches, / connected with the Subject; together with Extracts from the / Speeches of Mr. PITT, Mr. FOX, and Lord HAWKESBURY, / respecting Bonaparte and a Peace with France. /

Edited by WILLIAM COBBETT

[1801, London, *1st edition; 1802, Philadelphia (L. of C.).]

First published, in the main, in *The Porcupine*, 1801.

*1801 (November), [ii], 248 pp.+Appendix, lviii. Published by Cobbett and Morgan, Pall Mall, London. 8vo.

Cobbett was violently enthusiastic for the war with France, and a critical note appeared in his journal *The Porcupine* (q.v.) when peace negotiations began. Even after his windows were broken and his press damaged (10 October 1801) when he refused to join in the general illumination in honour of the Peace, he persisted in his unpopular opposition. *The Porcupine* suspended publication for two days and then resumed with the first of eight *Letters* to the Foreign Secretary, Lord Hawkesbury (1770–1828, Robert Banks Jenkinson, later 2nd Earl of Liverpool and Prime Minister, 1812–27). In these Cobbett trenchantly attacked the idea of peace, criticized the terms of the Treaty which he thought left France the mistress of Europe, and ranged himself with such opponents of the Government as William Windham (1750–1810), his special patron, and William Wyndham Grenville (1759–1834, later Baron Grenville). Cobbett was now in partnership with John Morgan, an English acquaintance of his Philadelphia days, and in November 1801 these *Letters*, together with other extracts from *The Porcupine*, were published by them in book form—see above. The *Letters*, but not the extracts, were republished in the following January in the second of two new editions, *Letters to the Right Honourable Lord Hawkesbury* (see [51]).

[51]   1802

LETTERS / TO THE / RIGHT HONOURABLE / LORD HAWKESBURY, / AND TO THE / RIGHT HONOURABLE / HENRY ADDINGTON, / ON THE / PEACE

WITH BUONAPARTÉ, / TO WHICH IS ADDED, / AN
APPENDIX, Containing a Collection (now greatly enlarged) of
all the Conventions, / Treaties, Speeches, and other Documents, /
connected with the Subject. /

Edited by WILLIAM COBBETT

[1802 (January), London, 1st edition: *Letters to the Right Honourable
Henry Addington* . . . (B.M.); 1802 (January), London, 2nd edition:
Letters to the Right Honourable Lord Hawkesbury . . .]

*1802 (January), 2nd edition, [iii], 259 pp.+Appendix, xcvi [+4 pp.
publishers' advts.]. Published by Cobbett and Morgan, Pall Mall, London.
8vo.

In January 1802 Cobbett followed up *A Collection of Facts and
Observations* (q.v.) with the publication of his three *Letters to the
Right Honourable Henry Addington* (B.M.). Addington (1757–
1844), later the first Viscount Sidmouth, had recently become Prime
Minister, and Cobbett warned him of the disastrous effects of a
Peace with France, on 'our Colonies, our Commerce, . . . our
manufactures, . . .and . . . our Constitution'. Nevertheless, he
disclaimed any intention to range himself 'in a systematic opposition
to his Majesty's Ministers, or to their measures'. In the same
month (January) as he published this first edition Cobbett issued a
second edition—see above—and included in it the *Letters* to Lord
Hawkesbury and some other material which had already appeared
in *A Collection of Facts and Observations* (see [50]).

[52]   1802
COBBETT'S POLITICAL REGISTER.

Edited by WILLIAM COBBETT

[Weekly periodical, 1802–35, 1836—London, various	ly entitled *Cobbett's
Annual Register*, *Cobbett's Political Register*, *Cobbett's Weekly Political
Pamphlet*, *Cobbett's Weekly Register*, *Cobbett's Weekly Political Register*.
1803 (only), a French translation, *Le Mercure Anglois*.]

*1802, vol. i, January to June 1802, 'Cobbett's Annual Register', xiv,
800 cols.+*Supplement*, cols. 801–1462, printed by Cox and Baylis, London.
8vo.

*1803, vol. ii, July to December 1802, 'Cobbett's Annual Register', viii,
[+12 pp. *Contents*], 896 cols.+*Supplement*, cols. 897–1936. Printed by

Cox and Baylis, and sold by E. Harding, Pall Mall, R. Bagshaw, Bow Street, London, J. Mercier, Dublin, and E. Sarjeant, New York. 8vo.

*1803, vol. iii, January to June 1803, 'Cobbett's Annual Register', ii, [+18 pp. *Contents*], 992 cols.+*Supplement*, cols, 993-3005. Printed by Cox and Baylis, and sold by John Budd, Crown and Mitre, Pall Mall, R. Bagshaw..., Richardson, Royal Exchange, Ginger, Piccadilly, London..., J. Mercer [*sic*], Dublin, J. Morgan, Philadelphia, and E. Sarjeant, New York. 8vo.

*1804, vol. iv, July to December 1803, 'Cobbett's Annual Register', [10 pp. *Contents*], 992 cols.+*Supplement*, cols. 993-2032 [+4 pp. *Index*]. Printed ... [&c., as in vol. iii]. 8vo.

*1804, vol. v, January to June 1804, [from issue of 7 January, entitled] 'Cobbett's Weekly Political Register'. [6 pp. *Contents*]. 1040 cols. Printed ... [&c., as in vol. iii]. 8vo.

*Vol. vi, July to December 1804, 'Cobbett's Weekly Political Register', [6 pp. *Contents*], 1073 cols. Printed ... [&c., as in vol. iii]. 8vo.

*1805, vol. vii, January to June 1805, viii pp., 1008 cols. Printed ... [&c., as in vol. iii]. 8vo.

*1805, vol. viii, July to December 1805, viii pp., 1040 cols. Printed ... [&c., as in vol. iii]. 8vo.

*1806, vol. ix, January to June 1806, viii pp., 992 cols. Printed ... [&c., as in vol. iii]. 8vo.

*1806, vol. x, July to December 1806, vi pp., 1040 cols. Printed ... [&c., as in vol. iii]. 8vo.

*1807, vol. xi, January to June 1807, viii pp., 1160 cols. Printed ... [&c., as in vol. iii]. 8vo.

*1807, vol. xii, July to December 1807, viii pp., 1040 cols. Printed ... [&c., as in vol. iii]. 8vo.

*1808, vol. xiii, January to June 1808, viii pp., 1040 cols. Printed ... [&c., as in vol. iii]. 8vo.

*1808, vol. xiv, July to December 1808, xii pp., 1032 cols. Printed ... [&c., as in vol. iii]. 8vo.

*1809, vol. xv, January to June 1809, xii pp., 1032 cols. Printed by T. C Hansard, Peterborough Court, Fleet Street, London. [Title-page, and all from the issue of 14 January 1808, printed by Hansard.] Published by Richard Bagshaw, Brydges Street, Covent Garden, London. 8vo.

*1809, vol. xvi, July to December 1809, [6 pp.], 1040 cols. Printed ... [&c., as in vol. xv]. 8vo.

*1810, vol. xvii, January to June 1810, [6 pp.], 1040 cols. Printed ... [&c., as in vol. xv]. 8vo.

[Bound with vol. xviii:]

*1810, vol. xviii, July to December 1810, [16 pp.], 1344 cols. Printed ... [&c., as in vol. xv]. 8vo.

*1811, vol. xix, January to June 1811, [24 pp.], 1632 cols. Printed . . . [&c., as in vol. xv]. 8vo.
[Bound with vol. xx:]

*1811, vol. xx, July to December 1811, [16 pp.], 832 cols. Printed . . . [&c., as in vol. xv]. 8vo.

*1812, vol. xxi, January to June 1812, [16 pp.], 832 cols. Printed by J. M'Creery, Black Horse Court, Fleet Street, and published by R. Bagshaw, London. [Title-page, and all from the issue of 4 April, printed by J. M'Creery.] 8vo.
[Bound with vol. xxii:]

*1812, vol. xxii, July to December 1812, [16 pp.], 832 cols. Printed . . . [&c., as in vol. xxi]. 8vo.

*1813, vol. xxiii, January to June 1813, [16pp.], 832 cols. Printed . . . [&c., as in vol. xxi]. 8vo.
[Bound with vol. xxiv:]

*1813, vol. xxiv, July to December 1813, [16 pp.], 832 cols. Printed . . . [&c., as in vol. xxi]. 8vo.

*1814, vol. xxv, January to June 1814, 832 cols. Printed and published by J. Morton, 94, Strand, London [from the issue of 16 April]. 8vo.
[Bound with vol. xxvi:]

*1814, vol. xxvi, July to December 1814, [4 pp.], 804 cols. Printed and published by G. Houston, 192, Strand, London. [All the issues actually printed and published by Morton.] 8vo.

*1815, vol. xxvii, January to June 1815, [4 pp.], 832 cols. Printed . . . [&c. as in vol. xxvi, although only from issue of 21 January 1815 are these numbers printed and published by Houston—up till then Morton is the printer and publisher, despite the title-page announcement]. 8vo.
[Bound with vols. xxviii and xxix:]

*1815, vol. xxviii, July to September, 1815, [4 pp.], 419 cols. Printed and published by G. Houston, 192, Strand, London. 8vo.

*1815, vol. xxix, October to December 1815, [2 pp.], 408 cols. Printed . . . [&c., as in vol. xxviii]. 8vo.
[Vols. xxvii, xxviii, and xxix contain a number of misplaced Title and Contents pages.]

*1816, vol. xxx, January to June 1816, 832 cols. Printed and published by and for Wm. Cobbett, Jun., 192, Strand, London [from issue of 27 January 1816]. 8vo.

*1816, vol. xxxi, July to December 1816, 832 cols. Printed . . . [&c., as in vol. xxx]. 8vo.

*1817, vol. xxxii [Part I]. January to March 1817, 416 cols.+32 cols. Printed and published by and for William Jackson, 11, Newcastle Street, and 192, Strand, London. [According to the title-page; actually the issue for 4 January 1817 was printed and published by Wm. Cobbett, Junior, and thenceforth, concluding with 29 March, all the numbers were printed by W. Molineux, 5, Bream's Buildings, Chancery Lane, and published by W. Cobbett, Junior. Only the last, the 'farewell number' of 5 April 1817, was published by Jackson.] 8vo.

[12 April to 5 July 1817—none issued in England.]

*1817, vol. 32 [Part II]. July to December 1817, 'Cobbett's Weekly Political Pamphlet', cols. 449–1216, printed and published by Wm. Jackson, 11, Newcastle Street, and 192, Strand, London. 8vo.

*1818, vol. 33, January to June 1818, 'Cobbett's Weekly Political Register'. [This title again used till 1821.] iv, 730 cols. Printed and published by and for Wm. Jackson . . . 192, Strand, London. 8vo.

[21 March and 2 May 1818—none issued.]   .

*1819, vol. 34, August 1818 to August 1819, iv, 1136 cols. Printed for and published by Thomas Dolby, 34, Wardour Street, London. 8vo. [According to the title-page; actually Dolby published only from the issue of 6 March 1819.]

[27 June to 15 August 1818, 17 October to 14 November 1818, 29 May to 14 August 1819—none issued, but see below *re* the last.]

*1820, vol. 35, August 1819 to January 1820, [iv], 788 cols. Printed and sold by William Benbow, 269, Strand, London. [According to the title-page; actually all of these numbers were published by Dolby.] 8vo.

[One of the issues omitted from vol. 34—14 August 1819—was included here. 16 October and 20 and 27 November, 1819—none issued.]

*1820, vol. 36, February to July 1820, [iv], 1320 cols. Printed and sold by William Benbow, 269, Strand, London. [According to the title-page; actually, until the issue of 8 April 1820, the publisher was again Wm. Cobbett, Junior; from 15 April to 27 May he was Charles Clement, 269, Strand, and from then on, Benbow.] 8vo.

[26 February to 18 March 1820—none issued.]

*1820, vol. 37, July to December 1820, [iv], 1704 cols. Printed and sold by William Benbow, 269, Strand, London. 8vo.

*1821, vol. 38, January to March 1821, [iv], 920 cols. Printed by C. Clement and published by John M. Cobbett, 1, Clement's Inn, London. 8vo. [According to the title-page; actually J. M. Cobbett and Clement succeeded Benbow from the issue of 20 January 1821.]

*1821, vol. 39, April to July 1821, iv, 1080 cols. Printed by C. Clement and published by John M. Cobbett, 1, Clement's Inn, London. 8vo.

[From 14 April 1821 until 1828, 'Cobbett's Weekly Register'.]

*1821, vol. 40, July to December 1821. [4 pp.], 1600 cols. [+8 cols. *Index*]. Printed . . . [&c., as in vol. 39]. 8vo.

*1822, vol. 41, January to March 1822, [2 pp.], 830 cols. [+4 cols. *Index*]. Printed and published by C. Clement, 183, Fleet Street, London.

8vo. [According to the title-page; actually Clement was the publisher from the issue of 23 February 1822.]

*1822, vol. 42, April to June 1822, [6 cols. *Index*], 832 cols. Printed and published by C. Clement, 183, Fleet Street, London. 8vo.

*1822, vol. 43, July to September 1822, [6 cols. *Index*], 832 cols. Printed . . . [&c. as in vol. 42]. 8vo.

*1822, vol. 44, October to December 1822, [2 pp.], 832 cols. [+6 cols. *Index*]. Printed and published by J. M. Cobbett, 183, Fleet Street, London. 8vo.

*1823, vol. 45, January to March 1823, [6 pp. *Index*], 832 cols. Printed . . . [&c., as in vol. 44]. 8vo.

*1823, vol. 46, April to June 1823, [2 cols.], 832 cols. [+6 pp. *Index*]. Printed . . . [&c., as in vol. 44]. 8vo.

*1823, vol. 47, July to September 1823, [2 cols.], iv pp., 832 cols. Printed . . . [&c., as in vol. 44]. 8vo.

*1823, vol. 48, October to December 1823, [6 cols. *Index*], 832 cols. [+ 4 pp. advts.]. Printed . . . [&c., as in vol. 44]. 8vo.

*1824, vol. 49, January to March 1824, [6 cols. *Index*], 832 cols. Printed and published by C. Clement, 183, Fleet Street, London. [According to the title-page; actually, only the numbers from 7 February 1824 were published by Clement.] 8vo.

*1824, vol. 50. April to June 1824, [6 cols. *Index*], 832 cols. Printed and published by C. Clement, 183, Fleet Street, London. 8vo.

*1824, vol. 51, July to September 1824, [6 cols. *Index*], 832 cols. Printed . . . [&c., as in vol. 50]. 8vo.

*1824, vol. 52, October to December 1824, [6 cols. *Index*], 832 cols. Printed . . . [&c., as in vol. 50]. 8vo.

*1825, vol. 53, January to March 1825, [6 cols. *Index*], 832 cols. Printed . . . [&c., as in vol. 50]. 8vo.

*1825, vol. 54, April to June 1825, [6 cols. *Index*], 832 cols. Printed . . . [&c., as in vol. 50]. 8vo.

*1825, vol. 55, July to September 1825, [6 cols. *Index*], 768 cols.+48 pp. *Big O. and Sir Glory* . . . . Printed . . . [&c., as in vol. 50, but *Big O. and Sir Glory* printed and published by John Dean, 183, Fleet Street, London.] 8vo.

[Last number of *Register* missing (cols. 769–832).]

*1825, vol. 56, October to December 1825, [6 cols. *Index*], 832 cols. Printed and published by W. Cobbett, 183, Fleet Street, London. [According to the title-page; actually it was published by Cobbett from the issue of 8 October 1825—No. 2.] 8vo.

*1826, vol. 57, January to March 1826, [4 cols. *Contents*], 832 cols. [8 cols. *Index*]. Printed and published by W. Cobbett, 183, Fleet Street, London. 8vo.

*1826, vol. 58, April to June 1826, [2 cols. *Contents*], 832 cols. [8 cols. *Index*]. Printed . . . [&c., as in vol. 57]. 8vo.

*1826, vol. 59, July to September 1826, [2 cols. *Contents*], 832 cols. [8 cols. *Index*]. Printed . . . [&c., as in vol. 57]. 8vo.

*1826, vol. 60, October to December 1826, [2 cols. *Contents*], 832 cols. Printed . . . [&c., as in vol. 57]. 8vo.

*1827, vol. 61, January to March 1827, [2 cols. *Contents*], 832 cols. [8 cols. *Index*]. Printed . . . [&c., as in vol. 57]. 8vo.

*1827, vol. 62, April to June 1827, [2 cols. *Contents*], 832 cols. [4 cols. *Index*]. Printed . . . [&c., as in vol. 57]. 8vo.

*1827, vol. 63, June to September 1827, [2 cols. *Contents*], 832 cols. [8 cols. *Index*]. Printed . . . [&c., as in vol. 57]. 8vo.

*1827, vol. 64, September to December 1827, [2 cols. *Contents*], 896 cols.+iv pp. Printed . . . [&c., as in vol. 57]. 8vo.

*1828, vol. 65, January to June 1828, [2 cols. *Contents*], 832 cols.+iv pp. Printed . . . [&c., as in vol. 57]. [From issue of January 1828—No. 1— "Cobbett's Weekly Political Register".] 8vo.

*1828, vol. 66, July to December 1828, [2 cols. *Contents*], 832 cols.+iv pp. Printed . . . [&c., as in vol. 57]. 8vo.

  * [Additional copy of No. 18, 1 November, sewn with *The Farmer's Wife's Friend*.]

*1829, vol. 67, January to June 1829, [2 cols. *Contents*], 832 cols. Printed and published by the Author at 11, Bolt Court, Fleet Street, London. 8vo.

  * [Additional copy of No. 9, 28 February 1829, sewn with *The Farmer's Wife's Friend*.]

*1829, vol. 68, July to December 1829, [2 cols. *Contents*], 832 cols. Printed . . . [&c., as in vol. 67]. 8vo.

*1830, vol. 69, January to June 1829, [2 cols. *Contents*], 842 cols. Printed . . . [&c., as in vol. 67]. 8vo.

*1830, vol. 70, July to December 1830, [2 cols. *Contents*], 1120 cols. Printed . . . [&c., as in vol. 67]. 8vo.

*1831, vol. 71, January to March 1831, [2 cols. *Contents*], 832 cols. Printed . . . [&c., as in vol. 67]. 8vo.

*1831, vol. 72, April to June 1831, [2 cols. *Contents*], 793 cols. Printed . . ; [&c., as in vol. 67]. 8vo.

*1831, vol. 73, July to September 1831, [2 cols. *Contents*], 832 cols. Printed . . . [&c., as in vol. 67]. 8vo.

*1831, vol. 74, October to December 1831, [2 cols. *Contents*], 832 cols. Printed . . . [&c., as in vol. 67]. 8vo.

*1832, vol. 75, December 1831 to March 1832. [2 cols. *Contents*], 896 cols. Printed . . . [&c., as in vol. 67]. 8vo.

*1832, vol. 76, April to June 1832, [2 cols. *Contents*], 832 cols. Printed . . . [&c., as in vol. 67]. 8vo.

*1832, vol. 77, July to September 1832, [2 cols. *Contents*], 832 cols. Printed . . . [&c., as in vol. 67]. 8vo.

*1832, vol. 78, October to December 1832, [2 cols. *Contents*], 832 cols. Printed . . . [&c., as in vol. 67]. 8vo.

*1833, vol. 79, January to March 1833, [2 cols. *Contents*], 832 cols. Printed . . . [&c., as in vol. 67]. 8vo.

*1833, vol. 80, April to June 1833, [2 cols. *Contents*], 832 cols. Printed . . . [&c., as in vol. 67]. 8vo.

*1833, vol. 81, July to September 1833, [2 cols. *Contents*], 832 cols. Printed . . . [&c., as in vol. 67]. 8vo.

*1833, vol. 82, October to December 1833, [2 cols. *Contents*], 828 cols. Printed . . . [&c., as in vol. 67]. 8vo.

*1834, vol. 83, January to March 1834, [2 cols. *Contents*], 828 cols. Printed . . . [&c., as in vol. 67]. 8vo.
[Bound with vol. 84:]

*1834, vol. 84, April to June 1834, [2 cols. *Contents*], 828 cols. Printed . . . [&c., as in vol. 67]. 8vo.

*1834, vol. 85, July to September 1834, [2 cols. *Contents*], 828 cols. Printed . . . [&c., as in vol. 67]. 8vo.
[Bound with vol. 86:]

*1834, vol. 86, October to December 1834, [2 cols. *Contents*], 828 cols. Printed . . . [&c., as in vol. 67]. 8vo.

*[Additional copies of No. 3, 18 October; No. 4, 25 October; No. 5, 1 November; No. 6, 8 November; No. 7, 15 November; and No. 8, 22 November 1834, bound in a volume entitled 'Cobbett's Trial. Normandy Farm, &c.' on the spine.] 8vo.

*1835, vol. 87, January to March 1835, [2 cols. *Contents*], 828 cols. Printed . . . [&c., as in vol. 67]. 8vo.
[Bound with vols. 88 and 89:]

*1835, vol. 88, April to June 1835, [2 cols. *Contents*], 828 cols. Printed . . . [&c., as in vol. 67]. 8vo.
* [Additional copy of issue of 13 June 1835, No. 11, bound in a volume entitled 'Cobbett's Register & Lectures' on the spine.] 8vo.

*1835, vol. 89, July to September 1835, [2 pp. MS. *Contents*], 624 cols. Printed . . . [&c., as in vol. 67 to the issue of 8 August 1835, No. 6, when William Cobbett, Junior, continued publication from 167, Fleet Street]. 8vo. [Ends with issue of 12 September 1835, No. 11; for continuation, see No. 12 below.]

*[Additional copy of No. 2, 11 July 1835, and No. 3, 18 July 1835, bound in a volume entitled 'Cobbett's Register & Lectures'; additional

copy of No. 6, 8 August; No. 7, 15 August; No. 8, 22 August; No. 9, 29 August; and No. 10, 5 September 1835, bound in a volume entitled 'Cobbett's Trial. Normandy Farm, &c.' on the spine.]

*[1836 (January),] 32 pp. 'Renewal of Cobbett's Register . . . The History of Normandy Farm.' Printed at 11, Bishop's Court, Old Bailey, and published at 21, Lowther Arcade, Westminster, by William Cobbett. [Bound in a volume entitled 'Cobbett's Trial. Normandy Farm, &c.' on the spine.] 8vo.

*1836, No. 12, 20 February 1836, cols. 625–688. Printed . . . [&c., as in '. . . History of Normandy Farm' above. 8vo. [Bound in a volume entitled 'Cobbett's Trial. Normandy Farm, &c.' on the spine.]

The *Political Register*, Cobbett's weekly periodical which he established in 1802, and which he conducted until his death in 1835, ranks as one of his greatest achievements. He wrote a great part of it himself, overcoming even such obstacles as prison or exile, and under his hand (although there were frequent changes in publisher and printer until 1821—see list above), it became a pioneer of Radical journalism, and a power to be feared. The *Register* was begun in January 1802, when Cobbett was still a Tory and a protégé of William Windham. Windham and his friends had advanced the necessary funds, as they had done in the case of the unlucky *Porcupine* (q.v.), recognizing, however, that their bright young recruit, who had already won his spurs in America, loved his independence too much to become a mere hack (see *Political Register*, 4 January 1817). His first efforts, unlike those of later years, must have pleased his backers. The *Register*, begun as a fortnightly with only 300 subscribers (*Political Register*, 31 December 1803), became a weekly with the third number. In 1803 (only), *Le Mercure Anglois*, a French version of parts of the paper, appeared in London; by 1804 the *Register* had attained a circulation of 4,000 (ibid.), and in 1806 and 1809 sales were still rising (1806—Bodl. MS. Engl. Hist. c. 33; B.M. Add. MSS. 37853, f. 197; 1809—Smith, *William Cobbett* . . . ii. 102, possibly 'to nearly 6,000'). Cobbett had then dropped the weighty *Supplement* of Parliamentary Debates and other political information attached to the first four half-yearly volumes (he began printing the *Parliamentary Debates*—q.v.—as a separate work in 1804), and in 1809 the price, which had usually been 10*d*., was raised to 1*s*. (the stamp tax and the cost of paper had both risen steeply). Cobbett had now parted company with his old political friends and had begun his progress as a Radical, a change reflected in the *Register*. In 1810 an article on flogging in the army, published in the previous year, brought him a prison sentence and heavy fines, but the *Register*, as well as other works, were increasingly distributed (see **Paper against Gold*). Indeed, for nearly nine months (12 September 1810–22 June 1811) it was now issued twice a week, the price of each number still a shilling, and the paper much more completely under Cobbett's own control after he had quarrelled with his old manager, John Wright (see the **Book of Wonders*, 1821). This improvement in circulation seems to have been checked as the Reform Movement declined after the rigorous suppression of the riots of 1811 and 1812. Moreover, foreign affairs, at least until 1815, crowded out the Reform question, and Cobbett, now more Radical than ever, was constantly losing some of his middle-class subscribers, although at the close of 1815 he spoke with praise of 'perhaps a hundred clubs' where workmen met to hear the paper read (*Political Register*, 23 December 1815). In 1816 *The Times* rashly professed surprise to hear that the *Register* still appeared. Cobbett retorted in the same year by turning to the working class with a twopenny *Register*, produced alongside the regular stamped number (since 2 September 1851 this had been sold at 1s. 0½d.). The success of the cheap *Register* was immediate and overwhelming (see [84] for the first of these—the **Address to the Journeymen and Labourers*, 2 November 1816). Aided by liberal discounts to sellers, it rocketed up to a circulation of forty to fifty thousand copies a week, despite the many semi-official obstacles put in its way (see **Address to the Journeymen and Labourers*) and the promotion of 'loyal *Registers*' (see **Anti-Cobbett*). Cobbett's influence was now tremendously high, and his journal, with a circulation many times that of any other newspaper, brought him an income of £1,500 a year (*Political Register*, 26 July 1817) and penetrated into every meeting-place of the people from the pious Sunday school to the convivial public-house (Home Office Papers, 42/156, 159). Cobbett was not allowed to enjoy this triumph overlong, and a determined effort was now made to crush the *Register* and shackle its editor (see **Mr. Cobbett's Taking Leave* [89]). Humbler individuals were, of course, more savagely harried. The parson-magistrate who informed Sidmouth that he had flogged two distributors of the *Register* in a Shropshire village (Home Office Papers, ibid.) may have been exceptional even for the time, but undoubtedly such repression had its effect. If a spy's story is to be believed, sales had fallen to 8,000 a week in October 1817 (Home Office Papers, 42/170). But it was no easy task to silence a man like Cobbett. Even the suspension of Habeas Corpus, his enforced flight to America (where an *American Political Register* [83]q.v.—had already been tried), and all the repression of the time, failed to cripple the *Register*. Cobbett now conducted it from across the Atlantic, sending his articles home to his publisher, and, apart from the first three months' gap (12 April to 5 July 1817), rarely missing an issue. (Cobbett's interest in America persisted all his life, and in 1832 a New York *Register* was established—see *Political Register*, 30 June 1832.) On 20 November 1819, after an absence of two and a half years, he returned to England, and a week later the Government introduced the first of the notorious 'Six Acts', all six of which became law in the first week of 1820. It was the last of these which succeeded where other methods of repression had failed. Entitled *An Act to subject certain publications to the duties of stamps upon newspapers* . . . (60 Geo. III, cap. 9) it imposed the newspaper tax of fourpence a copy on all pamphlets and papers of a certain size published more often than once a month and costing less than sixpence. The large circulations so daringly built up now melted rapidly away. On 6 January 1820 the last number of the old 'Twopenny Trash' appeared, and in the following week the price was raised to sixpence. Cobbett himself later complained that the Act had brought down his sales to perhaps 'a tenth part' of their former state (*Twopenny Trash*, July 1830). The stamped *Register*, abandoned since Cobbett's departure for America, was reintroduced in April 1821 (see *Political Register*, 28 April 1821), and at last, alongside the sixpenny edition, a more expensive paper sold at a shilling was available for free delivery through the post—a privilege associated with the stamp. From this time onwards Cobbett made many energetic but not altogether successful efforts to recover the lost circulation of his twopenny *Register*. He tried and failed to establish a daily paper, *Cobbett's Evening Post* (it ran from 29 January to 1 April 1820, see [105]); he threatened a Dublin plagiarist, who printed a *Weekly Register*, with empty threats of prosecution (*Political Register*, 3 August 1822, 27 September 1823, 25 December 1824—an earlier *Ulster Register* appears to have had his blessing); he argued with the Stamp Office over his insertion of news (*Political Register*, 24 November 1827); he constantly printed lists of newsmen from whom the paper could be obtained (e.g. *Political Register*, 8, 15 December 1827); and he tried unsuccessfully to interest enough of his readers in a proposal to republish the whole of the *Political Register* from its commencement in a cheap edition (*Political Register*, 2 February 1828). Nevertheless, Cobbett's immense political activity in this period won him many faithful adherents and new readers. So also did the many cheap reprints from the *Register*, which, like the *Poor Man's Friend*, 1826–7 ([144]), appeared in part in its columns. Such reprints appeared as long as the *Register* lasted (see Index of Titles). In 1828 Cobbett gave up his unstamped sixpenny paper completely and issued only the taxed *Register*. He now increased its contents whilst maintaining its size, and raised the price to sevenpence, explaining that he had rejected the more profitable course of a shilling paper, since that would have excluded many poorer readers (*Political Register*, 29 December 1827). In fact, the stamped shilling copy had then been finding only 400 readers a week (*Political Register*, 1 December 1827). The strength of the *Register* still lay in the many obscure clubs, or 'great societies', whose members, as the Attorney-General complained at Cobbett's trial in 1831, clubbed together to read it (see *Full... Report*, 1831 [182], and *State Trials...*, n.s. ii. 855). Between 1830 and 1832 Cobbett made another attempt to recapture his success with the cheap *Registers*. This was the publication of the *Twopenny Trash* (q.v.), a reprint of some of his best articles from the *Register*, together with original numbers, which were very widely read. Shortly before their introduction Cobbett implied that the circulation of the *Register* was then about 5,000 a week (in an appeal for a £10,000 election fund—*Political Register*, 10 April 1830). In 1830 (30 October), during the 'rural war' and later, Cobbett issued only the one stamped shilling *Register*, and at his trial in 1831 he cited this fact as proof that he was not seeking to incite the labourers to acts of violence and arson. Actually he had also doubled its size, and when in 1831 (8 January) he raised the price to 1s. 2d., he gave as a reason the inclusion of work on which he had spent, or was going to spend 'two years of ... enormous labour' (*Political Register*, 8 January 1831). This was in part a reference to Cobbett's proposed autobiography—a swan song with which he planned to close the

Register in a further two years. It was a promise already once postponed, destined to be renewed again, and yet never fulfilled, for Cobbett, like a true war-horse, died in full harness in 1835, still the editor of the *Register*. His paper did not long survive him. His sons, especially the eldest, William Cobbett, junior, tried hard to continue it, but lacking their father's journalistic ability and faced with many financial difficulties, including William's bankruptcy in 1836, they managed to maintain only an intermittent flickering life in the *Register* (see the last number, 20 February 1836, above).

[53]
1802
LETTER TO LORD AUCKLAND ON THE ABUSES IN THE GENERAL POST OFFICE.

By *WILLIAM COBBETT*

Reprinted from *Cobbett's Annual [Political] Register*, 27 November 1803.

A sharp complaint by Cobbett addressed to Lord Auckland (1744–1814), the Postmaster-General, alleging that the circulation of *The Porcupine* (q.v.) had been hampered in 1801 by unfair Post Office charges. Auckland offered him no redress, and Cobbett published their correspondence in the *Register* (27 November 1802) and reprinted the article as a pamphlet.

[54]
1802
A TREATISE ON THE CULTURE AND MANAGEMENT OF FRUIT TREES, IN WHICH A NEW METHOD OF PRUNING AND TRAINING IS FULLY DESCRIBED. TOGETHER WITH OBSERVATIONS ON THE DISEASES, DEFECTS, AND INJURIES IN ALL KINDS OF FRUIT AND FOREST TREES; AS ALSO, AN ACCOUNT OF A PARTICULAR METHOD OF CURE, MADE PUBLIC BY ORDER OF THE BRITISH GOVERNMENT ... BY WILLIAM FORSYTH. TO WHICH ARE ADDED, AN INTRODUCTION AND NOTES, ADAPTING THE RULES OF

THE TREATISE TO THE CLIMATES AND SEASONS
OF THE UNITED STATES OF AMERICA. BY
WILLIAM COBBETT.

*By WILLIAM FORSYTH; introduction and notes by WILLIAM
COBBETT*

[1802–18, London, 1st–6th editions (B.M.); 1802, *Introduction*, &c., by
Cobbett, Philadelphia (L. of C.); 1803, '*An Epitome of Mr. Forsyth's
Treatise*', Philadelphia (L. of C.); 1803, Albany (L. of C.).]

Cobbett added an introduction and notes, intended for the American
reader, to the Philadelphia edition of this popular *Treatise* by
William Forsyth (1737–1804), a superintendent of the Royal
Gardens. It was Cobbett's first effort to provide advice for agri-
culturalists, a labour he frequently undertook in later years (see
A Year's Residence in the United States, 1818).

[55]   1802

NARRATIVE OF THE TAKING OF THE IN-
VINCIBLE STANDARD . . . .

By WILLIAM COBBETT

Reprinted from *Cobbett's Annual [Political] Register*, 25 December 1802.

Cobbett's eulogistic account of the bravery of Antoine Lutz, a
French private soldier of the Queen's Regiment, who was said
to have captured a Napoleonic standard single-handed. Cobbett's
account was published in the *Register* (25 December 1802) and
reprinted as a pamphlet, to the great indignation of the officers of
the 42nd Royal Highland Regiment, who revived the story of
The Soldier's Friend (see [1]) and accused Lutz of having stolen
the trophy from a wounded Highlander (see their *Invincible
Standard* . . . 1803, B.M.).

[56]   1803

THE EMPIRE OF GERMANY DIVIDED INTO
DEPARTMENTS UNDER THE PREFECTURE OF
THE ELECTOR OF * * * * * BY JEAN GABRIEL

PELTIER. TO WHICH IS PREFIXED, A MEMOIR ON
THE POLITICAL AND MILITARY STATE OF THE
CONTINENT, WRITTEN BY THE SAME AUTHOR.
TRANSLATED FROM THE FRENCH, BY WILLIAM
COBBETT.

By *JEAN GABRIEL PELTIER; translated by WILLIAM
COBBETT*

[1803, London (Bodl.).]

A translation by Cobbett of *L'Empire Germanique divisée en
Departments* . . ., a work attributed to Jean Gabriel Peltier (1760?–
1825), a French *émigré*-journalist in London who, much to
Cobbett's annoyance, was tried and found guilty (21 February
1803) of a libel on Napoleon. Peltier was not called up for judge-
ment, however, and when the short uneasy Peace of Amiens was
abruptly terminated, nothing more was heard of the charge.
Cobbett's edition included his own preface dated 18 January 1803
and also the translation of a *Memoir*, written in 1801 by Peltier;
this *Memoir* he also published in the *Supplement* to vol. ii of his
**Annual [Political] Register* (see B.M. Add. MSS. 37853, f. 68,
**Annual [Political] Register*, vols. ii and iii, 1802, 1803). *The Empire
of Germany* was issued by E. Harding, who had taken over Cobbett's
business in Pall Mall; a week earlier John Stockdale had published
another translation, *The Germanic Empire reduced into Departments* . . ., which seems to have been taken from a French translation of a German work first printed in Hamburg.

[57]   1803
LE MERCURE ANGLOIS.

Edited by WILLIAM COBBETT

[Monthly periodical; 16 February–? May 1803, London.]

A French version of parts of the *Political Register* issued monthly
in London from 16 February 1803, but given up after a few issues
(see **Political Register*).

1803

FOUR LETTERS TO THE CHANCELLOR OF THE EXCHEQUER ON THE FINANCES; EXPOSING THE DECEPTION OF HIS FINANCIAL STATEMENTS AND SHOWING THE FATAL TENDENCY OF THE PEACE OF AMIENS WITH RESPECT TO THE PUBLIC CREDIT. SUBMITTED TO THE STOCK-HOLDERS OF GREAT BRITAIN.

By WILLIAM COBBETT

[1803, London (Library Company, Philadelphia).]

Reprinted from *Cobbett's Annual [Political] Register*, 9, 16, 23, 30 April 1803.

Four letters to Addington reprinted from the *Register* (9–30 April 1803) and republished by Harding, in which Cobbett attacked the claim that the Peace of Amiens had brought large savings in public expenditure.

[59] # 1803

IMPORTANT / CONSIDERATIONS / FOR THE / PEOPLE OF THIS KINGDOM. /

Anonymous [By WILLIAM COBBETT]

Published in the *Political Register*, 30 July, 1803.

*[1803], 16 pp. Published by the Association for preserving Liberty and Property, sold by J. Downes, Temple Bar; J. Spragg, King Street; ... J. Asperne, Cornhill; and J. Hatchard, Piccadilly, London. 'Price 2d., or 1s. 6d. per Doz.' 12 mo. [This copy is bound with two other pamphlets in a volume entitled 'Answer to Paine—Suisse 1802—Reeves' on the spine.]

This violent denunciation of the French was written by Cobbett after the Peace of Amiens, which he violently opposed (see *A Collection of Facts* [50]), had been shattered by Napoleon's renewal of the war. The pamphlet appeared in the *Political Register* (30 July 1803) without any indication of its origin. In the same month it was issued by the Government, headed with the Royal arms, and sent to the officiating minister of every English and Welsh parish for display and distribution in the churches. It was ascribed to many authors, among them John Reeves, whose Association republished it in this edition, but Cobbett did not disclose his authorship until nearly six years had passed (see *Political Register*, 17 June 1809).

THE / POLITICAL PROTEUS. / A VIEW / OF THE / PUBLIC CHARACTER AND CONDUCT / OF / R. B. SHERIDAN, Esq. / AS EXHIBITED IN / I. Ten Letters addressed to him; / II. Selections from his Parliamentary Speeches from the Commencement / of the French Revolution; / III. Selections from his Speeches at the Whig Club, and at other Public / Meetings. /

By WILLIAM COBBETT

Taken largely from the *Political Register of 1803.

> *1804, 388 pp. Printed by Cox, Son, and Baylis, 75, Great Queen Street, London; sold by Budd, Crown and Mitre, Pall Mall; Bagshaw, Bow Street, London; Mundell, Edinburgh; Mercier, Dublin; Morgan, Philadelphia; and Sarjeant, New York. 8vo.

In 1803, when Cobbett was associated with Windham as an enemy of Reform, the latter had risen in the Commons (4 August 1803) to defend Cobbett and his paper, the *Political Register*. The attack had come from Sheridan, who in a debate on the National Defence Bill had insinuated that the editor had incited a mutinous spirit in the Navy and had laboured to produce a 'national bankruptcy'. This was partly a revival of the old charges concerning *The Soldier's Friend* ([1]), and it had drawn from Windham, an opponent of the Government, a eulogy in which he had declared that Cobbett deserved 'a statue of gold'. Cobbett himself, in a series of nine letters (12 August 1803–21 November 1803) in the *Political Register*, replied to such effect that Thomas Sheridan (the dramatist-politician's son), according to his own account, vainly challenged him to a duel, and to the sound of a furious journal war Cobbett claimed to have thrashed John Heriot, editor of the *True Briton* (see *Political Register*, 20 August 1803, and the *True Briton*, 15–22 August 1803). The nine letters, together with another (15 March 1803) from the *Political Register* and extracts from Sheridan's earlier speeches in favour of Reform and the French Revolution, made up this volume, which was published in January 1804.

[61]   # 1804

COBBETT'S / PARLIAMENTARY DEBATES, / . . .

[and]

[62]

COBBETT'S / Parliamentary History / OF / ENGLAND. / FROM THE NORMAN CONQUEST, IN 1066 / TO / THE YEAR, 1803. / FROM WHICH LAST-MENTIONED EPOCH IT IS CONTINUED / DOWNWARDS IN THE WORK ENTITLED, / 'COBBETT'S PARLIAMENTARY DEBATES.' /

> *Edited jointly by WILLIAM COBBETT and JOHN WRIGHT until 1811; thereafter by JOHN WRIGHT.* [In progress as Hansard.]

Cobbett's Parliamentary Debates
> *1804–14, vols. 1–27; vol. 1 printed by Cox and Baylis, vol. 2 printed [also] by J. J. Brettell, vols. 3–9 printed by J. Brettell, vols. 10–27 printed by T. C. Hansard; vols. 1–17 published by R. Bagshaw . . . ., vols. 18–27, published by Longman, Hurst, Rees, Orme & Browne . . . London. Vols. 23–27 entitled *The Parliamentary Debates* . . . .

Cobbett's Parliamentary History. [Complete]
> *1806–20, vols. 1–36; vols. 1–36 printed by T. C. Hansard; vols. 1–7 published by R. Bagshaw . . ., vols. 8–36 published by Longman . . . London. Vols. 13–36 entitled *The Parliamentary History* . . . .

On 7 June 1804 Cobbett published the first volume of his *Parliamentary Debates*, a report of the speeches in the previous session of Parliament. This was the first attempt to provide a complete report of parliamentary proceedings, and it has survived to this day. In 1812, when Cobbett was worried by debt after a serious quarrel with his fellow-editor, John Wright (see *Paper Against Gold*), he sold the publication to T. C. Hansard (1776–1833), who had printed the work since 1808. In 1818 the reports became known as *Hansard's Parliamentary Debates*, and they continue today as the more familiarly known official *Hansard*. In 1806 Cobbett began the publication of the *Parliamentary History*, a companion series and a vast compilation of the available records of political proceedings from 1066 up to 1803, the date at which the *Parliamentary Debates* began (for the sources used in the *History*, see H. H. Bellot, *Bulletin of the Institute of Historical Research*, x, 1932–3, 171–7).

This, too (like another venture, Cobbett's [later, T. B. Howell's] *Complete Collection of State Trials*—q.v.), passed out of his hands in 1812. Although most of the actual work involved in these massive undertakings was done by Wright and others, Cobbett deserves much credit for the initiative and public spirit which rescued many public documents from oblivion and established a work which has become a national institution.

[63]   1805

COBBETT'S / SPIRIT OF THE / PUBLIC JOURNALS. / VOL. I. / FOR THE YEAR / 1804. /

Edited by WILLIAM COBBETT

*[1805], xx, 1220 cols. [1320 cols.]. Printed by J. Brettell, Marshall Street, Golden Square and published by J. Budd, Pall Mall, R. Bagshaw, Bow Street, Covent Garden . . . London. 8vo.

This was a collection of over 450 articles extracted from the leading English, American, Irish, and French newspapers in 1804. Cobbett admitted that the title he had chosen was not a new one (*Political Register*, 26 January 1805), but claimed that his work was far superior to earlier undertakings in France and England in point of size, seriousness, and impartiality. It was published on 1 February 1805, 'elegantly half-bound in Russia leather' at the price of £1. 7s., and although Cobbett hoped that it would prove as 'productive of great utility' as its companions the *Political Register* and the *Parliamentary Debates*, it failed to win wide support and was not continued.

[64]   1806

STRICTURES / ON / COBBET'S [*sic*] UNMANLY OBSERVATIONS, / RELATIVE TO THE / DELICATE INVESTIGATION: / AND / A REPLY TO THE ANSWER / TO / AN ADMONITORY LETTER / TO / H.R.H. the Prince of Wales, / . . . .

By the Author of the Admonitory Letter

*1806, 32 pp. Printed by Dewick and Clarke, Aldersgate Street, London, for Tipper and Richards, Leadenhall Street, London. 'Price Two Shillings.' 8vo.

Cobbett, the passionate defender of Caroline against the Prince of Wales in 1813 and 1820, was cautious in embracing her cause in 1806 when the 'delicate investigation' was first undertaken. His desire to await more evidence and his attacks on the *Morning Post*, then prominent in defence of the Princess, roused the writer of this anonymous pamphlet, who abused Cobbett as a 'vain contemptible slanderer' (see also *An Admonitory Letter to The Prince of Wales*, 1806—by the same author—and '*The Book*', 1813, Cole Collection).

1806
[65]

A / LETTER / TO / MR. COBBETT / ON / HIS OPINIONS / RESPECTING THE / SLAVE-TRADE. /

By the REV. THOMAS CLARKE

*1806, 114 pp. [+2 pp. publisher's advts.]. Printed for J. Hatchard, 190, Piccadilly, opposite Albany House, London. 8vo. [This copy is bound with other works by the same author in a volume entitled 'Clarke's Sermons' on spine, the others being *A Letter to the Proclamation Society and the Society for the Suppression of Vice*, 1805, 36 pp., and *Sermons*, and *Addresses*, 1812, 84 pp., 19 pp.; the volume has a title-page dated 1812 and an *Advertisement* of 4 pages by the author's son, Richard Clarke.]

The author, a prebendary of Hereford, upbraided Cobbett for his support of the Slave Trade and expressed his strong disapprobation of negro slavery. Cobbett had recently treated a private letter of his somewhat contemptuously in the *Register* (9 March 1805), and the author, whilst noticeably exercising forbearance, deplored his opponent's wide influence. Cobbett's attitude to negro slavery was straightforward enough. In 1801 he had defended the Slave Trade because its abolition would have been prejudicial to British commerce (*Political Register*, *Supp.*, p. 917), and in 1807, while he no longer defended the trade, he thought it was a matter about which no 'reflecting man' cared (*Political Register*, 2 May 1807). From the first he condemned what he saw as the hypocrisy of those who sighed for the blacks abroad and ignored the cries of the 'factory slaves' at home (see [118], note to *American Slave Trade*, 1822; also his 'Letter to Wilberforce', *Political Register*, 30 August 1823), and he was always contemptuous of those who saw a common humanity between white and black. Subsequently Cobbett supported the emancipation of negro slaves in the British Colonies (although without compensation to the slave-owners), but he retained to the end his fierce dislike of 'canting saints' like Wilberforce.

[66]   1806

MR. PAULL'S / LETTER / TO / Lord Viscount Folkestone; *As it appeared in* / THE POLITICAL REGISTER. /

By JAMES PAULL

*[1806], 16 pp. Printed and published by W. Glindon, 48, Rupert Street, Haymarket, London. (Price threepence.) 8vo.

This letter, exposing the misgovernment of India, observed by the writer, James Paull (1770–1808), whilst resident as a trader in Lucknow, appeared in Cobbett's *Political Register* on 25 October 1806. A few weeks later the author, like Cobbett a new-comer to the Reformers, unsuccessfully contested Westminster as a Radical. In the following year he stood again together with Sir Francis Burdett (1770–1844), but quarrelled violently with his fellow candidate and retired after both had been seriously wounded in a duel—Paull dangerously. By then Cobbett had transferred his support, as had most of the other members of the committee, to the two successful Radicals, Burdett and Cochrane.

[67]   1809

COBBETT'S / COMPLETE COLLECTION OF / State Trials / AND / PROCEEDINGS FOR HIGH TREASON AND OTHER / CRIMES AND MISDEMEANOURS / FROM THE / EARLIEST PERIOD TO THE PRESENT TIME. /

Edited until 1812 by WILLIAM COBBETT, JOHN WRIGHT, and THOMAS BAYLEY HOWELL, thereafter by T. B. HOWELL

[1809–26, 33 vols., London.]
*1810, vol. viii only. [This volume has the title-page and contents page of vol. vii at the front; it is also incorrectly entitled 'VII' on the spine.] [viii], 1576 cols. Printed by T. C. Hansard, Peterborough-court, Fleet Street, published by R. Bagshaw, Brydges-Street, Covent Garden, London. . . . 8vo.

*1814, vol. xx, *A Complete Collection . . . with Notes . . . by T. B. Howell . . .*, [vi], 1400 cols. Printed by T. C. Hansard . . . for Longman, &c., London. 8vo.

This series was begun in 1809 under the nominal joint editorship of Cobbett, John Wright, and Thomas Bayley Howell (1768–1815), although the latter was actually engaged as editor. Howell, a barrister, incurred Cobbett's suspicion, chiefly because of his 'college insolence' (B.M. Add. MSS. 22907, ff. 87–88), but he remained in this position until Cobbett's break with Wright in 1812 (see *Cobbett's Parliamentary Debates and Parliamentary History*), when he acquired control of the publication and renamed it *Howell's . . . State Trials*. In this form it was continued by him and his son, Thomas Jones Howell (d. 1858), until 1826.

[68]   1809

ELEMENTS OF REFORM, / OR / AN ACCOUNT OF / THE MOTIVES AND INTENTIONS / OF THE / ADVOCATES / FOR / PARLIAMENTARY REFORMA- TION. /

By WILLIAM COBBETT; edited anonymously

Extracts from Cobbett's writings selected to discredit him.

*1809, 37 pp. Printed and published by T. Gillet, 7, Crown Court, Fleet Street, London, 'Price, Two Shillings'. 8vo.

This pamphlet, sold at two shillings, was one of the many hostile publications issued by Cobbett's enemies giving extracts from his earlier anti-Reform writings. *Elements of Reform* also appeared in London in 1809 in a sixpenny edition, published by J. Gold (B.M.); in 1816 as *Parliamentary Reform*, it was reprinted in Manchester by J. Gleave (Oldham Public Library) and in Bolton by J. Gardner (Arnold Muirhead Collection). Cobbett wrote a spirited reply to these charges of inconsistency, mentioning in particular this 1809 pamphlet (see *Political Register*, 27 May 1809). By then he had decisively broken with his old patrons and friends, and was vociferously demanding Parliamentary Reform, and condemning such current scandals as that which connected the Duke of York, Mrs. Clarke, and the sale of army promotions. Soon his activity brought him a two-year prison sentence (see *Political*

Register, 14 July 1810), nominally because of an anti-flogging article in the *Political Register* (of 1 July 1809), and Cobbett now conducted an even more influential *Register* from Newgate.

[69]   1809

PROCEEDINGS / OF A / GENERAL COURT MARTIAL / HELD AT THE HORSE GUARDS, / On the 24th and 27th of March, 1792, / FOR THE TRIAL OF / Capt. RICHARD POWELL, Lieut. CHRISTOPHER SETON, / and Lieut. JOHN HALL / OF THE 54th REGIMENT OF FOOT; / On Several Charges preferred against them respectively / By WILLIAM COBBETT, / Late Serjeant-Major of the said Regiment; / TOGETHER WITH SEVERAL CURIOUS LETTERS / ... AND / VARIOUS OTHER DOCUMENTS ... /

ANONYMOUS

*1809, 32 pp. Printed and published by J. Gold, Shoe Lane, Fleet Street, London. Price sixpence. 8vo.

A publication intended to damage Cobbett's reputation by suggesting that in 1792 he had brought malicious and unfounded charges against his late superior officers in the army, from which he had then, but recently, obtained an honourable discharge (see *The Soldier's Friend*, 1792 [1]). He had accused them of widespread corruption and had brought back from his service abroad some evidence of their dishonesty. At length the court martial was held, but, almost at the last moment, Cobbett, warned of the danger in which he stood if he persisted in these attacks, fled to France. In his absence the three officer prisoners were duly acquitted, and when Cobbett became a Radical in later years his enemies published such reports as this pamphlet (there was also a 2s. 6d. edition), made much of his allegedly false charges, and cited his failure to appear at the trial (Cobbett's spirited reply is in the *Political Register*, 17 June 1809). The pamphlet includes correspondence between Cobbett and Sir Charles Gould, the Judge-Advocate-General.

Cobbett's Oppression!! / PROCEEDINGS / ON / THE
TRIAL OF AN ACTION / BETWEEN / WILLIAM
BURGESS, / A poor Labouring Man! / AND / WILLIAM
COBBETT, / A Patriot and Reformer!! / FOR EMPLOY-
ING / WILLIAM ASLETT, AND JOHN DUBBER, / *To
Assault and Falsely Imprison the Plaintiff.* / TRIED BEFORE /
MR. JUSTICE LAWRENCE ... / ... on ... the 20th of /
July 1809. / TAKEN IN SHORTHAND. /

ANONYMOUS

*1809, iv, 26 pp. [+2 pp. publisher's advts.]. Printed and published by
T. Gillet, 7, Crown-court, Fleet Street, and sold by Sherwood, Neely and
Jones, Paternoster-row, ... London. 'Price One Shilling.' 8vo.

In 1809, in the midst of a bitter struggle with the Government,
soon to lead him to Newgate, Cobbett found himself the target of
malicious attacks from many sides. Such was the garbled report of
his military trial in 1792 (see *Proceedings of a General Court
Martial*, 1809 [69]), and such also was this pamphlet report of his
trial for events arising from the alleged ill-treatment of one of his
farm-boys, dissatisfied only because he had to get up too early in the
morning at Botley. The boy, Jesse Burgess, had run away after
receiving his wages in advance, and his brother William, the plaintiff, who seems to have aided his escape, as well as the boy's mother,
had been wrongfully detained by two persons employed by Cobbett.
Burgess was awarded ten pounds damages, although he had asked
for a thousand, but the story of Cobbett's 'cruelty' and 'oppression'
was assiduously spread, not only by this pamphlet, but also by
placards extensively posted on the walls of London at a great cost.
In 1820, when Cobbett contested Coventry, the story was revived,
only to be rebutted by Jesse Burgess himself (see *Political Register*,
29 July 1809, and J. M. and J. P. Cobbett, *Selections from ...
Political Works*, iii. 280). Cobbett's 1808–10 farm account book
(now in Nuffield College, see [281]) gives a favourable picture of
him as an employer (see also 'Cobbett and his Men', by M. L.
Pearl, in *The Countryman*, vol. xliv, No. 1, 1951).

THE / LIFE / OF / WILLIAM COBBETT. / BY HIM-
SELF. / INTENDED AS AN ENCOURAGING EX-
AMPLE / TO / ALL YOUNG MEN OF HUMBLE
FORTUNE; / BEING A PROOF OF WHAT CAN BE
EFFECTED / BY STEADY APPLICATION AND
HONEST EFFORTS. /

By WILLIAM COBBETT; edited anonymously

Slightly abridged version taken from *The Life and Adventures of Peter Porcupine*, 1796.

>*1809, '2nd edition', 61 pp. Printed by B. McMillan, Bow Street, Covent Garden; for T. Purday & Son, No. 1, Paternoster Row, London. 'Price Two Shillings and Sixpence.' 8vo.

See note to *The Life and Adventures of Peter Porcupine*, 1796 [17].

COBBETT'S REMARKS ON SIR F. BURDETT'S
LETTER TO HIS CONSTITUENTS. . . .

By WILLIAM COBBETT

>[1810, London (Goldsmiths' Libr., London).]

Reprinted from the *Political Register*, 24 March 1810.

A reprint from the *Register* (24 March 1810) of Cobbett's defence of Sir Francis Burdett during the political crisis which led to the arrest of the Radical baronet. Within the next fortnight Burdett defied a vote of the House of Commons accusing him of a breach of privilege after he had championed John Gale Jones (1769–1839), a Radical orator imprisoned by the House. Burdett's celebrated speech in defence of Jones (said to have been written by Cobbett) was published in the same *Register* and also reprinted in very large numbers (see *Sir Francis Burdett to his Constituents*, 1810, &c.; BURDETT, Cole Collection).

AN ESSAY ON SHEEP, INTENDED CHIEFLY TO
PROMOTE THE INTRODUCTION AND PROPAGA-
TION OF MERINOS IN THE UNITED STATES OF
AMERICA, BY PROVING, FROM ACTUAL EXPERI-
MENTS, THE GREAT ADVANTAGE THEREOF TO
AGRICULTURE AND MANUFACTURE. BY R. R.
LIVINGSTON ... WITH A PREFACE AND EXPLANA-
TORY NOTES BY WILLIAM COBBETT.

*By R. R. LIVINGSTON; edited with a preface and notes by
WILLIAM COBBETT*

[1809, 1810, New York; 1813, New Haven, Conn. (L. of C.); 1811,
London, first with *Preface*, &c., by Cobbett (B.M.).]

This work by Robert R. Livingston (1743–1813), an American
politician, had first been published in New York in 1809, when
both Houses of the State Legislature had ordered it to be printed at
the public expense. In 1811 Cobbett reissued it in this new edition,
to which he added a preface 'to the English Reader', from the
'State Prison, Newgate, 3rd April, 1811'. In it he admitted the
change in his 'opinion [of] about three years ago', when he had
thought 'that the Americans never could do without *wool* from
other countries'. Since then he had learned how sheep were kept
folded 'at house' during the European winter; the Napoleonic
invasions had broken up and redistributed the wealth of Spain,
including her famous flocks of sheep; and America was 'becoming,
if not actually become, independent of England'. This, Cobbett
thought, was an event to be welcomed, for the mutual happiness of
both countries was not dependent on the 'exchange of English
clothing for American *food*'. Intercourse between nations ought to
grow, for it was 'the source of an increase of knowledge', but
'maritime commerce', said Cobbett, brought only large seaport
towns full of 'vice and wretchedness'. Moreover, 'a great monopoli-
zing, combining, speculating, taxing, loan-jobbing commerce' was
even worse, for it was 'hostile to everything that is patriotic, liberal
and just'. From 1807 Cobbett had been severely attacked for his
reiteration of the cry 'Perish Commerce' which he supported in the
Register by long quotations from *Britain Independent of Commerce*

(1807), a physiocratic work by William Spence (1783–1860) (see *Political Register*, 7 November 1807, and Cole, **Life*, ch. x).

[74]   1812

THREE LETTERS TO THE INDEPENDENT ELEC-
TORS OF THE CITY OF BRISTOL.

                                    By WILLIAM COBBETT
    [1812, Bath (Bodl.).]

Reprinted from the **Political Register*, 4 July, 1, 15 August 1812.

Written in support of Henry Hunt's candidature at Bristol and reprinted by M. Gye of Bath.

[75]   1812

            HAMPSHIRE FARMERS' ADDRESS.

                                            By W. C.
[In volume entitled: REJECTED ADDRESSES: OR THE NEW THEA-
TRUM POETARUM, 1812, 1839, 1st–19th eds.]

                    By HORATIO ('Horace') and JAMES SMITH
Parody of Cobbett.

    *1839, Rejected Addresses: or, The New Theatrum Poetarum, 19th edition,
    [port. illus.], xxix, 170 pp. Published by John Murray, Albemarle Street,
    London. [Cobbett: 'Hampshire Farmer's Address', 29–30 pp.] 8vo.

An able parody of Cobbett's style by the brothers Smith (Horatio or 'Horace', 1779–1849, and James, 1775–1839). It was first published in October 1812 in connexion with a competition for an address to mark the opening of the new Drury Lane Theatre to replace the old house which had been destroyed by fire. The authors parodied the supposed writers, whose addresses had been rejected, and Cobbett was made to object (not quite fairly) 'to the gewgaw fetters of *rhyme* (invented by the monks to enslave the people)'. In the main, however, the work is an excellent and affectionate parody which indicates the warm regard for Cobbett common among wide sections of people at this time. *Rejected Addresses* was a highly successful work which had reached this 19th edition in 1839 (see also **Rejected Articles*, by P. G. Patmore, 1826 [145]).

1814

LETTER TO THE INHABITANTS OF SOUTHAMPTON ON THE CORN BILL.

By WILLIAM COBBETT

[1814, London (Southampton Public Libr.).]

Reprinted from the *Political Register*, 4 June 1814.

Cobbett's attempt to prove to his 'worthy but deluded neighbours' of Southampton that a petition they were about to frame against the Corn Bill was a 'mass of heterogeneous matter, the offspring of ignorance and the source of delusion'. This reprint was published by J. Morton, then also the publisher of the *Political Register*. Cobbett agreed with the petitioners in their opposition to the Corn Bill, but took issue with them on their 'blindness' to the 'real causes' of high prices—'the taxes and the depreciation of our currency'.

[77]

1815

FIVE LETTERS TO LORD SHEFFIELD ON HIS SPEECH AT LEWES WOOL FAIR, 26 JULY 1815 . . . .

By WILLIAM COBBETT

[1815, London (Goldsmiths' Libr.).]

Reprinted from the *Political Register*, 26 August 1815.

These five letters made up a whole double number of the *Register* and were intended as a reply to Lord Sheffield (1735–1821, previously John Baker Holroyd), who had deplored the depressed state of the wool-trade. Cobbett claimed that the distress was not 'to be looked for' in low prices, and he pleaded for freer trade between this country and America. In an *Appendix* he added 'Lord Sheffield's Report' of 1811 to show the error of its 'prophecies'.

[78]

1815

LETTERS / ON / THE LATE WAR / BETWEEN THE / UNITED STATES AND GREAT BRITAIN: /

TOGETHER WITH / OTHER MISCELLANEOUS WRITINGS / ON / THE SAME SUBJECT. /

By WILLIAM COBBETT

Except for last letter, first published in the *Political Register*, 1811–15.

* 1815, vii, 407 pp. Published by J. Belden and Co. Van Winkle & Wiley, Printers, New York. 8vo.

A collection of Cobbett's writings on the war with America, all of which with one exception had appeared in the *Political Register* (31 August 1811–5 August 1815; the exception was the last item in the book, a letter from Cobbett to the Earl of Liverpool, dated Botley, 20 March 1815, which the editor claimed to have received in MS.). Some of the *Letters* had first been published in a series in the *Register* (e.g. *Letters to the Prince Regent*, the first three of which were republished in a 'pamphlet by some gentleman of the City of London'—*Political Register*, 20 June 1812—and 'Letters to the Earl of Liverpool'). A number were taken from Cobbett's correspondence in the *Register*, with American and English friends, some anonymous (e.g. 'Aristides', *Political Register*, 12 November 1814), and most of the material seems to have re-appeared in the American Republican press (*Political Register*, 3 June 1815) or occasionally as a pamphlet (e.g. Cobbett's *An Address to the Clergy of Massachusetts*, originally *Letters to the Cossack Priesthood of Massachusetts*, Boston, 5,000 sold in 'several editions'—*Political Register*, 12 July 1815—see [79]). Cobbett was uncompromising in his opposition to the war with America and his prophecies that it would end with Great Britain giving up all the points of substance were justified by events. He infuriated the Tories at home by his advocacy of the American cause (cf. *The History of the Regency and Reign of George the Fourth*, 1834), but he made many new friends in America who could overlook his old Toryism (see, for instance, the preface to this work, published in New York).

[79]   1815

AN ADDRESS TO THE CLERGY OF MASSACHU-SETTS. WRITTEN IN ENGLAND, NOV. 13, 1814. BY WILLIAM COBBETT. WITH A PREFATORY

EPISTLE TO CERTAIN PRIESTS, BY JONATHAN, ONE OF THE PEOPLE CALLED CHRISTIANS...

By WILLIAM COBBETT

[1815, Boston (B.M.).]

First published in the *Political Register*, 10 December 1814. Included in *Letters on the Late War . . .*, New York, 1815.

In November 1814 a report reached Cobbett that the clergy of Massachusetts had been celebrating the fall of Napoleon and the entry of Cossack troops into Paris. Thereupon he wrote for the *Register* (10 December 1814) a bitter article entitled 'To the Cossack Priesthood . . .' In the following July, when his American admirers sent him a suit of clothes as a gift, he was able to report with 'still greater pleasure' that his *Letter* had been republished at Boston and 'five thousand copies had in several editions been sold' (*Political Register*, 22 July 1815).

[80]   1815

THE PRIDE OF BRITANNIA HUMBLED, OR THE QUEEN OF THE OCEAN UNQUEEN'D, 'BY THE AMERICAN CORK BOATS,' OR 'THE FIR-BUILT THINGS, WITH BITS OF STRIPED BUNTING AT THEIR MAST HEADS'—(AS THE RIGHT HON. MR. CANNING, IN THE BRITISH PARLIAMENT, CALLED OUR AMERICAN FRIGATES). ILLUS-TRATED AND DEMONSTRATED BY FOUR LETTERS ADDRESSED TO LORD LIVERPOOL, ON THE LATE AMERICAN WAR. BY WILLIAM COBBETT, ESQ. INCLUDING A NUMBER OF HIS OTHER MOST IMPORTANT LETTERS AND ARGUMENTS IN DEFENCE OF THE AMERICAN REPUBLIC. TO WHICH IS ADDED, A GLIMPSE OF THE AMERICAN VICTORIES, ON LAND, ON THE LAKES, AND ON THE OCEAN. WITH A PERSUASIVE TO POLITICAL MODERATION, MOST RESPECT-FULLY ADDRESSED TO THE PERSONS COMPOSING THE TWO GREAT PARTIES IN THE UNITED STATES IN GENERAL, AND TO THE POLITICIANS

OF CONNECTICUT AND MASSACHUSETTS IN PARTICULAR.

By WILLIAM COBBETT

[1815, Philadelphia (B.M.); New York, 1817, Cincinatti (L. of C.).]

Like Cobbett's *Letters on the Late War*, 1815 (q.v.), this collection was drawn in part from the *Political Register*. It is said to have been edited by Thomas Branagan.

[81]   1815

PAPER AGAINST GOLD AND GLORY AGAINST PROSPERITY. OR, AN ACCOUNT OF THE RISE, PROGRESS, EXTENT, AND PRESENT STATE OF THE FUNDS, AND OF THE PAPER-MONEY OF GREAT BRITAIN; AND ALSO OF THE SITUATION OF THAT COUNTRY AS TO ITS DEBTS AND OTHER EXPENSES; ITS NAVIGATION, COMMERCE AND MANUFACTURES, ITS TAXES, POPULATION, AND PAUPERS; DRAWN FROM AUTHENTIC DOCUMENTS AND BROUGHT DOWN TO THE END OF THE YEAR 1814.

By WILLIAM COBBETT

[1815, London, 2 vols. (B.M.); 1817, in parts and *one vol.; *1821, 1822, London, 4th edition (B.M.); *1828, London; 1834, 1846, New York (Boston Public Libr.); 1841, Manchester (Brotherton Libr., Univ. of Leeds).]

First published in the *Political Register* 1810–15; afterwards in 2 vols., 1815 (B.M.); in parts, 1817; and then issued under different titles:

COBBETT'S / PAPER AGAINST GOLD: / Containing the History and Mystery of the Bank of England, / the Funds, the Debt, the Sinking Fund, the Bank / Stoppage, the lowering and the raising of the value of / Paper-Money: and shewing, that Taxation, Pauperism, / Poverty, Misery and Crimes have all increased, and ever / must increase, with a Funding System. /

*[1817], viii cols., 470 cols. Printed by W. Molineux, 5, Bream's Buildings, Chancery Lane; Published by W. Cobbett, Jun., 8, Catherine Street, Strand; and retailed at 192, Strand, London. 8vo. [This copy is bound with two other items—not by Cobbett—in a volume entitled 'Paper against Gold' on the spine.]

*[Another copy bound with 8 pp. publisher's (Clement's) advts. at end.]

*[1821, '4th edition' PAPER AGAINST GOLD; / OR, / The *History*

and Mystery / OF THE / BANK OF ENGLAND. / viii cols., 470 cols. Printed by Plummer and Brewis, Love Lane, Little Eastcheap. Sold by John Cobbett, 1, Clement's Inn, London. 8vo. [This copy is bound with other works by Cobbett, the first of which is his *Too Long Petition*.]

*1828, 'PAPER AGAINST GOLD; / OR / The History and Mystery of the Bank of England, of the / Debt, of the Stocks, of the Sinking Fund, and of all / the other tricks and contrivances, carried on by the / means of Paper Money.' / [With 'dedication' to the Duke of Wellington.] xviii, 332 pp. Printed and published by Wm. Cobbett, 183, Fleet Street, London. 'Price 5s., bds.' 12mo.

Paper against Gold is a collection of thirty-two 'letters' or articles (first published in the *Political Register*, 1 September 1810–30 September 1815), all but the last three of which Cobbett proudly addressed from the 'State Prison, Newgate'. (He was then serving a two-year sentence, nominally for libel, 9 July 1810–9 July 1812—see *Political Register*, 14 July 1810 and note to *Elements of Reform*, 1809 [68].) Cobbett in prison, however, was almost as active as Cobbett free. He lived well, if at a burdensome cost, and with all his other work even managed to supervise the management of his farm and the education of his children (see, for instance, *Advice to Young Men . . .*, 1829). Meanwhile, with the gradual progress of the Reform Movement, his paper prospered. For nearly nine months it was now issued twice a week (12 September 1810—22 June 1811) and it fell more completely under his control after he had quarrelled with his old manager, John Wright (1770?–1844; see [110], note to *The Book of Wonders . . .*, 1820). Cobbett later claimed (*Political Register*, 20 July 1822) that a day after his confinement began, following on a talk with one of his American friends, a 'Mr. Dickins', probably Asbury Dickins (1780–1861), he planned *Paper against Gold* as an effort to 'trace the paper-money system to its deadly root'. With the end of the war still not in sight, he believed peace would bring back sanity to a nation 'made as mad as the March hare'—then, and not till then, would this exposure of the system be really effective. In fact Cobbett, some years earlier, had begun to see the growth of paper-money and the debt as twin evils which could bring a national catastrophe, and in the six weeks in Newgate before this series began he had already written some powerful articles on 'Paper-Money' for the *Political Register* (for his 1803–6 writings, cf. [113] *Preliminary Part of Paper against Gold*, 1821; for the seminal effect of Paine's[1] *Decline and Fall of the English System of Finance*, 1796, see *Paper against Gold*, Letter XXV). The country was then awaiting the Report of the Bullion Committee, and as soon as this appeared Cobbett followed up these scattered articles with the more formal *Paper against Gold*. His 'series of letters', addressed to the 'tradesmen and farmers in and near Salisbury' (where a country bank had recently failed with the usual attendant ruin), provided his readers with an intensely graphic view of the whole financial system. Cobbett started with the common origin of the Bank of England and the National Debt. Paper money, he held, had been used to pay the interest on the debt, largely inflated by the war, and the nation groaned under the load of taxation it had thus incurred. Cobbett saw a fatal causality between the rise of a new governing class of stockjobbers and fundholders and the growth of pauperism. The vast increase in paper was no sign of national prosperity, and the nature of the bubble was illustrated by the suicide of Goldsmid, a Jewish banker, whose death,

---

[1] [82]

* *The Decline and Fall of the English System of Finance*, by Thomas Paine, 1796, Paris, Philadelphia, London, Venice, &c.

    *1796, 3rd edition, 44 pp., Paris, reprinted for D. I. Eaton, 74, Newgate Street, London.

    *1796, another edition, 16 pp., Paris, reprinted for T. Williams, Broadway, Blackfriars, London.

    *1819, another edition, 26 pp., published by R. Carlile, 55, Fleet Street, London.

    *1844, in *The Political Works of Thomas Paine*, published by Dugdale, London.

This important work by Paine, dated Paris, 8 April 1796, had won him fresh laurels throughout Europe. It was warmly greeted by the French Government, and the Ministry of Foreign Affairs promptly ordered a thousand copies. France, in the throes of violent inflation, believed to be aggravated by Pitt's 'forged *assignats*', looked with favour on this attack on the credit of England, and the pamphlet was said to have been translated into 'all the languages of the continent' within six or seven weeks of its first publication. Thereafter a number of writers, some at Pitt's behest, sought to rebut Paine's arguments, and one, Ralph Broome, in his *Observations . . .* rashly asserted the absolute security of the Bank. Among others, George Chalmers, already the author of a malicious *Life of Thomas Pain*, published a *Pamphlet* against *The Decline and Fall* (see PAINE, Cole Collection). Perhaps the most unexpected result of Paine's pamphlet was the effect it had seven years later on Cobbett. Paine's work was first published when Peter Porcupine was repeating Chalmers's scurrilities in America, but in 1803 a more thoughtful Cobbett, seeking his way in England through 'all the pamphlets of the . . . financiers', discovered Paine's 'twenty-five pages'. From his Newgate jail in 1811 he recalled the incident with some exaggeration. 'Here,' he wrote, 'I saw to the bottom at once. Here was no bubble, no mud to obstruct my view; the stream was clear and strong: I saw the whole matter in its true light, and neither pamphleteers nor speech-makers were, after that, able to raise even a momentary puzzle in my mind' (*Paper Against Gold*, Letter XXV).

Cobbett scornfully noted, had thrown the 'Pillars of the City' into a panic. Moreover, the 'funding system', in itself a cause of war, was bound up with the whole system of a corrupt, unreformed Parliament. Cobbett, in *Letter* XXIX, the last he wrote in Newgate, calls for a 'just compensation' for the Fundholders, and before a 'courtier ... and a Parson ... with claws distended' prepare 'to lay hold' of his cheek, he hastens to explain that he does not mean anything so severe as the selling of plate or the confiscation of church lands. (For his later similar views on the debt, see *Four Letters to ... Wortley*, 1833 [204]; *Manchester Lectures*, 1832 [188]. *Paper against Gold* was first published in book form in 1815, when three additional letters, which had appeared in the *Political Register* (23, 30 September 1815), and a long appendix were included. This was a two-volume edition sold at the 'retail price' of '20s. in Paper-Money'. At the beginning of 1817 Cobbett was offering to sell the remainder of this issue at half price (*Political Register*, 4 January 1817), and a few weeks later he announced two one-volume editions, one upon 'fine large paper' at 10s., and the other 'for the use of schools, and of *young persons* in general' at 4s. (*Political Register*, 1 February 1817). Ultimately this latter cheap edition appeared in twopenny numbers (No. 1, 24 February 1817—No. 15, 29 March 1817) and was sold at 3s. a volume. These 1817 editions, also an 1821 '4th edition'—see above—appeared under a slightly altered title and contained an introduction dated 'Botley, 8th February, 1817'. In the same year Cobbett said that altogether 150,000 had been sold (*Political Register*, 12 July 1817), and of these, he claimed in 1828, 30,000 had been 'in the two-penny trash form' (*Political Register*, 26 January 1828). On the other hand, he more modestly put forward a total sale of 40,000 in 1824 (*Political Register*, 27 March 1824). An 1828 edition—see above —which was sold at 5s. retained the altered title, omitted the last three letters (Nos. XXX–XXXII), and included a mock dedication to the Duke of Wellington (which also appeared simultaneously in the *Political Register*, 10 May 1828; see also *Preliminary Part of Paper against Gold*, 1821 [113]). Another edition, 'condensed by Margaret Chappelsmith', was published by A. Heywood in Manchester in 1841 (Brotherton Libr., Univ. of Leeds).

1816

COBBETT'S / AMERICAN / POLITICAL REGISTER. /

Edited by WILLIAM COBBETT

[Weekly periodical, New York, January–June 1816, May 1817–January 1818 (L. of C.).]

*1816, 'volume XXX. From January to June, 1816, Inclusive'. iv cols., 812 cols.+Index pp. 813–18. Published by H. Cobbett and G. S. Oldfield, No. 19, Wall Street. Van Winkle & Wiley, Printers, New York. 8vo.

This was an American publication intended at first as a collection of letters from correspondents which Cobbett considered unsafe to print in England and planned to publish in America as a quarterly or half-yearly volume called the *Collection of Suppressed Communications* (*Political Register*, 27 January 1816). This idea he abandoned, and the weekly *American Political Register* published by his nephew, Henry Cobbett, and G. S. Oldfield is nearly all his own work and contains some of his best political writing, most of it specially written for American readers. An exception was the series called the 'American Packet', which described parties and politics in the United States and had already appeared in the English *Register*. Despite its lively, entertaining style, the *American Political Register* was not a financial success, and it had expired by the time Cobbett arrived in America in flight from his political enemies at home. It was then revived and continued, to cover the period May 1817 to January 1818, as 'volumes 2 and 3 American' (with vol. 1—the same as vol. xxx above—in Library of Congress; vols. 2 and 3, American, are described as the equivalents of vols. 33 and 34, English). The pamphlet, *Our Anti-Neutral Conduct Reviewed*, (New York?), 1817, (L. of C.) appears to have been taken from the *American Political Register* (cf. a 'Letter To Major Cartwright' in the English *Political Register*, 14 February 1818).

1816

[Address] TO THE / JOURNEYMEN / AND / *Labourers* OF / *England*, / WALES, SCOTLAND AND IRELAND. /

By WILLIAM COBBETT

First published in the *Political Register*, 2 November 1816.

*1816, 16 pp. Printed for the Proprietors, by J. Molineux and Co., Riding's Court, St. Mary's Gate, Manchester. 8vo.

This *Address* was the famous 'No. 18' of the *Political Register* (2 November 1816), which Cobbett republished as an open sheet for twopence, an event which marked his emergence as a great working-class leader. This copy, however—see above—is not one of those which Cobbett reprinted himself—it had been immediately republished in Manchester by a group of sympathizers and sold 'below cost' for 1½*d*. Cobbett put a stop to this sort of action later when, beset by faked cheap *Registers*, he withdrew permission for any republication except in a newspaper (*Political Register*, 11 January 1817.) The price of his journal was then 1*s*. 0½*d*., and it had commonly been read by groups of working men, meeting in public houses and clubbing together to buy a copy (cf. *Political Register*, 16 November 1816, and Home Office Papers, 42/156). In a time of post-war political tension, however, the paper faced many difficulties. Publicans, for instance, were frequently threatened with the loss of their licences if they permitted the sale of 'seditious pamphlets' on their premises, and fake but 'loyal' *Registers* abounded when Cobbett gave all and sundry permission to reprint his writings. The way to overcome some of these obstacles was found when Cobbett, urged on by his friend and neighbour, Lord Cochrane (1775–1860), decided to publish a popular statement of his Reform policy at the cheapest possible price. The vehicle chosen was this *Address*, a brilliantly written article in the *Register* which put forward a moderate enough case for Reform, stressing the non-violent, constitutional character of the programme—it called for the suffrage for direct taxpayers only—but reminding its audience that all wealth was derived from labour. Even these fairly moderate propositions were dangerous, and Cobbett later recalled how his misgivings had prompted him to send his son John to London to try to stop the publication. By then, however, it was too late, and the twopenny No. 18 had been published, 6,000 having been sold on the first day (*Political Register*, 2 August 1817). There was no stopping its progress now. In a week a sale of 20,000 had been reported, and as if to show that he would not retreat, Cobbett announced that he had accepted Major Cartwright's plan of universal suffrage. From now on also, starting from No. 15 (the issue of 12 October 1816), he would publish a weekly cheap *Register* on an open sheet, alongside the ordinary stamped number; a few weeks later the sheet had been abandoned for an octavo pamphlet on which a small tax was paid in bulk (*Political Register*, 23 November, 14 December 1816). By 30 November, sales of No. 18 were said to be 40,000, and similar quantities of the other numbers of the cheap *Register* were soon being sold (cf. B.M. Add. MSS. 30121, f. 201, Sir Robert Wilson to Lord Grey, 8 November 1816, 'one bookseller sold 40,000 . . . above half a million . . . distributed' and *Monthly Magazine*, January 1817, '40,000 to 50,000' a week). Cobbett himself claimed a sale of 200,000 of No. 18 in two months (*Political Register*, 2 August 1817), and much later spoke of a 'prodigious' circulation, 'forty or fifty thousand copies a week' (*Political Register*, 10 April 1830). Whatever the real figure, the cheap *Register* first dubbed 'twopenny Trash' by its enemies (see note to *Cobbett's Two-Penny Trash*, 1831 [183]) was undoubtedly the most widely read publication of its time, its circulation several times larger than that of any other newspaper. This achievement was all the more remarkable since many obstacles continued to be placed in its way. It could not be sent by post, there was some harrying of booksellers and especially hawkers (see *Political Register*, 21 December 1816, 1 February 1817), and official encouragement was often given to 'loyal' publications (see *Anti-Cobbett*, 1817, and Aspinall's *Politics and the Press*, 155). Despite this general atmosphere of depression the twopenny *Register*, sold by innumerable obscure working men— one, held up as an example, had earned himself £3. 15s. by selling 1,800 copies (*Political Register*, 7 December 1816)—continued to prosper. Cobbett said that even on the morrow of 'Sidmouth's Circular' (addressed to the Lord-Lieutenants, 27 March 1817, against the 'circulation of blasphemous and seditious pamphlets') 20,000 copies had been sold in one day (*Political Register*, 2 August 1817). Cobbett's writings at this time played an enormous part in moulding working-class opinion (see Bamford's *Passages . . . of a Radical*), and although ultimately repression became so severe that he had to flee the country (see his *Taking Leave* [89] and *A History of the Last Hundred Days of English Freedom*), he had the satisfaction of knowing that by that time he had created a political weapon which he could wield even from across the Atlantic.

1816

A LETTER ADDRESSED TO MR. JABET, OF BIRMINGHAM.

By WILLIAM COBBETT

[1816, Coventry (Birmingham Reference Libr.).]

Reprinted from the *Political Register*, 9 November 1816.

An attack, reprinted by J. Aston of Coventry, on Richard Jabet (d. 1826?), a Birmingham printer, who was said to have provoked a riot by republishing a Bolton *Address* supporting the Government.

[86] ## 1816

THE / LIFE / OF / WILLIAM COBBETT, / AUTHOR OF THE / *Political Register.* / WRITTEN BY HIMSELF. /

By WILLIAM COBBETT; edited anonymously

Slightly abridged version taken from *The Life and Adventures of Peter Porcupine*, 1796.

> *1816, '9th edition', 16 pp., printed by Macdonald and Son, 46, Cloth Fair, for W. Hone, 55, Fleet Street and 67, Old Bailey, London. 'Price fourpence'. 8vo.

See note to *The Life and Adventures of Peter Porcupine*, 1796 [17].

[87] ## 1817

COBBETT'S NEW YEAR'S GIFT TO OLD GEORGE ROSE.

By WILLIAM COBBETT

[1817. (Sutton and Son), Nottingham (New York Public Libr.).]

Reprinted from the *Political Register*, 4 January 1817.

A famous article from the *Register* reprinted in Nottingham. George Rose (1744–1818), a powerful sinecurist for many years, had become the favourite butt of the Radicals when they attacked the system of political corruption. Cobbett estimated that he and his well-placed sons had, between them, drawn half a million pounds of public money (cf. *Extraordinary Red Book*, 1817, 2nd edition, which stated that Rose himself had pocketed over a million as Treasurer of the Navy).

1817

ANTI-COBBETT, / OR / THE WEEKLY PATRIOTIC PAMPHLET. / EXTRACTED FROM THE DAILY MORNING PAPER / 'THE DAY AND NEW TIMES'. /

ANONYMOUS

[Weekly periodical. March 1817, London.]

*1817, Vol. I, Nos. 4, 5, 6, cols. 97–192. [Printed by John Knight, Lane's Court, Great Warner Street, Clerkenwell.] Published at 112, Strand, London, and sold by Effingham Wilson, 88, Royal Exchange, London; R. Jabet, Birmingham; W. Bulgin, Bristol; M. Wright, Leeds; and Hough and Son, Gloucester. 'Price Three Halfpence'. 8vo.

This was one of the many hostile works aroused by Cobbett when he published his tremendously successful cheap *Register* in 1816 (see *To the Journeymen and Labourers*). There were many imitation Cobbett journals published at Norwich, Romsey, Oxford, London, and other places in this period, a number of them receiving small grants and other aid from the Government (see Home Office Papers, 41/1/490–1, 42/158–60). This particular pamphlet, *Anti-Cobbett*, was composed of articles taken from *The Day and New Times*, a daily journal owned by Dr. (later Sir) John Stoddart (1773–1856), more commonly known as ' "Dr. Slop", the leader of the "Bridge Street Gang" ' (see William Hone's *Slap at Slop*, 1821, HONE, Cole Collection). According to Cobbett, this weekly pamphlet was advertised in 300 newspapers, endless reams of placards announced it, and 200,000 circular letters were addressed to individuals by name, urging them to aid its circulation—a campaign which Cobbett estimated could not have cost less than £20,000 (*Political Register*, 2 August 1817). Whether this was true or not, frantic efforts were certainly being made at this time to nullify the effects of the cheap *Registers*—often with little enough results. This *Anti-Cobbett*, for instance, although published for 1½d. seems to have lasted for only eight issues, and a similar *Brunswick Weekly Political Register*, published at Norwich, had an equally short life (see Home Office Papers, 42/160).

MR. COBBETT'S / TAKING LEAVE OF HIS COUNTRYMEN. /

By WILLIAM COBBETT

First published in the *Political Register*, 5 April 1817.

*[1817], 32 cols. Printed by Hay and Turner, 11, Newcastle Street, Strand, and published by the Proprietor, Wm. Jackson, 192, Strand, London. 'Price Two-pence.' 8vo.

*Another copy bound in a volume of pamphlets entitled 'Westminster Election Tracts' on spine, this being the 36th item in the volume.

Early in 1817, when his cheap *Register* had become a powerful agitator for Reform (see *To the Journeymen and Labourers*), Cobbett decided to escape from under the heavy hand of the Government. Burdened by large debts, one of the intended victims of various hastily enacted 'gagging' laws and the suspension of the Habeas Corpus Act (4 March 1817), he foresaw a menacing alliance of his political enemies and certain of his creditors, and prudently decided to continue his fight from afar. When Sidmouth, through an emissary, according to Cobbett, sent an offer of 'compensation' if he would give up writing, Cobbett made no answer, and hastened his departure for the United States. Having written this pamphlet and entrusted it to his friends, he sailed secretly from Liverpool (27 March 1817). It appeared in the next number of the *Political Register* (5 April 1817) as a farewell address, under the date 'Liverpool, 28th March 1817', and was reprinted as a pamphlet —see above. In it Cobbett explained the reasons for his departure, announced the suspension of the paper, and promised its reappearance in 'about three months'. A pledge which he kept, for it resumed publication on 12 July 1817, with Cobbett regularly sending his articles across the Atlantic.

COBBETT'S ADDRESS / TO THE / *Americans.* /

By WILLIAM COBBETT

*[1817], 7 pp. [+1 p. publisher's advts.]. Printed by Hay & Turner, 11, Newcastle Street, Strand, and published by J. Duncombe, 19, Little Queen

Street, Lincoln's Inn Fields, London. 'Price three halfpence.' 8vo. [This copy is bound with other items in a volume entitled 'Westminster Election Tracts', this being the 37th item in the volume.]

A letter dated 'Jamaica, Long Island, May 9, 1817', addressed 'to the People of America', in which Cobbett appealed to 'those Gentlemen who are Proprietors or Editors of Newspapers in the United States' to aid him in breaking the 'close connexion . . . between the hired prints of London and the Aristocratic prints here, and thus expose the string of atrocious falsehoods', which he said had already been spread in America about his flight. The object of these slanders, he believed, was to make the people of both countries believe that he had fled from England because of his debts and not because of his politics. An additional note, dated New York, 14 May 1817, explained the reasons for the stoppage of *Cobbett's American Register* (see [83]).

[91]   # 1817

MR. COBBETT'S ADDRESS TO HIS COUNTRYMEN ON HIS FUTURE POLITICAL WORKS; AND ON THE STATE OF THEIR POLITICAL AFFAIRS.

By WILLIAM COBBETT

[1817, London (B.M.).]

This Address, dated 'Jamaica, Long Island, May 11, 1817' was published by Richard Carlile (1790–1843), the Radical free-thinker, from his Fleet Street shop. It announces Cobbett's intention to resume his 'literary labours without loss of time' and says that the form of his future writings against 'the boroughmongers' would be announced in an advertisement published in 'a few days' by his nephew Henry Cobbett, 'who will have the sole management of the business'. This is probably a reference to the 'Prospectus' announced in *Cobbett's Address to the Americans*, 1817 (see [90]).

[92]   # 1817

A History of the Last Hundred / Days of English Freedom, / By WILLIAM COBBETT, / With an Introduction, / 'Main

99

Events of Cobbett's Life', and a Biographical Index / By J. L. HAMMOND. /

> By WILLIAM COBBETT; edited, with an introduction, &c. by J. L. HAMMOND

First published intermittently in *Cobbett's Weekly Political Pamphlet (The Political Register), 26 July 1817–18 October 1817.

> *1921, [iii], 114 pp. Published by the Labour Publishing Company, Ltd., 6, Tavistock Square, and George Allen and Unwin, Ltd., London. (In Labour Classics, No. 2.) 8vo.

Cobbett wrote these extremely effective articles for the *Register* (then called the *Weekly Political Pamphlet*) shortly after he had begun his two and a half years' exile in America (see *Mr. Cobbett's Taking Leave of his Countrymen, 1817, and *A Year's Residence in America, 1818, 1819). In them he recounted the events that had led to the notorious 'Gagging' laws and the suspension of Habeas Corpus, casting ridicule on the attempts to incriminate the Spencean Societies and Hampden Clubs as revolutionary organizations (cf. *The Trials at Large of . . . Thistlewood . . . Watson, &c., 1817, Cole Collection). In 1921 these articles were first republished in book form at Cole's suggestion by J. L. Hammond (1873–1949) the historian, who added a short historical introduction and a biographical index.

1818

[93]

[LONG ISLAND PROPHECIES]
COBBETT'S / TOO LONG PETITION, Nov. 1817—
LETTER TO TIERNEY, July 1818. / LETTER TO THE
REGENT ON THAT WILD AND VISIONARY PRO-
JECT, / PEEL'S BILL, SEPT. 1819. /

> By WILLIAM COBBETT

First printed in the *Political Register, 7 February, 1 July 1818, 30 October 1819.

> [1822, London, various issues; also entitled (caption): Long Island Prophecies (Harvard Libr.).]

> *[1822], 54 cols. Printed and published by C. Clement, 183, Fleet Street, London. 8vo. [Bound with Cobbett's Preliminary Part of Paper against Gold and Paper Against Gold.]

These articles, written by Cobbett during his exile in America (see *A Year's Residence [94]), first appeared in the Political Register —the Petition (dated 20 November 1817) on 7 February 1818, the Letter to Tierney (dated 1 July 1818) on 12 September 1818, and the Letter to the Regent (dated 5 September 1819) on 30 October 1819. Cobbett often referred with pride to these writings, calling them his 'prophecies' and a 'warning' of the fate that would overtake England unless there was a reduction in interest payments on the debt, and in 'salaries, pensions, sinecures, and public pay of all sorts' (e.g. Political Register, 27 April, 20 July, 15 September 1822). The Petition, one of the many Cobbett composed, was ultimately not presented to the House of Commons for a curious reason. It had been offered to the friendly Lord Folkestone (later the third Earl of Radnor, 1779–1869), only to be politely declined by him with the explanation that the House usually rejected petitions 'when extending through several sheets of paper'. The chance was too good to miss and for ever afterwards it was the 'too long petition' (Political Register, 7 February 1818). The Letter to Tierney, occasioned by the passing of the Bank Restriction Act (58 Geo. III, c. 37) in May 1818, with its accompaniment of distress and repression, recalled the warnings of *Paper Against Gold (see note to [81], and attacked George Tierney (1761–1830), 'the most able man' in the House, for his part in the debate (Political Register, 12 September 1818). The Letter to the Regent, written shortly after 'Peel's Act' (59 Geo. III, c. 49) had been passed, similarly inveighed against the 'paper-money system' scoffed at the gradual resumption of cash payments, called for Parliamentary Reform, and warned the 'deceived' Prince that never before was he 'surrounded with dangers so great as now menace you and our country' (Political Register, 30 October 1819). Cobbett republished these three articles as a pamphlet, in at least five issues, the last of which was advertised at sixpence, 'as Six-Acts command' (Political Register, 20 April 1822), and addressing the 'boroughmongers', he boasted, 'these three papers will live, and long live, in proof of my superiority over you all' (Political Register, 27 April 1822). One issue (Harvard Libr.) has the caption title, Long Island Prophecies; the publication was advertised as such in *Mr. Cobbett's Publications, c. 1822 (see *Cobbett's Sermons, 1822 [112]); for the original MS. of the Letter to Tierney see [274]).

A / YEAR'S RESIDENCE / IN THE / UNITED STATES OF AMERICA. / Treating of the Face of the Country, the Climate, the Soil, / the Products, the Mode of Cultivating the Land, the Prices / of Land, of Labour, of Food, of Raiment, of the Expenses / of House-keeping, and of the usual manner of Living; of / the Manners and Customs of the People; and of the / Institutions of the Country, Civil, Political and Religious. / IN THREE PARTS. /

By *WILLIAM COBBETT*

[1818–19, New York, 1st edition, London, another edition (B.M.); London, *2nd edition, 1818, Belfast, another edition (Trinity College Libr., Dublin); 1822, London, 3rd edition, 1828, London, another edition (B.M.).]

*1818, 1819, viii, 9–610 pp. [with Index to Pt. I—no Index to Pts. II and III—no map]. Published by Sherwood, Neely and Jones, Paternoster Row, London. 8vo.

*[1922] . . . 'ornamented by Martin Travers' . . . with introduction by John Freeman. xx, 276 pp. Published by Chapman & Dodd, . . . London. 8vo. (In the *Abbey Classics*, No. 5.)

Cobbett, who had left America in 1800 as a Tory, returned in 1817 (5 May) as a Radical and a political refugee (see his *Taking Leave*, 1817 [89]). He was to remain in America for more than two years, and although he was neither forgotten nor unknown in the United States (see *Letters on the Late War between the United States and Great Britain*, 1815 [78], and *American Political Register*, 1816), he took little part this time in American public affairs. Instead he promptly leased a farm at Hyde Park, near North Hempstead, Long Island, and busied himself with its management and the writing of articles for the *Political Register* at home. Out of this experience grew *A Year's Residence*, a collection of articles which Cobbett had sent to England to be published in three parts during his absence, and which reached several editions on both sides of the Atlantic. Although written in this disjointed fashion, *A Year's Residence* is remarkable for its living, smoothly flowing style. Indeed, it is the first book in which Cobbett found that happy combination of political pamphlet, daily journal, travelogue, and farming treatise so vividly exploited in the later *Rural Rides*. Cobbett's love of the land appears very strongly in this work, and with it his admiration of the advantages enjoyed by the American farmer and citizen, but there are also some characteristic notes of criticism. Thus he is concerned at the lack of graceful gardens (see *The American Gardener*, 1821); opposes, in a friendly fashion, the notion of Morris Birkbeck (1764–1825), an English settler in Illinois who had claimed that the Western Prairies were ripe for colonization by groups of Englishmen (*Political Register*, 6–13 February 1819, reprinted in Part III—above); and is aghast at the American habit of spirit 'tippling'. Cobbett devotes a whole chapter to an account of the cultivation of the *Ruta Baga*, the Swedish turnip, or swede, which he did much to popularize in England, and then turns to abuse the potato, that 'lazy root' favoured by the political economists. This is part of his campaign against the fashionable cults of the day and, similarly, he trounces Milton for his absurd theology, and Shakespeare for his 'puns and smut'. Perhaps the most vituperative writing is reserved for Henry Bradshaw Fearon (see Fearon's *Sketches of America . . .*, 1818),[1] an English traveller, who, much to the joy of the Tories (see *Quarterly Review*, January 1819), claimed to have seen Cobbett's farm, dirty and in disrepair. Cobbett wrote a great deal during his exile in America (see, for instance, *Grammar of the English Language*, 1818 [96]; *The American Gardener*, 1821 [114]), and no doubt a hired farm fell a little below his usual standards, but he was happy enough, judging by the felicitous *Year's Residence*, and he does not appear to have been thinking of an early return to England until a disastrous fire on 20 May 1819 destroyed his house and much of the equipment. The non-renewal of the suspension of Habeas Corpus in January 1818 had cleared the way for his return, and, taking Paine's bones with him, Cobbett arrived at Liverpool on 20 November 1819.

---

1   1818

[95]

Sketches of America. | A | NARRATIVE OF A JOURNEY | OF FIVE THOUSAND MILES | THROUGH | THE EASTERN AND WESTERN STATES OF AMERICA | . . . | WITH | REMARKS ON | MR. BIRKBECK'S 'NOTES' AND 'LETTERS'. | *1818, 2nd edition, xi, 454 pp. Printed for Longman, Hurst, Rees, Orme, and Brown, Paternoster Row, London. 8vo.

Fearon, something of a Radical, visited America between 1817 and 1818 on behalf of some potential emigrants from England, and on his return published these highly critical *Sketches* . . . . An enraged Cobbett immediately took his revenge in an appendix to his *Year's Residence in the United States . . .* entitled 'Fearon's Falsehoods'.

1818

A / GRAMMAR / OF THE / ENGLISH LANGUAGE, / IN A SERIES OF LETTERS. / Intended for the Use of Schools and of Young Persons in / general; but, more especially for the Use of Soldiers, / Sailors, Apprentices, and Plough-boys. /

By WILLIAM COBBETT

[1818, New York (L. of C.); London ('1819'), *1st edition; 1819, 2nd, 3rd editions; 1820, 4th edition; numerous other issues and editions: 1823, with *Six Lessons*; 1824; *1826; *1829, Andover printed; 1831; 1833; 1835; *1836; *1840; 1842; *1844; 1847; 1850; 1852; 1863; 1865; 1866; 1866, another edition by J. P. Cobbett with 'additional chapter'; 1880, edited by J.M.; &c.; New York, 1832; 1833; 1837; 1846; 1883; 1884, edited by A. Ayres; &c.; 1824, Berlin, 1825, Jena, 1839, Leipzig (German trans.); 1852, Philadelphia; &c.]

*1819, 1st edition, iv, 5–186 pp. [ii]. Published by Thomas Dolby, 34, Wardour Street, London. 12mo.

*1826, 'TO WHICH ARE ADDED SIX LESSONS INTENDED TO PREVENT STATESMEN FROM USING FALSE GRAMMAR AND FROM WRITING IN AN AWKWARD MANNER.' [iv], [pp. unnumb.], XXIV Letters. Published by W. Cobbett, Fleet Street, London. 12mo. [Inscribed by Cobbett and J. Y. Akerman.]

*1829, iv, [pp. unnumb.], XXIV Letters; stereotyped and printed by B. Bensley, Andover, and published by the Author, 183, Fleet Street, London. 12mo. [Bound with *A French Grammar*, 1825, Paris.]

*1836, [iv], [pp. unnumb.], XXIV Letters. Published by Anne Cobbett, 10, Red Lion Court, Fleet Street, London. 12mo. [Bound with *List of Mr. Cobbett's Books* at end.]

*1840, [iv], [pp. unnumb.], XXIV Letters. Published by Anne Cobbett, 10, Red Lion Court, Fleet Street, London. 12mo. [Bound with *List of Mr. Cobbett's Books* at end.]

*1844, [iv], [pp. unnumb.], XXIV Letters. Published by A. Cobbett, 137, Strand, London. 12mo. [Bound with *List of Mr. Cobbett's Books* at end.]

*[1923 ?] 'Cobbett's Easy Grammar;' 'with preface by the Rt. Hon. J. R. Clynes, M.P.': 'revised and brought up to date'; vi, 128 pp., published by W. Foulsham & Co. Ltd., 10 and 11, Red Lion Court, Fleet Street, London. 12mo. ['Foulsham's Shilling Series.']

The Grammar of the English Language ranks as one of Cobbett's greatest works. It was written in America in the form of letters (two of these are in the B.M., Add. MSS. 22169) to his third son, James Paul Cobbett (1803–81), who, at fourteen, copied them from the manuscript in accordance with his father's ideas on education and became 'a grammarian at once' (*List of Mr. Cobbett's Books, c.* 1834). Cobbett's whole life was an example of what a self-taught peasant could achieve, and in addressing the Blanketeers in 1818 he stated that it was a finely written but ungrammatical letter from a Nottingham stocking-weaver which had made him recall his own efforts and had impelled him to write the *Grammar* (*Political Register*, 21 November 1818; see also his 'Letter to Benbow', *Political Register*, 6 December 1817). Characteristically, he trounced the 'grammar books most in vogue . . . those of a Mr. Lindley Murray', who was accused of copying his definitions from Bishop Lowth (Lowth's *Short Introduction to English Grammar*, 1762 (see [2]), had been Cobbett's guide when he was a raw army recruit—see his *Life and Adventures of Peter Porcupine*). This new project would not do, however, if it was simply a book of grammar and nothing else. Cobbett impregnated it with the political struggle that was now part of his life. 'By the writing of [it]', he says, 'I might possibly be able to create numerous formidable assailants of our insolent high-blooded oppressors' (*Political Register*, 21 November 1818). In this task Cobbett succeeded brilliantly. His colourful political examples of the rules of grammar, his ability to make the working-class reader feel at ease, his earnest and serious tone (children should never be addressed in a childish way, explained Cobbett), even his contempt for the 'learned languages'—all this endeared the book to its readers and ensured an enormous circulation. Published on 7 December 1818 in London (an earlier American edition was registered for copyright in New York on 17 July 1818), the first issue of 5,000 copies was sold out in a fortnight (*Political Register*, 9 January 1819), a 'second edition' of another 5,000 followed on 4 January, and a third on 23 February. Cobbett claimed that over 13,000 had been sold in six months (*Political Register*, 14 August 1819), and a fourth edition on 30 November 1820 was dedicated to Queen Caroline in place of William Benbow (*Political Register*, 25 November 1820—it was published by Benbow, who since 8 June 1820 had also become the publisher of the *Register*). At the close of 1822 Cobbett estimated that the total sale of the *Grammar* was about 50,000 in England and

America, and he announced a fifth edition to appear on 1 January 1823. This new edition was to contain an additional 'six lessons intended to prevent statesmen from using false Grammar and from writing in an awkward manner'; it was to be published by Cobbett's second son, John Morgan Cobbett (1800–77)—there had been a quarrel with Benbow—and the price was now raised from 2s. 6d. to 3s. (*Political Register*, 21 December 1822, 4 January 1823). Cobbett's fortunes were now somewhat more prosperous than they had been, and keeping the publication in the family was one way of ensuring this (the early profits on the *Grammar* had first been used to pay off his old debts—see 'Letter to Tipper', 20 November 1817, quoted Melville, ii. 99). From 1824, when the copyright assigned to John Hinxman in 1818 was repurchased by Cobbett (see *Faithfull MSS. [289]), the *Grammar* must have proved very profitable. In 1826 another issue was published by Cobbett himself (see above copy, with his signature and that of his one-time secretary John Yonge Akerman, 1806–73), and in 1828 the total sale was said to be 55,000 without ever having been mentioned 'by the old shuffle-breeches blackguards who call themselves reviewers' (*Political Register*, 19, 26 January 1828). There had been some criticism of the book,[1] but Cobbett seems to have thought this beneath contempt. By 1834 he claimed that more than 100,000 had been sold (*List of Mr. Cobbett's Books*, c. 1834, attached to *History of George the Fourth*), and there were many pirated editions in odd parts of the world (e.g. a Madras edition, whose publisher Cobbett threatened to prosecute—*Political Register*, 27 September 1823).

---

[1]

1819

[97]

A / CRITICAL EXAMINATION / OF / COBBETT'S / ENGLISH GRAMMAR; / IN / *A Letter to a Friend:* / SHEWING / THE ERRORS AND INCONSISTENCIES CONTAINED IN THAT / WORK, AND THE ABSURDITY OF THE AUTHOR'S PRO- / POSED CHANGES IN THE ESTABLISHED GRAM- / MATICAL TERMS AND USAGES OF THE / ENGLISH LANGUAGE./

By X

* 1819, 65 pp. Printed for W. Wright, 46, Fleet Street, London. 12mo.
This was one of the earliest attempts to ridicule Cobbett's highly successful *Grammar*. The anonymous writer, who professed not to have 'read any other of this author's works', passed 'over in silence the absurd mass of personal and general invective with which the book is filled' and claimed to be concerned only with its 'confused' and 'inaccurate' instruction in English Grammar.

Even down to our own day, this *Grammar* has maintained its freshness, vigour, and utility. The *B.M. Catalogue* records at least twelve different editions after 1860, and the late J. R. Clynes, a Labour Home Secretary, in the preface to a 1923 edition—see above—paid a tribute to its stimulating and enduring influence on his own career.

[98] ## 1818

OBSERVATIONS / ON / COBBETT'S / TREMENDOUS AND ALARMING / *Scheme* / FOR THE ANNIHILATION OF THE / BANK OF ENGLAND / Paper System, / BY MEANS OF / FORGED BANK NOTES; / WITH / REFLECTIONS / ON ITS FATAL TENDENCY. /

ANONYMOUS

*[1818], 8 pp. Printed by and for J. Fairburn, 2, Broadway, Ludgate Hill, London. 'Price Twopence'. 8vo.

A sharp condemnation of Cobbett's half-jocular, half-serious proposal for a wholesale forgery and free distribution of banknotes, finally to discredit the paper money, destroy the Government, and ruin the fundholders. This 'scheme' had first appeared in two of the *Political Registers* (22, 29 August 1818) conducted by Cobbett during his American exile. John Fairburn, the publisher of this hostile pamphlet, inserted an advertisement for another of his publications, *The Gorgon*, a weekly paper of Radical and working-class tendency, but, since it was backed by Francis Place and Sir Francis Burdett, fiercely anti-Cobbett in tone (see *The Gorgon*, 1819, no. 41, in Cole Collection).

[99] ## 1818

THE TRIAL OF MISS MARY ANN TOCKER, FOR AN ALLEGED LIBEL ON R. GURNEY, JUN. VICE-WARDEN OF THE STANNARY COURT, IN THE COUNTY OF DEVON; WHICH TRIAL TOOK PLACE BEFORE MR. JUSTICE BORROUGH, ONE OF THE JUDGES OF THE COURT OF KING'S BENCH, ON WEDNESDAY, THE 5TH OF AUGUST, 1818, AT THE TOWN OF

BODMIN, IN THE COUNTY OF CORNWALL. TO WHICH IS PREFIXED A LETTER TO MISS TOCKER, AND TO WHICH IS ADDED AN ADDRESS TO JURY-MEN ON THEIR DUTIES AS JURORS, AND ESPECI-ALLY ON TRIALS FOR CRIMINAL LIBEL. BY WILLIAM COBBETT.

Edited anonymously; with a 'letter' and an 'address' by WILLIAM COBBETT

[1818, New York (New York Public Libr.); Boston (Harvard Libr.).]

Mary Ann Tocker, the sister of Henry Tocker, a solicitor of Plymouth, was sued in 1818 for a libel on Richard Gurney (1790–1843), a somewhat disreputable vice-warden of the Stannaries. Miss Tocker achieved great fame in Radical circles by the spirited manner in which she conducted her own defence and won her acquittal (see *Sherwin's Political Register*, 15 August 1818, and *The Black Dwarf*, 2 September 1818, Cole Collection), and the report of the trial was widely circulated in numerous editions. Cobbett, too, was delighted with 'Miss Tocker's triumph', particu-larly as it was achieved, in part, by her appeal to the jury over the head of the judge, the unpopular Sir James Burrough (1750–1839), whom Cobbett himself had faced in 1809 when Burrough was the leading counsel in the Burgess case (see *Cobbett's Oppression* 1809 [70]). He reprinted this pamphlet report of the trial as soon as he received it in New York, adding a 'letter' to Miss Tocker and an 'Address' to jurymen (see *Political Register*, 2 January 1819). Cobbett also published a letter 'to Judge Burrough' on the trial (*Political Register*, 2 January 1819), the original manuscript of which is in the Cole Collection (see [274]).

[100]   1819

CORRESPONDENCE BETWEEN MR. COBBETT, MR. TIPPER AND SIR FRANCIS BURDETT.

By WILLIAM COBBETT and SIR FRANCIS BURDETT; edited by RICHARD CARLILE.

[1819, London (B.M.).]

The Radical baronet, Sir Francis Burdett (1770–1844), had lent Cobbett a total of about £3,000 by 1816. This was made up of

£2,000 in 1812; £300, disclaimed by Cobbett, which had gone to John Wright in 1810; and a further £700 in 1816. Shortly afterwards Cobbett separated for political reasons from Burdett and his Westminster 'Rump', and these loans, which Cobbett regarded at times as a gift towards his political expenses, brought their quarrel to a head. On 20 June 1817 he wrote to Burdett from America, enclosing a copy of a letter to Tipper, a stationer and paper-maker, to whom he owed £3,000, stating his inability to pay at once, and even claiming that the failure of 'society' to give him the protection of the laws of property even justified him in a refusal, which he would not claim, to pay at all. This correspondence, with Burdett's indignant reply (31 January 1818), was published in *The Examiner* (3 January 1819) as part of a campaign to discredit Cobbett (see also *Quarterly Review*, vol. xxi, 136, where an inaccurate list of his debts is given); in defence of him, Richard Carlile (1790–1843), the Radical free-thinker, published this reprint of the correspondence, adding his opinion that Burdett's action was inspired by a fear of Cobbett's exposure of the electoral manoeuvres of the 'Rump' (see also *A Defence of Mr. Cobbett Against the Intrigues of Sir Francis Burdett . . .*, 1819 (B.M.), and *Political Register*, 10 April 1830, 5 October 1833).

[101]   1819

A / LETTER / TO / MAJOR CARTWRIGHT, / IN JUSTIFICATION OF THE WRITER'S CONDUCT AT THE LATE ELECTIONS / FOR WESTMINSTER; AND, IN ANSWER TO THE CALUMNIES / SPOKEN AND PUBLISHED AGAINST HIM / *By Cobbett, Hunt, and Thelwall,* / AND CERTAIN MEMBERS OF MR. HOBHOUSE'S COMMITTEE./

By THOMAS CLEARY

*1819, 33 pp. Printed by Hay and Turner, 11, Newcastle Street, Strand, and published by Onwhyn, 4, Catherine-Street, Strand, ... London. (Price six-pence.) 8vo.

Thomas Cleary was an Irish law student who had been the honorary secretary of the Hampden and Union Clubs founded from about 1812 onwards under the inspiration of Major John Cartwright (1740–1824), the 'Father of Reform'. In June 1818 Henry Hunt (1773–1835), still an ally of Cobbett's, incurred the displeasure of Burdett and his followers by contesting the vacant Westminster seat. Cleary was then given by Francis Place a private letter from Cobbett to John Wright (1770?–1844), his former manager, which contained a brief scurrilous mention of Hunt, and this passage Cleary read out on the hustings. The letter had been written ten years earlier in 1808, and when news of the incident reached Cobbett in America, having forgotten the letter, he promptly declared it to be a forgery. Cleary and Wright were now bitterly attacked in the *Political Register*, and after Cobbett returned to England they both brought actions against him for libel. Cleary was awarded the almost derisory amount of forty shillings (4 December 1820), but, a week later, Wright was more successful and got a thousand pounds (see *The Book of Wonders*, 1821). This pamphlet defence of himself by Cleary, addressed to Major Cartwright, is dated 21 June 1819, and assails Cobbett, Hunt, Thelwall, and most of the members of the Westminster Committee, from whom Cleary had now separated. He later acted as honorary secretary of the Cartwright Club and in 1834 invited Cobbett to preside at the annual dinner in memory of the Major.

[102]   1819

THOMAS PAINE. A SKETCH OF HIS LIFE AND CHARACTER.

> By WILLIAM COBBETT, MARGARET BRAZIER DE BONNEVILLE, NICOLAS DE BONNEVILLE, and JAMES PAUL COBBETT

[1892, New York, London, 1st edition.]

In *The Life of Thomas Paine* . . . By Moncure Daniel Conway; Edited by Hypatia Bradlaugh Bonner, 1909. (1st ed. 1892.)

*1909, *The Life of Thomas Paine* . . . By Moncure Daniel Conway; edited by Hypatia Bradlaugh Bonner, xvi, 352 pp., published by Watts & Co., 17 Johnson's Court, Fleet Street, London. 8vo. ['Thomas Paine, A Sketch . . .', pp. 329–39.]

This *Sketch* was written by Cobbett in America in 1819 when he was anxious to do some service to the memory of the man he had once savagely attacked (see his * *Life of Thomas Paine*, 1796 [20]). It was compiled from the notes and recollections of the de Bonnevilles, a French couple, close to Paine in his last years. Cobbett is said to have paid Madame Margaret Brazier de Bonneville (1767–1846) a thousand dollars for her papers, and both she and her husband, Nicolas (1760–1828), as well as Cobbett's son, James Paul, then with him in America, added short passages to the final manuscript. In the event, Cobbett never published the *Sketch*, perhaps because Madame de Bonneville, who eventually became a Roman Catholic, made various stipulations which were not fulfilled. According to her own account, the thousand-dollar note was not met and she had to come to London to recover the manuscript from Cobbett. Richard Carlile (1790–1843), the Radical free-thinker, to whom she wrote to this effect in 1822, published her letter in *The Republican* (8 March 1822—see CARLILE, Cole Collection) and reprinted part of it in his hostile * *Life of William Cobbett* ([142]) in 1826. In 1892 Moncure Daniel Conway (1832–1907) obtained a copy of the manuscript from the Cobbett family, and published it for the first time in an *Appendix* to his *Life of Thomas Paine* (see PAINE, Cole Collection).

[103]   1819

REPORT OF THE ACTION, / WRIGHT v. CLEMENT, / FOR CERTAIN LIBELS PUBLISHED IN / COB- BETT'S POLITICAL REGISTER; / TRIED IN THE COURT OF KING'S BENCH AT WESTMIN- / STER, ON FRIDAY, THE 10TH OF DECEMBER, 1819, / BEFORE LORD CHIEF JUSTICE ABBOTT, AND A SPE- / CIAL JURY. /

Reported by GEORGE FARQUHARSON; *edited with preface by* JOHN WRIGHT

     *1819, xxii, [i], 55 pp. [+1 p. publisher's advts.] Printed [by T. C. Hansard] for J. Wright, No. 5, Panton Square, London. (Two shillings). 8vo.

John Wright charged William Innell Clement (d. 1852) with issuing two of Cobbett's libels on him in the *Register* (4 January 1817, 6 March 1819). Clement denied responsibility as a pub- lisher, a claim in which he was upheld by his brother, Charles, but the second of the two charges was successful and Wright was awarded £500. The trial caused a sensation by the production in court of a letter and an article written by Cobbett in 1810, but retracted after a few days, in which, in deference to the welfare of his family, he offered to discontinue the *Register* if the charge against him was dropped by the Government. Wright published the correspondence and the article in this *Report* in order to discredit Cobbett and to confirm the somewhat garbled accounts which had appeared in 1812 and 1816 in *The Times*.

[104] # 1819
A FULL REPORT OF THE PROCEEDINGS OF A PUBLIC MEETING...

Anonymous

[1819, London (Arnold Muirhead Collection).]

Cobbett's speech at a crowded London meeting (13 December 1819) in favour of a 'Plan' to abstain from 'excisable articles' in the interior of 'sobriety, frugality and good government'.

[105] # 1820
COBBETT'S EVENING POST.

Edited by WILLIAM COBBETT

[Daily periodical; Nos. 1–55, 29 January—1 April 1820, London, folio (B.M.).]

Cobbett was never very lucky in his attempts to found a daily newspaper, and this one, started at the end of January, lasted only just over two months. The project coincided with his determination to stand for Coventry, but both undertakings ended dismally and helped to bring about his bankruptcy in the same year. Undeterred, Cobbett was thinking of reviving the *Evening Post* and calling it *The Gridiron* at the end of the following year, although the plan never matured (*Political Register*, 22, 29 December 1820); instead, in 1822, he bought a large share in a daily newspaper, *The Statesman* (see note to [121]).

1820

THE / BEAUTIES OF COBBETT: / IN THREE PARTS. /

By WILLIAM COBBETT; edited anonymously

Extracts from Cobbett's writings selected to discredit him.

> *[1820 ?] 'Part the First. Life of Thomas Paine . . .' 16 pp., [portrs.]; 'Part the Second. The Torch of Truth: being I. . . . observations on the 'Age of Reason'. II. '. . . Mr. Cobbett's views upon religious subjects.' 16 pp., [portrs.]; 'Part the Third. Politics for the People.' 16 pp., [portrs.]. Printed by T. C. Hansard, Peterborough-court, Fleet Street, and sold by H. Stamman [*sic*], 68, Princes Street, Leicester Square, London. 'Price Twopence' [each part]. 12mo. [The three parts are sewn together.] *A reprint, 'sold by H. Stemman' . . . Part 3 only.]

A hostile selection from Cobbett's 12-volume edition of his Tory writings in America, *Porcupine's Works . . .*, 1801, embellished with portraits of Paine and Cobbett. It was sold in three twopenny numbers by Henry Stemman, who published a great deal of anti-Cobbett literature, and printed by Thomas Curson Hansard (1776-1833), who, in 1812, had acquired Cobbett's *Parliamentary Debates* [61], his *Parliamentary History*, and also his* State Trials ([67]). The three parts were constantly being reprinted in various forms in all parts of the kingdom.[1] In 1836, shortly after Cobbett's death, an edition of his Tory writings appeared, similarly entitled *Beauties of Cobbett* ([222], but, apparently, without any hostile intention on the part of the publisher.

---

[1] 1820   *The Beauties of Cobbett*, Parts 1-3, Dublin (Trinity College Library, Dublin).
[1819?]   slightly different versions:
        Politics for the People, Birmingham, printed by T. Knott (Birmingham Reference Library); another issue printed by W. Hodgetts, Birmingham (London School of Economics Libr.).
        Observations on Paine's 'Age of Reason', Birmingham (a 'dialogue' between Paine and Cobbett not in *The Beauties*) (Birmingham Reference Library). *Cobbett's Reflections on Religion, Number 1*, Sunderland (B.M.). This copy carries an advertisement for *Reflections on Politics*.
1819   *The Life of Thomas Paine . . .*, Durham (B.M.).
1822   (see *Cobbett's Gridiron* [119]).
1832   (see *Cobbett's Ten Cardinal Virtues*, Manchester [190]).

1820

COBBETT'S PARLIAMENTARY REGISTER.

Edited by WILLIAM COBBETT

[Weekly periodical: 6 May–December 1820, London (B.M.).]

Begun on 6 May 1820, this was another of Cobbett's shortlived journalistic ventures. During the parliamentary session this *Register*, containing a summary of the proceedings, was usually issued weekly, although in July more than one number was issued each week. Vol. i was published on 4 October 1820, and vol. ii in the following December—after which month no more numbers were issued.

1820

A LETTER FROM THE QUEEN TO THE KING

[*By WILLIAM COBBETT*] Signed 'Caroline, R'.

[1820, London, numerous editions.]

Printed in the *Political Register*, 19 August 1820.

Cobbett was prominent among the Radicals in his defence of Queen Caroline against George IV. He wrote this famous letter of remonstrance for her and penned many of the 'loyal addresses' as well as her 'replies'. The letter was widely reprinted, but Cobbett loyally kept his authorship secret, and even attributed it to Alderman Wood (see *Selections from Cobbett's Political Works*, vi. 32, —note by J. M. Cobbett; *The Champion*, 19 May 1838; and Anne Cobbett's MS. in Nuffield College [283]).

1820

AN ANSWER TO THE SPEECH OF THE ATTORNEY-GENERAL AGAINST HER MAJESTY THE QUEEN.

By WILLIAM COBBETT

Reprinted from the *Political Register*, 26 August 1820.

A defence of Queen Caroline which was published by Benbow.

THE / BOOK OF WONDERS: / IN FOURTEEN CHAP-
TERS. / CONTAINING, / In the compass of eighty closely
printed columns, a Mass of Information more / suited to the Present
Moment, and better calculated to open the Eyes of the People / of
England, than any work of a similar nature that has hitherto
appeared. / EMBELLISHED WITH ILLUSTRATIVE
ENGRAVINGS; / AND / DEDICATED TO HER MOST
GRACIOUS MAJESTY / QUEEN CAROLINE. /

Extracts from Cobbett's writings selected to discredit him.

THE / BOOK OF WONDERS: / PART THE SECOND. /
CONTAINING / A Report of the Extraordinary Exhibition
made in the Court of King's Bench, / at Westminster Hall, before
Lord Chief Justice Abbott, and a Special / Jury, on Monday,
the 11th of December, 1820, / BY / 'THE GREAT EN-
LIGHTENER OF THE PEOPLE,' / WILLIAM
COBBETT. /

Edited anonymously

*1821, Part I, 80 cols., [illus.]. Printed by T. C. Hansard, Peterborough-
Court, Fleet-street, published by H. Stemman, No. 68, Princes-street,
Leicester Square, London. 8vo.

*1821, Part II, 86 cols., [portr.] [+1 p. publisher's advts.]. Printed by
T. C. Hansard, Green Arbour Court, Old Bailey; Published by H.
Stemman, No. 68, Princes Street, Leicester Fields, London. 'One Shilling
and Sixpence. '8vo. [Parts I and II bound with other items in a volume entitled 'Hone & Cobbett' on the spine.]

One of the most effective of the many hostile compilations from
Cobbett's works assembled to discredit him by demonstrating his
inconsistencies, *The Book of Wonders*, like other works of a similar
tendency, was printed by Hansard and published by Stemman.
Part I, ably illustrated with cartoons by I. R. Cruikshank, exhibited
his many changes, whilst Part II told the story of Cobbett's trial
on 11 December 1820 for a libel on his former manager, John
Wright (1770?–1844), who had been awarded damages of £1,000
at this trial, and who may have been the anonymous editor of the
whole work. *The Book of Wonders*, cheaply priced at 1s. 6d. for
each part, achieved a wide circulation in the next few years and was
often peddled by Cobbett's enemies. When Cobbett contested

Preston in 1826, for instance, one of the candidates, the barrister, John Wood (1790–1838), industriously spread the work around the constituency, much to Cobbett's disgust (see *Cobbett's Poor Man's Friend*, 1826 [144], and *Political Register*, 1, 8 July 1826).

[111]   1821

THE QUEEN'S ANSWER TO THE LETTER FROM THE KING TO HIS PEOPLE

By WILLIAM COBBETT

[1821, London, Philadelphia (Boston Athenæum).]

Reprinted from the *Political Register*, 27 January 1821.

A mock 'answer' from the Queen which Cobbett addressed to the 'Mr. Parasite' who had written an equally fictitious *Letter from The King to his People* (see 26th edition, 1821; also another spurious *Letter from the Queen in Reply to the One from the King*, 1821, QUEEN CAROLINE, Cole Collection).

[112]   1821

COBBETT'S SERMONS / ON / 1. HYPOCRISY AND CRUELTY. / 2. DRUNKENNESS. / 3. BRIBERY. / 4. OPPRESSION. / 5. UNJUST JUDGES. / 6. THE SLUGGARD. / 7. MURDER. / 8. GAMING. / 9. PUBLIC ROBBERY. / 10. THE UNNATURAL MOTHER. / 11. FORBIDDING MARRIAGE. / 12. PARSONS AND TITHES. /

By WILLIAM COBBETT

[First issued in twelve monthly parts, 1821–22, London, *1822; 1823 (Arnold Muirhead Collection); 1828, Andover printed (B.M.).]

First published as *Cobbett's Monthly Religious Tracts*—No. 1, March 1821; title changed with No. 4 to *Cobbett's Monthly Sermons*.

*1821, 48 pp., 'vol. i, No. 2' only of *Cobbett's Monthly Religious Tracts*, printed by C. Clement and published by John M. Cobbett, 1, Clement's Inn, London. 'Price 3*d*.' 12mo. [This copy is bound with other items in a volume entitled 'Cobbett' on the spine.]

*1822, 'stereotype edition', [i], 295 pp. Printed and published by C. Clement, 183, Fleet Street, London. 12mo. [Bound with and preceded by (4 pp.) *Mr. Cobbett's Publications* (1822).]

Indignant with the tract writers who preached passivity and piety to the poor, irritated by the charge that he was a blasphemer, and quick to seize a loophole left in the last of the 'Six Acts', Cobbett issued the first of a series of *Monthly Religious Tracts* in March 1821. After the third number he pointedly changed the title to *Cobbett's Monthly Sermons*, for '*Sermons* the public call them . . . *Tract* is beneath the thing described' (*Political Register*, 26 May 1821), and continued the series (no February *Sermon* appeared) in twelve numbers to March 1822, when a title-page dated 1822 and a contents leaf were included for those readers who wished to bind their own sets. The collected series, advertised at first for 4s. (*Political Register*, 23 March 1822), was soon reduced in price to 3s. 6d., and in 1823 a new edition followed, replacing the many mixed sets (several editions of the separate numbers had been issued). The work, which contains some of Cobbett's best writing, undoubtedly enjoyed wide popularity—already by the fifth number Cobbett had claimed that the 'Tract Society' was 'beat . . . out of the water' by a sale of nearly 40,000, and that it 'would be hardly decent to describe' the purposes for which people take its pamphlets (*Political Register*, 21 July 1821). By the time the last *Sermon* had appeared, Cobbett was proudly acclaiming a translation into French and Italian and an English circulation of 100,000 (*Political Register*, 25 March 1822). Soon this was to rise to 150,000 (**Mr. Cobbett's Publications*, bound with *Cobbett's Sermons*, 1822), to 211,000 in 1828 (*Political Register*, 1 November 1828) when a 'new edition' (B.M.) was issued, and so on, until there were even 'some parsons who have the good sense and virtue to preach them from the pulpit' (**The Cobbett Library*, . . . c. 1830). A thirteenth *Sermon*, *Good Friday (q.v.), was published in 1830. Some of the original manuscripts of these *Sermons* are in the Cole Collection see [280].

[113]   1821

PRELIMINARY PART / OF / PAPER AGAINST GOLD; / The main object of which is to show the *Justice* and *Necessity* of / reducing the interest of that which is called the *National Debt*, in / order to rescue the rightful Proprietors of the Land from the / grasp of the devouring race engendered by Paper-money. /

By *WILLIAM COBBETT*

117

First published in the *Political Register*, 21 May 1803–17 September 1806.

> *1821, vi (8 paras.), 202 cols. (194 paras.) [+1 p. publisher's advts.].
> Published by John M. Cobbett, 1, Clements Inn, London. 8vo. [This copy
> is bound with Cobbett's *Paper against Gold* and *Too Long Petition* . . .].

This was a collection of early articles from the *Political Register* (21 May 1803–27 September 1806) showing Cobbett's long opposition to paper-money and the 'funding system'. It was published on 26 May 1821 at the price of 3s. 6d. as an accompaniment to *Paper against Gold*, republished in January of the same year (see note to [81]). Cobbett was now more than ever convinced of the infamy of 'this accursed system of paper-money'. 'Many, indeed, are the subjects on which I have written', he says in the preface to this *Preliminary Part* . . ., 'but . . . in relation to this, all other matter has been in the way of episode . . .', and in advertising the work (*Political Register*, 19 May 1821) he called for 'the justice and necessity of reducing the Interest of the Debt . . . [for] . . . Cash-payments and the interest of the Debt *in full*, cannot go on together'.

[114]   1821

THE / AMERICAN GARDENER; / OR, / A TREATISE /
On the Situation, Soil, Fencing and Laying-Out of / Gardens; on
the making and managing of Hot- / beds and Green-houses; and on
the Propagation / and Cultivation of the several sorts of Vegetables, /
Herbs, Fruits and Flowers. /

By WILLIAM COBBETT

> [*1821, London; 1826, Corfu (in Italian) *Il Giardinere Americano*
> (Massachusetts Horticultural Society, Boston); numerous American editions:
> 1823, Baltimore; (1832 ?), Claremont; 1835, New York, also 1841, 1844,
> 1846, 1856, &c.; 1842, Concord; 1852, Philadelphia; &c.].
> *1821, 'stereotype edition', [pp. unnumb.], 391 paras. [+ 6 pp. Index].
> Published by C. Clement, 1, Clement's Inn, London. '5s. Boards.' 12mo.

Cobbett, who had worked as a gardener's boy in the south of England, never lost his enthusiasm for a well-kept plot of ground, and this book, finished in 1819 during his second sojourn in America, was intended for the American farmer, who, however admirable in other respects, neglected the beauty and utility of the garden. Cobbett published the book in 1821 after his return to England and subsequently revised it as *The English Gardener*, 1829 (see [150]). *The American Gardener* is dedicated to Mrs. Tredwell of Salisbury Place, Long Island, a friendly neighbour in America, and Cobbett afterwards complained that a 'vile wretch who pirated it there had the baseness to leave out the dedication' (*The Cobbett Library*, 1832–4).

1821

[115]

COTTAGE ECONOMY: / CONTAINING / Information relative to the brewing of BEER, making / of BREAD, keeping of COWS, PIGS, BEES, EWES, GOATS, / POULTRY and RABBITS, and relative to other matters / deemed useful in the conducting of the Affairs of a / Labourer's Family. /

By WILLIAM COBBETT

First issued in seven monthly parts, August 1821–March 1822.

[1822, London, *1st (book) edition; other London editions: *1823, 1824 (B.M.); 1826 (L. of C.); 1828, 1831 (B.M.); 1835, 'new edition'; 1838, '15th edition', Anne Cobbett (Oldham Public Libr.); 1843, '16th edition' (University Libr., Nottingham); 1850, '17th edition' (B.M.); [1865?] *'19th edition'; *1916, *1926; New York editions: 1824 (Yale); 1833 with *The Poor Man's Friend* as an appendix (Library Company, Philadelphia).]

*1821 [Nos. 1 and 2 only—No. 1, August 1821, 'Introduction', 1–24 pp.; No. 2, September 1821, 'Brewing Beer', 25–48 pp.]. Printed and published by C. Clement, 1, Clement's Inn, London. 12mo. [These copies are bound in a volume entitled 'Cobbett' on the spine, and are the last items in that collection.]

*1822, 207 pp., 208 paras., [illus.]. Printed and published by C. Clement, No. 183, Fleet Street, London. 12mo. [pp. 167–8 are publisher's advts.]

*1823, 'A new edition', '. . . added, instructions / relative to the selecting, the cutting and the bleaching / of the Plants of ENGLISH GRASS and GRAIN, for the / purpose of making HATS and BONNETS.'/ [illus.] [pp. unnumb.], 236 paras. Printed for J. M. Cobbett, [183] Fleet Street, London. 12mo.

*[1865?] '19th edition', 'with recipes for using Indian Corn Meal in the Making of Bread, &c.' 224 pp. [incl. Index]. 264 paras. [illus.]. Published by Charles Griffin and Company, Stationers' Hall Court, London. 8vo.

*1916, 'with an introduction by G. K. Chesterton' [reprint of 17th edition, published by Anne Cobbett, 137, Strand, London, 1850]. vi, 195 pp. [incl. Index], 265 paras. [+ 1 p. publisher's advts.], [illus.]. Published by Douglas Pepler, Hampshire Hog Lane, Hammersmith, London. 8vo.

*1926, 'with a preface by G. K. Chesterton', x, 220 pp. Published by Peter Davies, London. 8vo.

First published in seven monthly numbers from August 1821 to March 1822 (six at 3*d.*, the seventh, a double, two-monthly number at 6*d.*), this very popular work was quickly reissued in book form for 2*s.* 6*d.* Monthly publication at 3*d.* had been decided on because of the 'Six Acts' (*Political Register*, 21 July 1821), and the subject-matter—the reconquest by self-taught labourers of country crafts retreating before the factory system—was one close to Cobbett's heart. He began with instructions on home-brewing (the advertisement for the series had reported the prosecution of a publican for adulterating beer—*Political Register*, 28 July 1821), deplored, in some famous passages, the use of tea, 'a weaker kind of laudanum', and passed on to deal with the baking of home-made bread. Then followed many valuable hints on cottage management, including advice on the rearing of live-stock. Even before the series was complete, *Cottage Economy* had made a considerable stir all over the country. Cobbett reported a sale of 30,000 after a few months (*Mr. Cobbett's Publications*, c. 1822–3), 50 sets up to No. 5 were ordered from France by December (*Political Register*, 8 December 1821), and even Henry Brougham in Francis Jeffrey's Whig *Edinburgh Review* praised the work (*Edinburgh Review*, February 1823). It was to attain a new celebrity in mid-1823, however, for Cobbett now began to interest himself closely in the cottage manufacture of 'Leghorn Bonnets' previously imported, sometimes in an unfinished state, from Italy. Domestic production from a freely obtained raw material by 'the wives and children of country labourers' was Cobbett's acknowledged aim. He assured his readers that the enterprise would have remained 'safely confined' in his own breast if he had thought that it might create a new class of capitalists and merchants—'bonnet lords to rival the calico lords'. But this possibility did not exist with this material, which 'in many cases can scarcely be denominated private property' (*Political Register*, 31 May 1823). Cobbett's interest had first been aroused by some straw bonnets a Miss Woodhouse had sent to the Society of Arts from America. He set to work to disprove the notion that only foreign grasses could be used, and soon discovered that some kinds of common English wheat and grass were eminently suitable for the purpose. His researches won him the medal of the Society of Arts, and on 31 May 1823, treating of his 'discovery', he published No. 8 of *Cottage Economy* as a separate shilling pamphlet with an illustration of three grasses. It may have been included with the other numbers in a new edition by the end of August, for then Cobbett writes of meeting a cripple in Kent, who, after reading his 'little book', was supporting himself by plaiting straw (*Political Register*, 6 September 1823). This may have been the (new) edition—see above—which alone included the engraved grasses and a title-page dated 1823. Its actual date of publication remains uncertain, and it was not advertised in the *Political Register*, which as late as 3 January 1824 refers to No. 8. Sales were booming, however, and a new edition called the '6th', still at 2s. 6d., appeared on 11 September 1824, with much new material on 'straw bonnets' (*Political Register*, 4 September, 13 November 1824). On 16 December 1826 another edition with a chapter on 'Ice-houses' (illustrated) was issued at the old price (the 'Ice-houses', incidentally, might in case of failure, 'serve all generations to come as a model for a pig-bed') and by 1828 sales of 45,000 and 'pretty nearly 50,000' had been reported (*Political Register*, 15 September 1827, 19 April 1828). A year or so later Cobbett was claiming that *Cottage Economy* had even been translated into Greek (*Political Register*, 11 April 1829), and in 1831 came a new edition with more instructions for cottage crops. From 1838 onwards (see above) Anne Cobbett published various editions, adding her mother's advice for using the 'meal and flour of Indian corn' ('Cobbett's corn'); by 1850 the 17th edition had been reached, and as recently as 1926 the book has been reissued with a preface by G. K. Chesterton.

[116]   1821

THE FARMER'S FRIEND. TO THE FARMERS OF
THE KINGDOM.
                                By WILLIAM COBBETT

[1822, London (Birmingham Reference Libr.).]

Reprinted from the *Political Register*, 15 December 1821, 5 January 1822, with some additions.

During the agricultural distress of 1821 and 1822 Cobbett was making a special appeal to farmers against the protectionist agitation of George Webb Hall (1765–1824), who, as the secretary, since

1820, of the Board of Agriculture, was prominent in the organization of opinion in favour of a high fixed duty on imported wheat and duties on a wide range of other foods. In this widely distributed two-penny reprint of two articles in the *Register* (15 December 1821 and 5 January 1822, together with some short additional matter), Cobbett vigorously attacked Hall's protectionist views, and called on the farmers to petition for a 'reduction of rents' instead of a 'Corn Bill' (see also note to *The Farmer's Wife's Friend*, 1822 [120]).

[117]   1821

COBBETT'S WARNING TO NORFOLK FARMERS. PROCEEDINGS AT THE DINNER GIVEN BY THE RADICAL REFORMERS AT NORWICH ON THE 22ND DECEMBER 1821, TO MR. COBBETT.

By *WILLIAM COBBETT*

[1822, London (Norwich Public Libr.).]

Reprinted from the *Political Register*, 29 December 1821 and 5 January 1822.

A report of a dinner (22 December 1821) given to Cobbett by his supporters in Norwich, which the local newspaper, the *Norwich Mercury*, failed to publish. It was sold at threepence, and issued by C. Clement, who also published the *Register*. A year later Cobbett carried an immense Norwich county meeting with him on his proposals for an 'equitable adjustment' (see [126] *Norfolk Yeoman's Gazette*, 1823), and the editor of the *Norwich Mercury*, Richard Mackenzie Bacon (1775–1844), published an indignant *Reply to Mr. Cobbett* (1823, Norwich, 4th, 5th editions, Norwich Public Library) explaining his refusal to publish Cobbett's report and deploring 'a triumph which no man of common sense could have anticipated'.

[118]   1822

AMERICAN SLAVE TRADE; OR, AN ACCOUNT OF THE MANNER IN WHICH THE SLAVE DEALERS TAKE FREE PEOPLE FROM SOME OF THE UNITED STATES OF AMERICA, AND CARRY THEM AWAY, AND SELL THEM AS SLAVES IN OTHER OF THE

STATES; AND OF THE HORRIBLE CRUELTIES
PRACTISED IN THE CARRYING ON OF THIS IN-
FAMOUS TRAFFIC; WITH REFLECTIONS ON THE
PROJECT FOR FORMING A COLONY OF AMERICAN
BLACKS IN AFRICA, AND CERTAIN DOCUMENTS
RESPECTING THAT PROJECT. BY JESSE TORREY,
JUN. PHYSICIAN. WITH FIVE PLATES. TO WHICH
ARE ADDED NOTES AND A PREFACE BY WILLIAM
COBBETT.

By *JESSE TORREY, jun.; preface by WILLIAM COBBETT*
[1822, London (B.M.), originally published as a *Portraiture of Domestic Slavery*, Philadelphia, 1817 (L. of C.).]

Early in 1822 Cobbett's son, John Morgan, published this illustrated London edition of *American Slave Trade*, a violent attack
on negro slavery in the United States. Cobbett himself added a
preface dated 'Kensington, 18 Sept., 1821', in which he referred to
the author, Jesse Torrey (*fl.* 1787–1834), an American physician,
as 'public-spirited' and 'humane'. In this preface he gave a clue to
some of his reasons for republishing the book which had first been
issued in 1817 in Philadelphia as *A Portraiture of Domestic Slavery*
. . . . 'We ought not to be incessantly railing against West India
Slave Holders', he wrote, 'while we see Slavery existing to such an
extent, and the Slave Trade carried on with such shocking cruelty
in a country which, throughout the world, is famed for its freedom.'
It would be foolish 'to abolish Slavery', he went on, 'merely because
the thing is called for by a set of missionaries, or, what is worse, by
a set of hypocrites', and he instanced the futile attempts of the
abolitionists in America as an example of the magnitude of the task
(see Clarke's *Letter to Mr. Cobbett*, 1806 [65], for Cobbett's
earlier attitude to negro slavery).

[119]   1822

COBBETT'S GRIDIRON: / WRITTEN TO WARN /
FARMERS OF THEIR DANGER; / AND TO PUT /
LANDHOLDERS, MORTGAGERS, / LENDERS, BOR-
ROWERS, THE LABOURING / AND INDEED / ALL

CLASSES OF THE COMMUNITY / ON THEIR GUARD. /

Edited anonymously

Extracts from Cobbett's writings selected to discredit him.

> *1822, 32 pp., [illus.]. Printed [by T. C. Hansard] for Henry Stemman, 68, Princes Street, Leicester Square, London. 'Price, Sixpence.' 8vo.

> *[Another copy bound with *Cobbett's Book of the Roman Catholic Church*, which it follows.]

> *[Another copy bound with other items in a volume entitled 'Hone and Cobbett' on the spine.]

One of the many anti-Cobbett publications of the time, this six-penny pamphlet was published by Stemman and printed by Hansard (cf. *Beauties of Cobbett*, 1820, and *Book of Wonders*, 1821). It consisted of maliciously chosen extracts from his writings calculated to discredit him, and it was much copied by other opponents. Cobbett himself cautions his readers against two pamphlets with this title, and remarks of the 'forgers and cheats' who had compiled them, that 'any stray dog . . . you meet is more worthy of a bit of bread' (*Political Register*, 23 March 1822; an undated, unidentified newspaper cutting is attached to one of the bound copies—above—giving the text of this warning with the editorial comment that 'the *broiling* makes him wince'; see also *Cobbett's Ten Cardinal Virtues*, 1832). The 'Gridiron' was derived from the famous undertaking which Cobbett had made in the *Political Register* (13 November 1819), here reproduced together with a satirical cartoon. Confident that the resumption of cash payments promised in 'Peel's Act' was an impossibility unless the debt interest was reduced and taxes cut, Cobbett had offered, if found wrong in his predictions, to be broiled on a gridiron by Castlereagh 'while Sidmouth stirs the fire, and Canning stands by, making a jest of my writhing and my groans'. In the event, cash payments were gradually resumed at the Bank and the system did not collapse, largely because of the great expansion of the economy. Cobbett, however, claimed, with some justice, not to have been proved wrong, and to the end of his days he maintained his 'gridiron prophecy' against such gibes as those in this pamphlet. Thus in 1821 (*Political Register*, 29 December 1821) he proposed to revive his old *Evening Post* as *The Gridiron* (a project which never matured) and there were 'Feasts of the Gridiron' at different times all over the country (e.g. at Norwich, Bolton, and

London in 1826; *Political Register*, 1, 8, 15 April 1826). The Gridiron even became a symbol which appeared at the head of some copies of the *Register* as late as 1835, and in 1838 it was adopted as such by the near-Chartist Cobbett Club of London (see **A Political Tract*, 1839 [227]).

1822

[120]

THE FARMER'S WIFE'S FRIEND. /

By WILLIAM COBBETT

Reprinted from the **Political Register*, 23 March 1822.

> *1822, 29 cols. Printed and published by C. Clement, 183 Fleet Street, London. 'Price 3*d*.' 8vo. [Stitched with two numbers of the *Political Register*, 1 November 1828 and 28 February 1829.]

Republished (29 March 1822) as a threepenny pamphlet a week after it had first appeared in the *Political Register* (23 March 1822), this was a sequel to Cobbett's,'Letter to the Farmers of this Kingdom' and a short 'Letter to Webb Hall' (*Political Register*, 15 December 1821, 5 January 1822), 30,000 of which, he claimed, had already been circulated as a twopenny pamphlet entitled *The Farmer's Friend* (see [116]). Both pamphlets were sold at a 50 per cent. minimum profit to the retailer, and Cobbett urged 'Gentlemen' to give parcels to 'labourers out of work', who might then earn 2*s*. 5*d*. for selling 20—'no bad day's wages' (*Political Register*, 18 January 1822). This, like the careful mingling of practical advice with political appeal in the *Register* and elsewhere, was all part of Cobbett's campaign among the countrymen, soon to bear fruit in the great 1823 movement of the smaller landowners and farmers. (For the important Norfolk agitation, the highlight of Cobbett's influence amongst the agriculturalists, see *Political Register*, 11 January 1823, and [126] note to *The Norfolk Yeoman's Gazette*, 1823, a short-lived weekly in which Cobbett played a big part.)

1822

[121]

THE STATESMAN.

Articles by WILLIAM COBBETT

> [Daily evening periodical; 1806–24 incorporated in *The Globe and Traveller*, 1824, London (B.M.).]

This was an old-established evening paper in which Cobbett acquired a large share from March 1822 to about May in the following year. He wrote political articles and summaries of parliamentary proceedings in its columns and later claimed, when accusing Brougham of plagiarism, that he had been paid £10 a week for these (*Political Register*, 31 March 1832). The paper had been active in the struggle against the Constitutional Association (the 'Bridge Street Gang') even before Cobbett's advent, but at some time in May he differed with his fellow proprietor (? R. Wardell, jun.; see A. Aspinall, *English Historical Review*, July 1950, 'Statistical Account of London Newspapers, II, 1800–1836') and broke off his connexion with it (see **Cobbett's Collective Commentaries*, 1822, where a large number of the articles were reprinted).

[122]   1822

THE / HORSE-HOEING HUSBANDRY: / OR, / A TREATISE on the Principles of TILLAGE and VEGETATION, / wherein is taught a method of introducing a sort of VINEYARD / CULTURE into the CORN FIELDS, in order to increase their / Product and diminish the Common Expense. / BY JETHRO TULL, / . . . / TO WHICH IS PREFIXED, / An INTRODUCTION, explanatory of some Circumstances connected / with the History and Division of the Work; and containing an / Account of certain Experiments of recent date, / BY WILLIAM COBBETT. /

> By *JETHRO TULL*, edited *with an introduction by WILLIAM COBBETT*

[1822, London, 1st Cobbett edition (B.M.).]

*1829, another edition, xxiv, 466 pp. [incl. Index]. Published by Wm. Cobbett, 183, Fleet Street, London. 'Price, bds. 15s.' 8vo.

Cobbett's edition of the work of the famous agricultural improver, Jethro Tull[1] (1674–1741) contains a characteristic introduction

---
[1]   1731

Horse-Hoeing Husbandry: / OR, / An ESSAY on the PRINCIPLES / OF / Vegetation *and* Tillage. / Designed to introduce / A NEW METHOD OF CULTURE; / WHEREBY / The Produce of Land will be increased, and the / usual Expence lessened, /

dated Kensington, 20 April 1822. In this, on the grounds of his own experiments, Cobbett defends Tull's 'main principle . . . that Tillage will supply the place of manure', preaches a homily on the subjects of plagiarism and private property, and inveighs against the Game Laws and the Tithes. Cobbett's edition was, as he claimed, a great improvement on any that had gone before, and although he was rash to claim that it contained 'the foundation of all knowledge in the cultivation of the earth' (*The Cobbett Library, 1832–4), his motive was an honest enough intention to offer first practical, then political advice to the farmer.

1822

[123]
REDUCTION NO ROBBERY.

By WILLIAM COBBETT

[1822, London (B.M.).]

Reprinted from the *Political Register*, 22 June 1822.

A 'letter to the Men of Kent' on their petition for a reduction of the interest on the National Debt. It was sold as a threepenny pamphlet.

1822

[124]
COBBETT'S / COLLECTIVE COMMENTARIES: / OR, / Remarks on the Proceedings in the Collective Wisdom of the / Nation, during the Session which began on the 5th of February, / and ended on the 6th of August, in the 3rd year of the Reign of / King George the Fourth, and in the year of our Lord

---

Together with / Accurate DESCRIPTIONS and ACTS of the Instruments / employed in it.

By JETHRO TULL

[1731, *A Specimen of* . . ., 1733, 1st edition, 1743, 2nd edition (B.M.).]

*1751, 'third edition, very carefully corrected,' [illus.] xv, 432 pp. [incl. Index], printed for A. Millar, opposite Catherine Street, in the Strand, London. 8vo.

This was the third edition of Tull's famous work. It had first appeared as *A Specimen* . . . in 1731 and more completely in a first edition of 1733 which had aroused many attacks. Tull defended his theories in *A Supplement* . . . (1735), an *Addenda* . . . (1738), and *A Conclusion* (1739). After his death a second edition (1743) and a third (see above), incorporating these additional writings, were followed by the Cobbett edition of 1822.

1822; / being the Third Session of the First Parliament of that King. / TO **WHICH ARE SUBJOINED,** / A complete List of the Acts Passed during the Session, with / Elucidations; and other Notices and Matters; forming all to- / gether, a short but clear History of the Collective Wisdom for / the year. /

Edited by WILLIAM COBBETT

*1822, 320 pp. Printed for J. M. Cobbett, 183, Fleet Street, London. (Price '6s. od.'.) 8vo.

This was a collection of Cobbett's parliamentary articles (most of which had appeared in 1822 in an evening newspaper, *The Statesman*; see [121]), a description of the Acts passed in that year, (5 February–6 August), a list of Cabinet Ministers and Judges, and the Government's Income and Expenditure. In March 1822 Cobbett had purchased a large share in *The Statesman* and had begun a daily parliamentary summary, with occasional political articles which he intended to publish in a series of annual volumes (see preface to *Collective Commentaries*). In May in the following year, however, he differed with his fellow proprietor, and tiring of an occupation that hindered his desire to continue his 'rural rides', he severed his connexion with the paper and dropped his daily commentary. 'Collective' and 'Collective Wisdom' was retained, however, as a satirical soubriquet for Parliament (see, for example, *Political Register*, 9 August 1823).

[125]   1822

MR. COBBETT'S PUBLICATIONS. / PUBLISHED BY / J. M. COBBETT, 183, FLEET STREET, LONDON. /

*[1822] [4 pp., published by J. M. Cobbett, 183, Fleet Street, London, 8vo. bound with and preceding *Cobbett's Sermons*, 1822.]

A descriptive catalogue which was often reprinted as an advertisement in the *Register*, and bound with various editions of Cobbett's books. It also appeared around 1824 as *List of Mr. Cobbett's Publications* and there were later versions entitled *List of Mr. Cobbett's Books*, and *The Cobbett Library* (see note to [156]; also Index of Titles under these heads).

1823

THE NORFOLK YEOMAN'S GAZETTE.

Edited by WILLIAM COBBETT

[Weekly periodical; Nos. 1-13, 8 February-3 May 1823, Norwich.]

In a *Narrative* which was also separately published (*Political Register*, 11 January 1823), Cobbett related how, at a huge county meeting for Reform in Norwich (3 January 1823) he had prepared a 'Norfolk petition' which had been finally carried amid some disorder. This was his famous economic and political programme (see Cole's *Life*, 278), but the 'vile' *Norwich Mercury* and the London press had distorted what had happened; he therefore appealed for support for a new weekly to be called *The Norfolk Yeoman's Gazette*, 'which would be able to give you . . . something really interesting to yourselves'. The paper was duly started on 8 February but its life was short. Only thirteen numbers were issued until 3 May 1823, when it expired, despite frequent appeals in the *Register* and a regular weekly article from Cobbett himself (see also note to [117], *Cobbett's Warning to Norfolk Farmers*, 1821).

[127] **1823**

TO LORD SUFFIELD

[1823, London (Arnold Muirhead Collection).]

Reprinted from the *Political Register*, 1 February 1823.

An angry reply to Lord Suffield (1781-1835, Edward Harbord, the third Baron), a moderate Reformer, who had presided over a Norfolk meeting called in opposition to Cobbett's 'Norfolk petition' (see note to [126] *The Norfolk Yeoman's Gazette*, 1823).

[128] **1824**

THE / *Law of Turnpikes*; / OR, / AN ANALYTICAL ARRANGEMENT OF, AND ILLUSTRATIVE / COMMENTARIES ON, ALL THE GENERAL ACTS / RELATIVE TO THE TURNPIKE ROADS / OF ENGLAND: / . . .

By WILLIAM COBBETT, junior

*1824, iv, 196 pp. Published by Charles Clement, 183, Fleet Street, London. 12mo. [This copy is bound with, and preceded by, a 4-page *List of Mr. Cobbett's Publications, c.* 1824.]

In 1823 Cobbett and his sons were fighting the turnpike trusts (*Political Register*, 25 October, 11 November 1823). As part of this campaign his second son, John Morgan Cobbett (1800–77), a barrister, fought a lawsuit with one of the Sussex trusts, while his eldest son, William (1798–1878), produced this analytical commentary of all the Acts dealing with the turnpike roads.

1824

[129]

A RIDE / OF / EIGHT HUNDRED MILES / IN / FRANCE; / ... To which is added, / A GENERAL VIEW OF THE FINANCES OF THE KINGDOM. /

By JAMES PAUL COBBETT

*1824, vi, 202 pp. + 10 pp. Index. Printed for the author, and published by Charles Clement, 183, Fleet Street, London.

Cobbett's third son, James Paul Cobbett (1803–81), to whom he had addressed the series of letters forming the *English Grammar* (q.v.), undertook at his father's request a tour of northern and western France between October and November 1823, sending home his impressions in the form of a 'journal'. This was intended to form a series of articles for the *Register* which would describe the standards of living of the French people. Ultimately other matters crowded these out, and most of the 'journal' was left for this volume, which appeared in March 1824 and reached a third edition. James Paul wrote a 'Memoir' of his father which is in manuscript in the Cole Collection (see [282]).

1824

[130]

A / FRENCH GRAMMAR, / OR, / PLAIN INSTRUCTIONS / FOR THE / LEARNING OF FRENCH. / IN A SERIES OF LETTERS. /

By WILLIAM COBBETT

[*1824, London; *1825, Paris; *1829, London; 1832, New York (L. of C.);

1837, New York (Mercantile Libr. Philadelphia); 1848, New York (Harvard Libr.); 1832–82, numerous London editions.]

*1824, [iv], [pp. unnumb.], XXVIII Letters, 456 paras. Published by Charles Clement, 183, Fleet Street, London. 12mo. [Bound with, and preceded by, iv-page *List of Mr. Cobbett's Publications*.]

*1825, [iv], [pp. unnumbered, XVIII Letters, 456 paras. De l'imprimerie de Plassan, rue de Vaugirard, no. 15, . . . [Published] A la Galerie de Bossange Père, . . . rue de Richelieu, no. 60, Paris . . . [Bound with *A Grammar of the English Language*, 1829.]

*1829, 'new edition', [ii], [pp. unnumb.], XXVIII Letters, 456 paras. Printed by B. Bensley, Andover, and published by the author, 183, Fleet Street, London. 12mo.

*[Another copy entitled 'Cobbett's English [*sic*] Grammar' on the spine, and bound with *List of Mr. Cobbett's Books, c.* 1830, 12 pp., at end.]

*1851, 11th edition, [pp. unnumb.], XXVIII Letters, 456 paras., published by Anne Cobbett, 137, Strand, London. 12mo. [Bound with *List of Mr. Cobbett's Books, c.* 1842, 12 pp., at end.]

*[1862 ?], 15th edition, 'revised with additions and corrections by James Paul Cobbett', viii, 439 pp. [+ 4 pp. publisher's advts.]. Published by Charles Griffin and Company, Stationers' Hall Court, London. 12mo.

As far back as 1795 Cobbett had published in Philadelphia *Le Tuteur Anglais* (see [7]), a highly successful book for teaching 'French people English'. Thereafter it was constantly reprinted in France and elsewhere as *Le Maître Anglais*, ultimately reaching as many as 'Threescore editions . . . on the Continents of Europe and America' (*Political Register*, 5 October 1833—although in rebutting a French plagiarist Cobbett had once admitted that it had been a 'work of haste'—*Political Register*, 21 February 1818). His new *French Grammar*, addressed to English readers, was a more thorough piece of work, and Cobbett said in 1833 that he 'had been making the notes preparatory to it for several years' even though 'a considerable part' of the book had been written 'between three o'clock and breakfast time' (*Political Register*, 28 December 1833). It was published on 21 August 1824, sold for 5s., and was recommended, strangely enough, by Cobbett for its absence of political instruction. 'For once in my life', he wrote, 'I have written a book *without a word of politics in it* . . ., all will agree that the book cannot be the worse for such exclusion' (*Political Register*, 31 July 1824). It was written in the form of letters to his youngest child, Richard—a style in which he excelled—and Cobbett claimed a 'very great sale' in

England and France in 1828, when he had himself printed 'upwards of 10,000' and was awaiting a new edition in October (*Political Register*, 26 January, 27 September 1828). There were many other editions after Cobbett's death, some of them edited by his third son, James Paul Cobbett, who also published a book of ¹*Practical Exercises . . .*, 1834, to the *Grammar*. James Paul's 'fifteenth edition' (see above), with his revisions and corrections, has an advertisement by the publisher for yet another French primer by a member of the family—*French Verbs and Exercises*, by Miss Susan Cobbett (William Cobbett's youngest daughter, 1807–89).

1824

[132]

A HISTORY / OF THE / PROTESTANT 'REFORMATION', / IN / ENGLAND AND IRELAND; / Showing how that event has impoverished and degraded the main / body of the People in those Countries. / IN A SERIES OF LETTERS, / Addressed to all sensible and just Englishmen. /

By *WILLIAM COBBETT*

[1824–6, first published in parts.]

PART SECOND. / CONTAINING / A List of the Abbeys, Priories, Nunneries, Hospitals, and other Religious / Foundations, in England and Wales, and in Ireland, / confiscated, seized on, or alienated, by the Protestant / 'Reformation' Sovereigns and Parliaments. /

By *WILLIAM COBBETT*

[1827, 1st edition.]

ı

1834

[131]

PRACTICAL EXERCISES / TO / COBBETT'S FRENCH GRAMMAR: / WITH A KEY. /

By *JAMES PAUL COBBETT*

*1834, iv, 114 pp. [+ 2 pp. publisher's advts.]. Printed by G. Eccles, 101, Fenchurch Street, published at Bolt Court, Fleet Street, London. 12mo. [Bound at the end with 12 pp. *List of Mr. Cobbett's Books, c.* 1842.]

Intended by James Paul Cobbett as an accompaniment to his father's *French Grammar and published in March 1834. James Paul Cobbett (1803–81), a barrister, in a preface (dated January 1834) described himself as the 'editor' rather than the author of the work.

[Part I: *'1824' (1824–6), London; 1824?, Baltimore; 1825, (Mortimer) Philadelphia Univ. of Pennsylvania Libr.); 1825, Pittsburgh; 1825 London (also nos. 1–3 in French), n.d. (Fithian) Philadelphia, 1825 (nos. 1–17 in Italian) Rome, 1826 (Connolly) Philadelphia (Arnold Muirhead Collection); 1826, Baltimore, Paris, Geneva, Naples, &c.; Parts I and II: 1827, London (B.M.); 1827, Lugano (Bibliothèque Nationale, Paris); 1827–8 (in German), Offenbach (Univ. of Illinois Libr.); *1829, London; 1829, Paris; 1830, Carácas (B.M.); 1832, 1834, New York (New York Public Libr.); 1832, 3, 9, Aschaffenburg; 1834, Nagy-Varad (B.M.); 1836, 1841, Paris; 1841, Naples; 1844, Sydney (B.M.); 1829–1905, London, Dublin, New York, &c., numerous editions.]

*1824–6, '1826' [Part I], [pp. unnumb.], XVI Letters, 478 paras. Printed and published by Charles Clement, 183, Fleet Street, London. 12mo. [last 'Letter' 'printed by' Wm. Cobbett, 183, Fleet Street, London.]

*[Another copy of Letter II *only* (of Part I) bound with other items in a volume entitled 'Cobbett Tracts'.]

*1829, [Parts I and II], [pp. unnumb.], 2 volumes, XVI Letters, 479 paras. + index [12 pp.]; 52 paras. + 'List . . .' + Index [24 pp.]. Published by the Author at 183, Fleet Street, London. 8vo.

*1850, 'stereotyped edition', [Part I only], XVI Letters, 479 paras., 333 pp. [incl. Index]. Published by Anne Cobbett, 137, Strand, London. 12mo.

*[1853?] [Parts I and II], 'sterotyped edition, illustrated', xxxiv, 333; [ii], 192. Published by Catholic Publishing and Bookselling Co., Charles Dolman, Manager, 61, New Bond Street, and 6, Queen's Head Passage, London. 12mo.

*1867, [Part I], 284 pp., illus + 3 pp. [publisher's advts.]. Published by James Duffy, 15, Wellington-Quay, Dublin, and 22, Paternoster-Row, London. 12mo.

*[post 1894] [Part I only], 'new edition revised, with notes and preface by Abbot Gasquet, D.D., O.S.B.,' xix, 415 pp. [incl. Index]. Published by R. & T. Washbourne, Ltd., Paternoster-Row, London. 8vo.

This famous polemic in the cause of Catholic Emancipation was begun in 1824, when the Irish question and the subject of Catholic relief had become a fiery topic closely linked with British Radical politics. As far back as 1803, whilst still something of a Tory, Cobbett had clashed with the Government on Irish policy (see *Political Register*, 2 June 1804, and Cole, *Life*, ch. viii), but he does not appear to have paid much serious attention to the question until 1823, when the rise of Daniel O'Connell (1775–1847) and his Catholic Association offered the Reformers a new and powerful ally. Never in sympathy with Nonconformist 'tract-mongers' or 'tithe-eating parsons', resolutely opposed to any denial of popular freedom, harking back, moreover, to a past age, Cobbett determined to write a *History of the Protestant Reformation* which should show the iniquity of the attacks on the Catholics. Not that he ever came near to conversion—born and bred a Protestant, his testimony was all the more valuable on that account, and he indignantly rejected a proposal (defeated in any case) made at a meeting of the British Catholic Association to present him with a copy of the *History of England* (1819, vols. i–iii; completed 1830) by Dr. John Lingard (1771–1851). 'I am not to be *hallooed on* upon anybody', retorted Cobbett (*Political Register*, 30 October 1824). Nevertheless, Lingard's scholarly book, which he was then still reading, became his primer for the *History of the Protestant Reformation*. Mildly critical of the author, who, 'like the other historians, has not informed us of the *prices* of *labour* and of *food* in the several reigns', 'disappointed', also, with the absence of the 'names' of the 'Courtiers of the "Reformation" ', Cobbett, learning, in spite of this, all he could from Lingard, diligently prepared his *History*, confident that the work of the Catholic scholar could never 'produce a thousandth part of the *effect* that mine will produce in the space of three years' (ibid.). His aim, he announced, was not to proselytize, but to show how the 'Reformation had *impoverished* and *degraded* the main body of the people of England . . . to make us all feel less hostile towards our Catholic fellow subjects . . . and . . . to admit them to all the rights we enjoy ourselves' (*Political Register*, 27 November 1824). Cobbett, indeed, affirmed this thesis with all his skill, but upon it he also sketched his favourite theme—that the Reformation was the beginning of a great act of spoliation that had ousted a benevolent Church and had culminated in the present pauperism of the poor— victims of heartless stockjobbers and tithe-mongering clergy. The first number of the *History*, sold at 3*d*., duly appeared on 29 November 1824, and its bright yellow wrappers were soon a familiar feature on bookstalls and in shops. In the second number, a month later, Cobbett strikingly expressed his view on the objects of such a book. Not for him the 'battles, negotiations, intrigues of court, amours of kings, queens and nobles . . . the gossip and scandal of former times . . . the romances . . .' which made up 'the far greater part of those books which are called *Histories of England* . . .' 'The great use of history', explained Cobbett, 'is to teach us how laws, usages and institutions arose, what were their effects on the people,

how they promoted public happiness, or otherwise; and these things
are precisely what the greater part of historians, as they call themselves, seem to think of no consequence.' Cobbett never pretended
to be an 'impartial' writer, and his hard-hitting work, more of a
polemic than serious history, proved an instant success. The original
print of 10,000 of No. 1 was increased to 30,000 on 22 December
and 40,000 on 1 January. (*Political Register*, 25 December 1824,
1 January 1825.) Cobbett's large ideas of a French translation
issued side by side with the English edition for use as 'Exercise-Books'
(*Political Register*, 13 November 1824) were a little premature,
although by 22 January a French edition of No. 1 had already
appeared, and 40,000 of No. 2 had been printed in England. So it
went on, amid a bitter quarrel with O'Connell which began mildly
enough in the columns of the *Register* (19 March 1825), indignant
denials by Cobbett of his conversion to Rome, and malicious
editions, published by his enemies, of his earlier writings on the
Catholics (see, for instance, 1*Cobbett's Book of the Roman Catholic

---

1   1825

[133]

COBBETT'S BOOK / OF THE / *Roman Catholic Church.* / IN FOUR PARTS. /
BEING / A FAMILIAR INTRODUCTION / TO HIS / 'HISTORY OF THE
PROTESTANT REFORMATION.' / *Addressed to all sensible and just Catholics.* /

Edited anonymously

Extracts selected to discredit Cobbett.

[First published in parts, February–March 1825.]

*[1825] 4 parts, 64 pp. [Printed by] T. C. Hansard, Paternoster-row-Press, [and
Published by] H. Stemman, Princes Street, Leicester Square, London. 'Price
Threepence.' 8vo. [This copy is bound with *Cobbett's Gridiron*, which it precedes.]

One of the most widely circulated and effective of the many pamphlets and books called
forth by Cobbett's *History of the Protestant Reformation*. Printed by Hansard and published by Stemman (cf. *Book of Wonders*, &c.) in four numbers, each sold for threepence,
it was an able and extremely hostile compilation from Cobbett's earlier anti-Catholic
writings, designed to discredit both his *History* and his ability as an historian. Cobbett
himself referred to it as the publication of 'some base creature' (*Political Register*, February
1825), but the editor, unperturbed, announced that the numbers would be bound from
1 April and would be called 'Cobbett's Red Book' to distinguish it (he said) from the
yellow-wrapped *History of the Protestant Reformation* known to hawkers by 'the un-
dignified appellation of *Cobbett's Little Yellow History*'. Somewhat less circumspect in this
respect was the publication by Simpkin and Marshall of five numbers of *A True History
of the Protestant 'Reformation'* . . ., by 'a Protestant' (see Nos. i–v, 1825 in B.M.),
which, from its title and format down to its method of address and even its yellow
wrappers, was plainly intended as a hostile imitation of Cobbett, difficult to distinguish,
at first glance, from his *History*.

Church, 1825). Through part of this turmoil Cobbett, if his later memory is accurate, was seriously ill and writing sections of the *History* and the *Register* in bed (*Political Register*, 27 September 1828). The last number of the *History* (No. 16) appeared on 1 April 1826—a fortnight later the whole set was being sold for 4s 6d. bound, and Cobbett, whilst announcing his intention of publishing a second part in the near future, was proudly claiming a world-wide sale which included 'two stereotyped editions in the United States', one published in Philadelphia in Spanish for South America (cf. letter from J. Doyle, a New York bookseller, speaking of an American sale next to that of the Bible), and editions in Paris, Rome, and Geneva (*Political Register*, 31 December 1825; 15 April 1826; 13 March, 7 July 1827). This remarkable achievement spurred Cobbett on to new heights of description and endeavour. He now calculated that the print from his own shop amounted to 640,000 separate issues, equal in extent to 'Eighty English Statute acres and Sixty-seven rods'; he announced a forthcoming new edition on 'fine paper'; and he published his Part II on 14 July 1827 at 3s. 6d. Part II, apart from its *Introduction* (a vivid attack on the property of Church and State, simultaneously printed in the *Register*), consisted of a 'list of the monasteries and other objects of confiscation by Henry the Eighth and his successors'. Cobbett frankly stated later that this list was 'mere compilation . . . taken from Bishop Tanner . . .' by a Catholic priest, Rev. J. O'Callaghan, employed by Cobbett for the purpose (*Political Register*, 28 December 1833; for O'Callaghan see his *Usury, 1828 [151], with an Introduction by Cobbett). Meanwhile the circulation of the books was still expanding. By 1828 the total sale of Cobbett's own editions (of separate numbers) was said to be 700,000 (between 70,000 and 80,000 of the first volume), new foreign editions had appeared in Portugal, France, Spain, Holland (*Political Register*, 26 January 1828), an American circulation of over 100,000 copies was claimed, and in Paris there were said to be 'three different booksellers publishing three different translations' (*Political Register*, 27 September 1828). Even the 'Press of the Vatican' was printing his book, Cobbett boasted (*Political Register*, 26 January 1828), but he seems to have dropped his intention of calling his *Letter to . . . the Pope* Part III of the *History* . . . (this *Letter*, published in the *Register* of 15 November 1828, and separately—see [153]—has an interesting mention of Cobbett's Irish *Political Register* issued in Dublin at this time). Cobbett was fond of reminding his readers that this prodigious sale had been achieved, at least in England, in spite of the almost complete neglect of the book by fashionable reviewers. (A partial exception was the Whig *Morning Chronicle*, 9 June 1825, which aroused Cobbett's fury by suggesting that he had been bribed and was providing 'pig's meat' for the poor.) Despite this 'respectable' failure to notice the book, there is no doubt of its enormous influence. Perhaps Cobbett was claiming too much when, in 1829, Catholic Emancipation having been achieved, he wrote, 'it is this book that has caused the Catholic Bill to be carried' (*Political Register*, 11 April 1829), but this is what many of his working-class readers must have thought. His special appeal to the poor is illustrated finally by the fate of his elegant two-volume edition of the *History of the . . . Reformation*. Promised two years before, it had now appeared, variously advertized at £1. 10s. and £1. 11s. actually selling at £1. 11s. 6d., but finding few buyers. Soon Cobbett was offering it at 10s., admitting that he was 'out in' his 'estimate', and resolving 'never to publish a dear book again', for 'the quantity of piety was not always in a direct proportion to the length of purse' (*Political Register*, 23 October 1830). Subsequent low-priced editions of the *History of the Protestant Reformation* were often brought out by Roman Catholic publishers—the most famous of these cheap editions probably being that edited by Abbot F. A. Gasquet (see above) at the close of the nineteenth century, and there were not wanting, in turn, other replies by Protestant apologists (see below,[1] and list compiled by Smith, *William Cobbett, a Biography*, 1878, ii. 243).

---

[1]   1825

[134]

A BRIEF HISTORY / OF THE / PROTESTANT REFORMATION: / IN / A SERIES OF LETTERS, / ADDRESSED TO WILLIAM COBBETT, / IN VINDICATION OF THE / *Misrepresentations and Aspersions* / CONTAINED IN HIS / 'HISTORY OF THE PROTESTANT REFORMATION IN GREAT BRITAIN AND IRELAND.' /

By the Author of 'The Protestant'
[*WILLIAM McGAVIN*]

First published in the *Glasgow Chronicle*.

*1831, 'new edition corrected', 176 pp., W. R. M'Phun, Publisher, Trongate, Glasgow. 8vo.

These letters first appeared in the *Glasgow Chronicle*, where the author William

[137]   1825

THE CATHOLIC APPEAL.

By THE CATHOLIC ASSOCIATION OF IRELAND
Reprinted from the *Political Register, 26 February 1825.

An Appeal of the Catholic Association to the 'People of England'.
It was sold by Cobbett at a halfpenny.

McGavin (1773–1832), a prominent correspondent of that paper, regularly replied to each number of Cobbett's *History of the Protestant Reformation*. McGavin, a self-taught textile merchant and an ardent anti-Catholic, engaged in a great deal of religious and political controversy; and some of his articles, such as the popular series entitled *The Protestant* (1818–22), and a series attacking Robert Owen (1823), were subsequently republished in book form.

                    1826
[135]

A / BRIEF HISTORY / OF THE / BRITISH REFORMATION, / FROM THE RISE OF THE LOLLARDS TO THE DEATH OF / QUEEN MARY: / With Observations on modern Romanism./

                                    ANONYMOUS

*[1826?] Part I, 'The Lollards'; Part II, 'The Days of Queen Mary'; [ii], 324 pp., [illus.]; 336 pp., [illus.]. Published by the Religious Tract Society, and sold at the Depository, 56, Paternoster Row, London. 8vo.

One of the many attacks on Roman Catholicism occasioned by Cobbett's *History of the Protestant Reformation*. This one, published by the Religious Tract Society, had previously appeared in parts; each number, as in this volume, embellished with a grisly portrait illustrating scenes of 'Popish idolatry' and intolerance.

                    1869
[136]

A REPLY / TO / COBBETT'S / 'HISTORY OF THE PROTESTANT REFORMA-TION IN ENGLAND AND IRELAND.'/

                Compiled and edited by CHARLES HASTINGS COLLETTE

*1869, [ii], 347 pp. [+ 8 pp. publisher's advts.]. Published by S. W. Partridge & Co., 9, Paternoster Row, London. 8vo.

A defence of the Protestant Reformation, 'necessitated', according to the author, because of the reissue 'by Romanists', 'in an unprecedently cheap form', of Cobbett's *History of the Protestant Reformation*. The writer, or compiler, makes a great deal of use of the very effective *Cobbett's Book of the Roman Catholic Church*, 1825 (q.v.).

1825

[SPEECH OF MR. O'CONNELL TRANSLATED INTO FRENCH.]

By DANIEL O'CONNELL

A translation of an article in the *Political Register*, 5 March 1825.

O'Connell's speech at a meeting in London, 25 February 1825, reported in the *Political Register* (5 March 1825); the publication by Cobbett of a separate French translation (not in the *Register*) was announced at the same time, but may never have taken place because of their quarrel which began about a fortnight later (for an anti-Cobbett view of this quarrel see the mock *Trial of Daniel O'Connell*, 1825, 3rd edition, O'CONNELL, Cole Collection).

1825

LETTERS / FROM / FRANCE; / . . . / . . . and . . . / . . . part of / the Netherlands; commencing in April, and ending in / December, 1824. /

By JOHN MORGAN COBBETT

*1825, viii, 288 pp. Printed by Mills, Jowett, and Mills (late Bensley), Bolt Court, Fleet Street, London. 8vo.

Like his brother, James Paul (see his *Ride of Eight Hundred Miles*), John Morgan Cobbett (1800–77), the second son, also a barrister, made a journey in France to obtain for his father an account of the state of the country. His longer tour (of the northern, southern, and eastern districts and also part of the Netherlands) began after his brother's return, and took place between April and December 1824. His letters home were published in July 1825, and favourably impressed a reviewer in the *Morning Chronicle*, who amused Cobbett by declaring that he saw in them 'no traces of the waywardness which detract from the value of the writings of the father' (*Morning Chronicle*, 19 July 1825). John Morgan Cobbett, who attended the 1839 Chartist Convention as a delegate, later represented Oldham as an independent member from 1852 to 1865, and finally as a Conservative from 1872 to his death.

GOLD FOR EVER! REAL CAUSES OF THE FALL OF
THE FUNDS: ALSO, WHOLESOME ADVICE TO
HOLDERS OF FUNDS, SCRIP, SHARES, AND ALL
SORTS OF PAPER MONEY.

By WILLIAM COBBETT

[1825, London (B.M.).]

Reprinted in the *Political Register*, 10 September 1825.

Evoked by the crisis caused by the failure of many country banks;
published as a twopenny pamphlet a week before it appeared in the
Political Register.

[141]   1825

BIG O. AND SIR GLORY: / OR, / 'LEISURE TO
LAUGH.' / A COMEDY. / IN THREE ACTS. / BY MR.
COBBETT. /

By WILLIAM COBBETT

First published in the *Political Register*, 24 September 1825.

*1825, 48 pp., printed and published by John Dean, No. 183, Fleet Street,
London, 8vo. [Bound at end of vol. lv of the *Political Register* (July to
September 1825).]

Cobbett published the original edition of this play in the *Political
Register* of 24 September 1825, and a few days later he apologized
for the untidy manner in which, owing to shortness of time, it had
been printed. He expressed his 'deep mortification' at thus being
forced 'to contemplate the disfigured features of the firstborn of my
Dramatic Muse', and also at having left out 'several very interesting
incidents and even several characters'. The manager of his shop,
John Dean, once his farm foreman (see *The Countryman*, 1951,
vol. xliv, No. 1), now reprinted the play in a new edition, and
Cobbett added a preface, dated 'Kensington, 28th September, 1825'.
'Big O.' was Daniel O'Connell (1775–1847), the Irish leader;
'Sir Glory' was the Radical baronet, Sir Francis Burdett (1770–
1847); and *The Times* appeared in the shape of its 'proprietress',
Anna Brodie. 'Big O. and Sir Glory', with its long footnotes and
speeches, although amusing in parts, was far less of a real stage play

than *Surplus Population*, 1831 (see [180]), but Cobbett gave leave 'to all manner of companies' to act his comedy, and added permission for it to be reprinted and republished in Ireland.

[142]

1826

LIFE OF WILLIAM COBBETT / *Author of a Life of Thomas Paine, of a Life of Peter Porcupine* / (*himself*), *of various writings in America under the signature of* / *Peter Porcupine, of the Political Register in England, of the* / Republican *Political Register in America, of good works few,* / *of bad works many.* /

By RICHARD CARLILE

[Issued as No. 19, vol. 13, of *The Republican*, 12 May 1826.]

In *The Republican*, 12 May 1826, No. 19, vol. 13, pp. 576–608. Printed and published by R. Carlile, 135, Fleet Street, London. (Price sixpence.) 8vo.

Richard Carlile (1790–1843), the famous Radical free-thinker, who spent many years in prison in the course of his long struggle for the freedom of the press, was drawn into a sharp quarrel with Cobbett in April 1826. Up till then the two had been uneasy allies; Cobbett defending Carlile and his supporters when they were prosecuted by the Government for publishing 'seditious' or 'blasphemous' writings, but differing from him over his advocacy of Republicanism and 'atheism'. Towards the close of 1824 Carlile, in his weekly journal, *The Republican*, gave some hints of his support for 'a prudent check on conception'. In the following year, with the blessing of Francis Place, he went even farther and began to publish articles and handbills which openly instructed his readers in contraceptive methods. Cobbett, perhaps, was unaware of what was going on, or affected not to notice it. In 1826, however, when Carlile attended one of the 'Feasts of the Gridiron', an indignant correspondent wrote to Cobbett protesting at the presence of 'a Malthusian'. Cobbett responded immediately with a savage attack on Carlile and the 'beastly doctrine'. A group of 'Bolton Reformers' who had just toasted both leaders at their local 'Feast of the Gridiron' had to retract their toast to Carlile, in response to Cobbett's violent demand (although both sides claimed a majority of supporters —see *Political Register*, 29 April 1826; *The Republican*, 28 April 1826), and the *Register* was full of bitter abuse of those who sought 'to recommend to the wives and daughters of the labouring classes the means of putting Malthus's principle in practice. . . .' In retaliation, Carlile wrote this 'Memoir', which filled a whole number of *The Republican* (12 May 1826), gave his support to Cobbett's opponents in the Preston election then taking place, and promised an even larger 'memoir' of Cobbett, and a 'phrenological description of his head' (neither of these publications seem to have appeared). The 'memoir', or *Life*, written to show Cobbett's moral and political inconsistencies, pleased *The Times*, which called both writer and subject 'wretch' (17 May 1826), but it did little more than add a few new stories to the large number already circulated by Cobbett's enemies. Among these Carlile claimed to have proof that Cobbett had obtained by fraudulent means the then unpublished manuscript of his 1819* *Thomas Paine a Sketch of his Life and Character* (see [102]; first published in Moncure Conway's *Life of Thomas Paine* 1892; see also G. D. H. Cole's *Richard Carlile*, Fabian Biographical Series, CARLILE, Cole Collection).

1826

[143]

Cobbett at the King's Cottage. |

By WILLIAM COBBETT

First published in the *Political Register*, 5 August 1826.

*[1826], 8 pp. Printed and published by John Fairburn, Broadway, Ludgate Hill, London. 'Price Twopence.' 8vo.

A petition which Cobbett attempted to present to George IV at Windsor (29 July 1826), and an account of his vain efforts to obtain an audience with the King. Cobbett had recently been defeated at a corrupt, old-style election in Preston (9–26 June 1826), and in this pamphlet he expresses his determination to combine the 'people of Westminster or of . . . Middlesex' with the 'people of the North' in the movement for Reform and 'the total repeal and abolition of the Corn Laws'—the subject of the petition.

1826

[144]

COBBETT'S / POOR MAN'S FRIEND: / OR, / Useful Information and Advice for the Working Classes; / in a Series of Letters, addressed to the Working Classes / of Preston. /

First published in parts in 4 numbers, August–November, 1826; then 5th number added in October 1827; 1830, 'new edition' (3 numbers); and various collected editions henceforth issued.

*1826, 4 nos., [pp. unnumb.], 111 paras., printed and published by W. Cobbett, 183, Fleet Street, London. 'Price Two-pence' (each number). 12mo. [The four numbers are bound with three other works by Cobbett, in a volume entitled 'Cobbett' on the spine.]

*[post-1836] '. . . / OR, / A DEFENCE OF THE RIGHTS OF THOSE WHO DO THE / WORK AND FIGHT THE BATTLES.' / [reissue of 1830 edition], 3 nos., 72 pp., 73 paras., published by Anne Cobbett, 137, Strand, London. [Printed by W. J. Sears, Ivy Lane, London.] 'Price Eightpence.' 12mo. [Bound with other works by Cobbett in a volume entitled 'Cobbett Tracts' on the spine—this being the third item.]

These letters were written by Cobbett after his second attempt to enter Parliament, when, supported by Sir Thomas Branthwayt Beever (1798–1879, a young Norfolk landowner and baronet), he had contested Preston (10–20 June 1826). The contest at Preston,[1] violent and even more unfairly conducted than Cobbett's earlier struggle at Coventry (8–16 March 1820), resulted in the election of Edward Geoffrey Smith Stanley (1799–1869, the future 14th Earl of Derby and Prime Minister) and John Wood (1790–1838, a barrister, later unpopular with opponents of the newspaper tax for his chairmanship of the Board of Stamps). Cobbett, who had withdrawn after expressing his determination to petition Parliament against the election, was left at the bottom of the poll. Nevertheless, he characteristically expressed his pleasure in the fight—'I have not been so happy since the day of my marriage' (*Political Register*, 1 July 1826)—and wound up his campaign with a series of triumphant meetings in Lancashire. On 3 July Cobbett was back in Kensington, and on 1 August, in fulfilment of a promise

---

[1] See the papers relating to this disputed election in Lancashire Record Office, Preston. Among the most effective of the anti-Cobbett publications aroused by the election were eleven numbers of *The Political Mountebank* . . . (Nos. 2–9, Harris Public Library, Preston, with other election broadsheets and posters). This was an ably edited, locally published, daily broadsheet, consisting of examples of Cobbett's 'inconsistencies', together with many of the old hostile stories. Richard Carlile, then conducting his own war with Cobbett (see his *Life of William Cobbett*, 1826), recorded the receipt of ten numbers from 'a friend' and considered that *The Political Mountebank*, which contained a passage from his own indictment, had been the main cause of Cobbett's defeat (*The Republican*, 23 January 1826). *A Collection of Addresses, Squibs, Songs, etc.* . . ., Preston [1826] (Bodl.), contains eleven numbers of *The Political Mountebank* (the last number, undated, is in the Arnold Muirhead Collection).

he had made during the election, he published No. 1 of *The Poor Man's Friend*. Sold at 2*d*., originally intended to be completed in 'about six numbers', it was described as 'a Companion of the Working Classes . . . the means of teaching them how to avoid suffering from Hunger . . .' (*Political Register*, 5 August 1826). Cobbett announced, moreover, that he was going to '*give* one copy of each number to every working family in Preston' as a mark of his 'gratitude' and 'admiration'. By November, when the fourth number[1] had appeared, he had, in fact, bestowed 3,350 of each issue (*Political Register*, 4 November 1826) and a year later, the fifth number, promised by January or February (*Political Register*, 2 December 1826) but delayed, was distributed in the same way (see **Political Register*, 20 October 1827, where No. 5 first appeared). The set, now complete (Nos. 1–5, Goldsmiths' Libr., London) and sold for one shilling, became Cobbett's special pride. He described it variously as 'a really learned work' (*Political Register*, 26 January 1828), 'the most learned work that I ever wrote' (*Political Register*, 27 September 1828), and 'my favourite work—I bestowed more labour upon it than upon any large volume' (**The Cobbett Library*, *c.* 1830). There is indeed some excuse for his praise, for *The Poor Man's Friend* is one of Cobbett's most effective pamphlets, vigorous, lucid, direct, and losing nothing of its force by reason of its simplicity. Into it he poured all his scorn for the Government and its measures, and all his enthusiasm for a pre-Reformation England, 'the richest and most powerful and most admired country in Europe, . . . famed for many things, but especially for its good living, that is to say, for the *plenty* in which the whole of the people lived. . . .' This happy if half-mythical picture, drawn in part from his **History of the Protestant Reformation* ([132]), was contrasted with the contemporary misery. Proposing to show 'how there came to be so much poverty', Cobbett demanded the natural and legal right of every Englishman to enjoy a decent life, itself the prerequisite of freedom. 'Poverty', he wrote, '. . . is, after all, the great badge, the never failing badge of slavery. . . .' *The Poor Man's Friend*, from 1 November 1828, advertised with a new sub-title: 'Essays on the Rights and Duties of the Poor', continued to be sold at one shilling until October 1830 when a new

---

[1] The original MS. of this is in the Cole Collection (see [280]).

8*d*. edition of three numbers[1] was issued, omitting the first and last letters. Letter No. 2 in the first edition now became No. 1, the others were renumbered accordingly, and the sub-title was again altered to 'A Defence of the Rights of those who do the work and Fight the Battles'. In this new format *The Poor Man's Friend* remained a powerful agitational weapon and with some important changes was republished in another version in 1832 (see **Cobbett's Poor Man's Friend . . . Addressed to the Working Men of Scotland*, 1832 [195]). *The Poor Man's Friend*, 1826, published by Stemman, (Goldsmiths' Libr.) is an anti-Cobbett collection.

[145]

1826

RICH AND POOR. / A LETTER FROM WILLIAM COBBETT TO THE PLOUGHBOYS AND / LABOURERS OF HAMPSHIRE. /

ANONYMOUS. [*By PETER GEORGE PATMORE.*]

[In a volume entitled: REJECTED ARTICLES, containing thirteen pieces in imitation of different writers.]
Parody of Cobbett.

*1826. '2nd edition', 'REJECTED ARTICLES', 353 pp. Published by Henry Colburn, New Burlington Crescent. [Cobbett: 'Rich and Poor . . .', 31–63 pp.] 8vo.

A clever parody of an article by Cobbett. The anonymous author, Peter George Patmore (1786–1855), who later edited the *New Monthly Magazine* (1841–53), also parodied a number of other writers, among them the brothers Smith (Horatio or 'Horace', 1779–1849, and James, 1775–1839), who in turn had written highly successful imitations of leading writers and poets in their **Rejected Addresses*, 1812, 19th edition 1839 (see [75]). In this latter work an excellent parody of Cobbett by James Smith had given some indication of the warm affection and fame which the 'plain homespun yeoman' had now won. Patmore did not quite match up to the Smiths; nevertheless, his work was popular enough to reach two editions in 1826 and to be republished, as a fourth edition under another title, *Imitation of Celebrated Authors*, in 1844.

---

[1] In B.M. but wrongly catalogued as '[1826]'. It was published from 11 Bolt Court, premises leased by Cobbett in September 1830.

1827

CATALOGUE OF AMERICAN TREES, SHRUBS, PLANTS, AND SEEDS FOR SALE BY MR. COBBETT.

By WILLIAM COBBETT

[1827, London (University Botanic Garden Libr., Cambridge).]

Reprinted from the *Political Register*, 8 December 1827.

From about 1821, when he had acquired a small nursery ground at Kensington, Cobbett tried hard to interest his readers in the sale of American trees and plants (and even in 'American tulip-tree planks'). These efforts were redoubled between 1827 and 1830 when he leased a small farm at Barnes in Surrey (see *Faithfull MSS., including the printed, *Mr. Cobbett's Sale of Live and Dead Farming Stock, Barn Elm Farm* . . . 1830 [289]). In these years Cobbett printed numerous advertisements of his nursery business in the *Register*, some of which, containing advice on planting, he reprinted for sale or gave away to purchasers (see *Political Register*, 29 March 1826, *Catalogue* . . . ; 25 November 1826, *American Trees and Shrubs*; 10, 17 February 1827, *American Seeds*; 8 December 1827—above, &c.; see also *The Woodlands*, 1828 [148]).

[147]
1828

ELEMENTS OF THE ROMAN HISTORY, IN ENGLISH AND FRENCH, FROM THE FOUNDATION OF ROME TO THE BATTLE OF ACTIUM; . . . THE ENGLISH BY WILLIAM COBBETT; THE FRENCH BY J. H. SIEVRAC. [Separate title-page in French: *Élémens de l'histoire romaine* . . .]

By J. H. SIEVRAC; translated by WILLIAM COBBETT

AN ABRIDGED HISTORY OF THE EMPERORS . . . [(1829), Separate title-page in French: *Histoire abrégée des empereurs* . . .]

[1828, *Elements* . . ., London (B.M.); 1829 *An Abridged History* . . ., London (L. of C.).

Two works intended 'for the use of schools and for young persons in general'. They were printed with the French and English texts side by side, and Cobbett described the first as 'an excellent Exercise Book to my French Grammar' (see note to [130]). The author,

J. H. Sievrac, was also the translator of Cobbett's *History of the Protestant Reformation* (*Political Register*, 26 January 1828). About a year earlier, perhaps because of this, he had come under the vigilant eye of Canning, who suspected, quite unwarrantably, that Sievrac had brought French gold to kindle Cobbett's 'zeal for Catholicism and Spain' (Parker, *Sir Robert Peel*, i. 407–8). Some of Sievrac's memories of Cobbett are reported in *Fraser's Magaziue*, February 1862.

1828

[148]

THE WOODLANDS: / OR, / A TREATISE / On the preparing of ground for planting; on the planting; on the / cultivating; on the pruning; and on the cutting down of Forest / Trees and Underwoods; / DESCRIBING / The usual growth and size and the uses of each sort of tree, the seed / of each, the season and manner of collecting the seed, the manner / of preserving and of sowing it, and also the manner of managing / the young plants until fit to plant out; / THE TREES / Being arranged in Alphabetical Order, and the List of them, in- /cluding those of America as well as those of England, and the / English, French and Latin name being prefixed to the directions / relative to each tree respectively. /

By *WILLIAM COBBETT*

[First published in seven numbers—10 December 1825–29 March 1828.]

· *'1825' [actually 1828], [i], [pp. unnumb.], 601 paras. [+1 p. Index +2 pp. publishers' advts.]. Printed and published by William Cobbett, 183, Fleet Street, London. 8vo.

This was partly the fruit of the seed farm which Cobbett had established at Kensington in 1821. From 'four acres of ground walled in—a very beautiful place indeed' (B.M. Add. MSS. 31127, ff. 18–19), he conducted a successful nursery business, constantly advertising his products in the *Register*, and happily combining his politics with small farming. In December 1825 Cobbett announced the publication of a work entitled *The Woodlands* . . . 'at different times, the actual practice of my whole life', to be issued in 'eight or ten numbers . . . price 2s. each . . . with a wrapper of coloured paper . . . to preserve the numbers for binding . . .' (*Political Register*, 3 December 1825). The first number, dedicated to a close friend, William Budd (1758–1840) of Burghclere, a Hampshire Clerk of the Peace who had introduced Cobbett to Jethro Tull's writings (see Cobbett's edition of the *Horse Hoeing Husbandry*), duly appeared on 10 December 1825, but more than two years were to pass before another number appeared—an unusual delay for Cobbett and one for which he offered a variety of explanations. A year after the publication of the first number he blames the 'late panic' for the delay. This was a reference to the crop of country bank failures, which, he says, 'dragged me back by the hair of the head to the WEN' (*Political Register*, 9 December 1826). A few weeks later the Christmas holidays are said to have delayed publication, whilst in the following summer, quite unabashed, he 'rejoices' that experiments in his nursery grounds had made him delay the series (*Political Register*, 28 July 1827). Cobbett now had other nursery gardens at Barn Elm, near Barnes in Surrey; he boasted of his million 'seedling forest trees' at Kensington, and a more convincing, if unusually modest, excuse for the delay was offered in November when he admitted, 'the truth was . . . I still wanted a good deal of experience in . . . rearing the trees from the seed' (*Political Register*, 10 November 1827). He was now, in fact, winning some fame as a planter and improver of woodlands; in particular the popularity of the false-acacia or locust tree owed much to Cobbett, especially since it had been taken up by his friend the third Earl of Radnor (earlier, Lord Folkestone, 1779–1869). The time was at last ripe for the completion of the series. On 9 February 1828, No. 2 appeared and five more numbers rapidly followed (the seventh and last, 29 March 1828). The volume, now advertised as bound at 15s. (14s. in September 1828), appeared with the title-page misleadingly dated '1825' (see above), and Cobbett, 'laughing by anticipation at all the charges of egotism . . .', pronounced it to be '. . . the only complete one of its kind that ever appeared in print . . .' (*Political Register*, 29 March 1828). From about 1826 onwards Cobbett also produced several *Catalogues* advertising his American seeds (see [146]).

[149]   **1828**

NOBLE NONSENSE!/OR,/COBBETT'S EXHIBITION/ OF THE STUPID AND INSOLENT PAMPHLET OF/ LORD GRENVILLE. /

By WILLIAM COBBETT

First published in the *Political Register*, 3 May 1828.

*[1828], 32 cols. Printed and published by Wm. Cobbett, 183, Fleet Street, London. 'Price Twopence.' [This copy is bound with other works by Cobbett in a volume entitled 'Cobbett's Letters' on the spine, this being the third item in the volume.]

A trenchant attack first published in the *Register* (3 May 1828) and promptly reprinted, concerning a pamphlet by William Wyndham, Lord Grenville (1759–1834). Grenville, a former Prime Minister (1806–7), and himself once one of Pitt's followers, had come round to the position taken by Dr. Robert Hamilton (1743–1829) in his criticism of the Sinking Fund as a means of reducing the National Debt. In his pamphlet *An Essay on the Supposed Advantages of a Sinking Fund* (1828) Grenville admitted how far he and Pitt had been mistaken in accepting Dr. Price's theories (see PRICE, Cole Collection). This, however, was small comfort for Cobbett, who headed this reprint with the sign of the Gridiron and with pardonable irritation reminded the whole of 'The Pitt Crew' of his writings against these theories ever since 1803 (see note to *Paper Against Gold*, 1815 [81]).

1828

[150]

THE / ENGLISH GARDENER; / OR, / A TREATISE / On the Situation, Soil, Enclosing and Laying-Out, of Kitchen Gardens; on the / Making and Managing of Hot-beds and Green-Houses; and on the Propaga- / tion and Cultivation of all sorts of Kitchen-Garden Plants, and of Fruit Trees, / whether of the Garden or the Orchard. / AND ALSO, / On the Formation of Shrubberies and Flower-Gardens; and on the Propagation / and Cultivation of the several sorts of Shrubs and Flowers. / CONCLUDING WITH / A KALENDAR, / Giving Instructions relative to the Sowings, Plantings, Prunings, and other / labours, to be performed in the Gardens, in each Month of the Year. /

By *WILLIAM COBBETT*

[1828, 1st edition, London, Andover printed, '1829' London (B.M.); *1833 (interleaved); 1833 (B.M.); 1838; *1845; &c.]

*1833, 338 pp. [interleaved], [incl. Index], [illus.]. Published at 11, Bolt Court, Fleet Street, London. 8vo.

*1845, [iv], 405 pp. [+5 pp. incl. Index], [illus.]. Published by A[nne] Cobbett, 137, Strand, London. 'Price 6s.' 8vo.

A revised and enlarged form of the *American Gardener . . .*, 1821 ([114]), intended by Cobbett for his own countrymen, and dealing mainly with the kitchen garden, the flower garden, the shrubbery, and the orchard. It was a popular work first published in August 1828 at 6s., and it was followed by a further edition in 1833 (see above for an interleaved issue of 1833 with MS. notes and a hand-painted sketch).

[151]   **1828**

USURY; / OR, / LENDING AT INTEREST; / ALSO, / The Exaction and Payment of certain Church-fees, such as / Pew-rents, Burial-fees, and the like, together with Fore- / stalling Traffick; / ALL PROVED / TO BE REPUGNANT TO THE DIVINE AND ECCLESIASTICAL LAW, AND / DESTRUCTIVE TO CIVIL SOCIETY. / TO WHICH IS PREFIXED / A Narrative of the Controversy between the Author and Bishop Coppinger, and of the Sufferings of the Former in / consequence of his adherence to the Truth. / BY THE / Rev. JEREMIAH O'CALLAGHAN, Rom. Cath. Priest. / . . . / WITH A DEDICATION / TO THE 'SOCIETY OF FRIENDS,' / BY WILLIAM COBBETT. /

By Rev. *JEREMIAH O'CALLAGHAN; 'dedication' by WILLIAM COBBETT*

[1824, 1st edition, New York; 1824 (December), London; *1828, London, with 'dedication' by Cobbett.]

*1828, v, 230 pp. [incl. Index]. Published by William Cobbett, 183, Fleet Street, London. 12mo. [Bound at end with *List of Mr. Cobbett's Books*, c. 1830, pp. 7–11 missing; p. 12 cut.]

The Reverend Jeremiah O'Callaghan (1780–1861) was an Irish Catholic priest suspended from his benefice by his bishop for actively opposing the practice of usury. His appeal to the Pope long un-answered, he sailed to America and there published this book, a devout work attacking the taking of interest and exposing even 'simoniacal practices' within the Catholic Church. Urged by papal authority he returned to Ireland, but meeting with an unfriendly official reception, he travelled to Rome, leaving on the way a copy of his book at Cobbett's shop. Cobbett, at this time engaged in publishing *The History of the Protestant Reformation* ([132]), a work of similar tendency, expressed his thanks in the column of the *Register*, asked the author to call on him, and announced his intention of republishing the book, 'the most interesting work' that he had ever read, making it plain that any profits which accrued would be held for O'Callaghan. (*Political Register*, 13 November, 18, 25 December 1824.) No word of the author was heard, however, until the summer of 1825, when, returning destitute to London, and forbidden to officiate as a priest, he was taken in by Cobbett as a classical tutor to his two sons. Their friendship seems to have flourished—O'Callaghan followed Cobbett in his quarrel with O'Connell, he was paid 'forty sovereigns' for his work in compiling Part II of the *History of the Protestant Reformation*, and when Cobbett published a new 'benefit' edition of O'Callaghan's book in October 1828, he added a mock 'dedication to the "Society of Friends" ' and an eulogistic account of the author (*Political Register*, 23 December 1826, 11 October 1828, 28 December 1833). O'Callaghan returned to America in 1830, settling there and combining his zeal for the Catholic Church with a fierce spirit of anti-capitalism. He republished *Usury* in 1834 and 1856.

[152]   1828

FACTS / FOR THE MEN OF KENT. /

By *WILLIAM COBBETT*

First published in the *Political Register*, 25 October 1828.

*[1828], 6 cols. Printed by William Cobbett, 183, Fleet Street, London. 8vo. [Bound with other works by Cobbett in a volume entitled 'Cobbett's Letters' on the spine, this being the fourth item in the volume.]

A spirited open letter by Cobbett first published in the *Political Register* (25 October 1828) in which he warns the labourers of Kent that 'great efforts' will be made to divide them over Catholic Emancipation. He moves on from the theme he had developed in *The History of the Protestant Reformation* (q.v.) to demand 'the abolition of all clerical tithes' in England and Ireland, and the appropriation of the rest of the Church revenues to the relief of the distressed.

1828
A LETTER TO HIS HOLINESS THE POPE.
                                    By WILLIAM COBBETT
    [1828, London (B.M.).]

Reprinted from the *Political Register*, 15 November 1828.

An attack on the 'Catholic Aristocracy' of England and Ireland.

[154]   1828

A TREATISE / ON / COBBETT'S CORN, / Containing
Instructions for Propagating and Cultivating the / Plant, and for
Harvesting and Preserving the Crop; / AND ALSO / An Account
of the several Uses to which the Produce is / applied, with Minute
Directions relative to each mode of / application. /

                                    By WILLIAM COBBETT

*1828, [pp. unnumb.] [illus.], 203 paras. Published by William Cobbett,
183 Fleet Street, London. 12mo.

*1831, [2nd edition] '. . . WITH / an Addition, containing a Statement of
the result of / Experience up to the Harvest of 1831.' / vi, 242 paras. [illus.].
Published by William Cobbett, 11 Bolt Court, London. 12mo.

In this most entertainingly written treatise Cobbett skilfully
blended agricultural and political advice with fascinating remini-
scences. Contemptuous of his critics and enemies, he waxed lyrical
at the prospect of English farm-labourers seeing 'this beautiful crop
growing in all their gardens . . . instead of the infamous Potato'.
'Cobbett's Corn' was the maize he had seen growing in America
and Cobbett made many efforts to popularize it in this country. In
this he was less successful than with his locust tree or false-acacia
(see *The Woodlands*, 1828 [148]), although he was still full of con-
fidence in the future of 'Cobbett's Corn' in 1831 when he issued
the second edition of the treatise—(above). The first edition (above)
had had a 'title page and table of contents . . . printed upon *paper*
made of *husks* of the corn of my growth this year' (*Political Register*,
29 November 1828), as had also one complete issue of the *Register*
(10 January 1829). This happy feature appears to have gone in
1831, but a new section added to the unchanged text of the first
edition is as outspoken and uncompromising on the subject of
'Cobbett's Corn' as the earlier one had been.

LETTER FROM MR. WILLIAM COBBETT TO MR. HUSKISSON ON THE SUBJECT OF THE AMERICAN TARIFF, INTENDED AS A REPLY TO A SPEECH OF THE LATTER, IN THE BRITISH HOUSE OF COMMONS.

By WILLIAM COBBETT

[1828, London (?) reprinted Philadelphia, n.d. (Library Company, Philadelphia).]

Reprinted from the *Political Register*, 2 August 1828.

No *Letter* from Cobbett directly addressed to William Huskisson, the statesman (1770–1830), appeared in the *Register* in this period. On 2 August 1828 the main article was addressed 'To the Readers of the Register on Huskisson's Schemes . . .' and dealt in detail with Huskisson's speech of 18 July 1828 on American tariffs. Another article entitled 'American Tariffs', the original MS. of which is in the Cole Collection (see [274]), appeared in the next issue of the *Register*. The first of these articles became the text of this *Letter* which is stated to have been reprinted in Philadelphia by John Binns in 1828 from an earlier London edition (Joseph Sabin, *A Dictionary of Books relating to America*, 1871, iv. 184). This London edition has not been traced. The speech is given in *Huskisson's Speeches*, 3 vols., 1831 (Bodl.).

LIST OF / MR. COBBETT'S BOOKS, / PUBLISHED AT No. 183, FLEET STREET, LONDON; / And to be had of all Booksellers in the United Kingdom.

By WILLIAM COBBETT

*[1829], 12 pp. [pp. 5–8 missing]. Printed by Mills, Jowett and Mills, Bolt Court, Fleet Street. 8vo. [Bound with *The Emigrant's Guide*, 1829.]

A descriptive catalogue also entitled *The Cobbett Library*, printed variously, and frequently found (undated) at the end of books by Cobbett from 1828 onwards (see Index of Titles); various selections from the list appeared from time to time as advertisements in the *Political Register* (see also two articles, 'Cobbett's Egotism' and

'Cobbett Library', ibid., 26 January, 27 September 1828); an earlier four-page version, *Mr. Cobbett's Publications, is found from 1822 and a *List of Mr. Cobbett's Publications from 1824 (see note to [125] and Index of Titles under these heads).

[157]   1829
ENGLISHMEN, HEAR ME.

By WILLIAM COBBETT

Reprinted from the *Political Register, 21 February 1829.

Pro-Catholic placard issued by Cobbett and sold at a penny.

[158]   1829
THE / EMIGRANT'S GUIDE; / IN / TEN LETTERS, / ADDRESSED TO / THE TAXPAYERS OF ENGLAND; / CONTAINING / INFORMATION OF EVERY KIND, NECESSARY TO PERSONS WHO / ARE ABOUT TO EMIGRATE; / INCLUDING / Several authentic and most interesting Letters from English Emigrants, now in America, to their Relations in England. /

By WILLIAM COBBETT

*1829, 153 pp. Printed by Mills, Jowett and Mills, published by the Author at 183, Fleet Street, London. 12mo. [Bound with List of Mr. Cobbett's Books, c. 1829 at end; pp. 5–8 missing.]

*1830, 'a new edition', '. . . and an / Account of the Prices of House and Land, recently obtained from / America by Mr. Cobbett', / 168 pp. Printed by Mills, Jowett and Mills. Published by the Author. 12mo.

Cobbett, an old opponent of emigration schemes (see his *Year's Residence in America, 1818, 1819 [94]), was not being inconsistent when he published his Emigrant's Guide in 1829. Beset with constant requests for advice from families facing ruin at home, he decided, when the economic situation was rapidly worsening, to issue a Guide which would not only serve as an everyday handbook but would also warn intending emigrants of the folly, as Cobbett saw it, of Englishmen proceeding to any other place than the already culti-vated regions of America. His qualms about emigration never left him, however, and from the first to the last the *Guide* was advertised with a footnote which began 'it grieves me very much to know it to be my duty to publish this book...'. Similarly *Twopenny Trash* for March 1831 (q.v.) bitterly condemns a wholesale emigration scheme then being canvassed. *The Emigrants Guide*, published on 1 August 1829, and sold cheaply for 2s. 6d., succeeded so well that by May and October 1830 two new editions had been issued adding, respectively, a *Postscript* relating to property (original MS. in Cole Collection, see [280]) and a *List* of essential stores (*Political Register*, 1 August 1829, 15 May, 2 October 1830).

[159]   1829

French versus *Cobbett*. / COBBETT / ON / THE GRID-IRON!! / (GRILLED TO A CINDER!) / BEING AN ANSWER TO COBBETT'S REGISTER / OF OCTOBER 3, 1829. /

By *DANIEL FRENCH*

*[1829] 24 pp. Printed and published by Daniel French, No. 3, The Mall, Kensington Gravel Pits. Sold by John Fairburn, Broadway, Ludgate Hill, London. 8vo.

This pamphlet, a curious mixture of defamation and religious devotion, was the work of Daniel French, a Catholic barrister. He and Cobbett had not long since been good friends, especially since French had been expelled from the English Catholic Association, allegedly for 'rudeness', more probably for trying to combine the movement for Catholic Emancipation with that of the extreme Reformers (*Political Register*, 12 July 1828). His other activities and qualities had at first also commended themselves to Cobbett and his family. Although a good Latin scholar, he had apparently been passed over without any reason when he applied for a Latin Professorship at the 'Scotch' London University (*Morning Herald*, 30 July; *Political Register*, 8 August 1829), and he joined Cobbett in attacking O'Connell and in setting up the General Association of Friends of Civil and Religious Liberty (which soon became the Association of Friends of Radical Reform or the Radical Reform Association—see *Political Register*, 19, 26 July, 30 August 1828, 11 July 1829, and Carlile's *The Lion*, 9 October 1829). Cobbett published French's *Translation of the Celebrated Oration of Demos-*

thenes against Leptines (30 May 1829), and only a few days before their quarrel referred to the barrister as 'one of the most amiable and upright men that ever lived' (*Political Register*, 8 August 1829). What really happened to disrupt this friendship and what was said by both sides is still obscure. From French, a rather disreputable witness, there were dark rumours of Mrs. Cobbett's past attempt at suicide, 'a twelvemonth since', and her present suicidal mood, both induced, according to French's account of her conversation with him, by the unprintable 'goings on' committed by her husband and his secretary, Charles Mulvey Riley, at Barn Elms Farm, whilst the latter's wife was away (Riley was also the editor of *Radical Reports . . . of the Radical Reform Association*, published by Cobbett, August 1829, and the author of a *MS. *Life of William Cobbett*; see [273]). Cobbett in turn accused French of a 'base conspiracy' against the life of Mrs. Cobbett, and for good measure added a charge of adultery with Riley's wife. All these sordid insinuations became public when Cobbett's three sons assaulted French in the street. At their trial at Hicks' Hall (24 September 1829) they were found 'guilty . . . under strong provocation', and the moderate verdict (all were bound over and fined) was widely acclaimed as a triumph and a vindication of the Cobbett family (for the disturbed state of Cobbett's family relationships in these last years see Cole, **Life . . .*, 1947 ed., and a letter reprinted in *The Countryman, 1932; for the trial, see *Faithfull MSS. [289], and *The Singular and Unprecedented Trial . . .*, 1829, Arnold Muirhead Collection).

[160]   1829

MR. COBBETT'S FIRST LECTURE ON THE PRESENT PROSPECTS OF MERCHANTS, TRADERS, AND FARMERS, AND ON THE STATE OF THE COUNTRY, IN GENERAL, DELIVERED IN THE THEATRE OF THE LONDON MECHANICS INSTITUTION, ON THURSDAY, 26TH OF NOVEMBER, 1820.

[MR. COBBETT'S SECOND LECTURE. DELIVERED 10TH DECEMBER 1829.]

[MR. COBBETT'S THIRD LECTURE. DELIVERED 17TH DECEMBER 1829.]

[MR. COBBETT'S FOURTH LECTURE. DELIVERED
11TH FEBRUARY 1830.]

[MR. COBBETT'S FIFTH LECTURE. DELIVERED
18TH FEBRUARY 1830.]

By *WILLIAM COBBETT*

[1829, London (Arnold Muirhead Collection).]

A report of Cobbett's five lectures given at the London Mechanics'
Institution during the winter of 1829–30. They attracted a great
deal of attention at the time, and for once Cobbett expressed his
satisfaction with the fair comment they received in the London
press, particularly on the occasion of the third lecture, when a small
'party of Irishmen' unsuccessfully tried to provoke a riot. This
seems to have been an exceptional event occasioned by his feud with
Henry Hunt. For the most part the members of his audience, having
paid their shilling admission fee, were attentive and appreciative
(see a report in the *Morning Herald* cited in the *Political Register*,
19 December 1829, which speaks of his two and a quarter hour's
lecture delivered with the aid of very few notes). *Mr. Cobbett's
Third Lecture* was also republished in Birmingham by J. Russell,
as part of a broadsheet giving *A Summary Report* of the formation
of the Birmingham Political Union (B.M.).

[161]   1830

AN / ACCURATE REPORT / OF / MR. COBBETT'S /
LECTURE-SPEECH / ON THE / PRESENT DIS-
TRESSES OF THE COUNTRY, / AND THEIR REME-
DIES, / AS DELIVERED BY HIM IN THE THEATRE,
HALIFAX, / ON SATURDAY EVENING, JAN. 16TH
1830, / TO A MOST RESPECTABLE AND CROWDED
AUDIENCE. /

By *WILLIAM COBBETT*

*1830, 2nd edition, 16 pp. Halifax. Printed and sold by N. Whitley,
Chronicle Office, Halifax. Price 3*d*. 4to.

In the winter of 1829–30 Cobbett made his first 'Northern'
lecture tour of Lancashire, Yorkshire, and the Midlands (see
Rural Rides, Cole edition, 1930). His second meeting in Yorkshire, at Halifax, was a great success, although he found his friends

157

there in 'despair' because it was such an 'aristocratical place', and the meeting, due to take place in the evening, had been advertised only on the morning of the same day. Nevertheless, the 'very beautiful little theatre', granted gratuitously by the lessee, 'was filled chock-full', with a 'respectable' audience who listened to him 'attentively' for nearly three hours (*Political Register*, 23 January 1830). In his *Register* Cobbett made only a brief reference to his 'harangue', but this enlarged second edition of a *Report* published at the office of the *Halifax Commercial Chronicle* is a very full account and, in its completeness, gives a valuable and impressive picture of Cobbett's power as a lecturer.

[162]   1830

THREE LECTURES ON THE STATE OF THE COUNTRY DELIVERED AT THE MUSIC HALL, SHEFFIELD, BY MR. WM. COBBETT, JANUARY 28TH, 30TH, AND FEBRUARY 1ST, 1830.

By WILLIAM COBBETT

[1830, Sheffield (Sheffield Reference Libr.).]

Cobbett had caught a bad cold when he reached Sheffield on his 'Northern' lecture tour and, according to this report published locally by G. R. Burgin, he began by proposing 'to postpone the lecture to another evening or to go on, just as you please (cries of "go on" and "we can't hear")'. Cobbett interpreted this mixed reception in his own way: 'Gentlemen, as it appears to be the desire, on I go . . .'; and he went on to such good effect that at the end of the last lecture, in appreciation of his 'severe hoarseness', 'three cheers were given . . . by a numerous company.'

[163]   1830

MR. COBBETT'S ADDRESS / *To the Tax-Payers of England and Scotland, on the subject of the* / SEAT IN PARLIAMENT. /

By WILLIAM COBBETT

Reprinted from the **Political Register*, 10 April 1830 with some additions.

*[1830] 'new edition enlarged', 16 pp. Printed by William Cobbett, Johnson's court; and published by him, at 183, Fleet-street, London. (Price 2*d*.) 8vo.

A proposal to raise a fund of £10,000 in order to place Cobbett in Parliament. The original manuscript of this appeal is in the Cole Collection (see [274]). Cobbett reprinted it at once as a twopenny pamphlet (not in '1832' as *B.M. Catalogue*) and added fresh details to its long autobiographical section.

[164]   1830

GOOD FRIDAY; / OR, / THE MURDER OF JESUS CHRIST / BY THE JEWS. /

By WILLIAM COBBETT

[*1830, London; American edition in *Thirteen Sermons* . . .: 1834, New York; n.d. Philadelphia; 1846, New York.]

*1830, 24 pp. Published by the Author, 183, Fleet Street, London. 12mo.

Cobbett always expressed the strongest antipathy to Jews, who, he thought, were cursed for their past history, their religion, and their profession of usury (although sometimes he thought Quakers were even worse). In this pamphlet, or sermon, published on 15 May 1830, he violently condemns any movement for 'liberality' towards them, and whilst uttering a warning against persecution, he repeats even the stupid slander which alleged a Jewish blood rite. The pamphlet, partly aroused by a Bill to remove Jewish disabilities, was a sequel to Cobbett's successful *Sermons* (see [112]), previously published in 1822. It does not appear to have been ordinarily issued in a collected form with these in England (cf. A. M. Muirhead, *The Library*, xx, No. I, June 1939), although *The Cobbett Library*, c. 1833–4 . . ., q.v., and the *Register*, 25 January 1831, advertised one such issue, possibly in error. In America, however, it was included in three different editions, entitled *Thirteen Sermons with an Address* . . . . Cobbett often referred to *Good Friday*, and in 1833 he reprinted it in the *Register* (9 March 1833). The manuscript of the pamphlet is in the Cole Collection (see [280]).

A / GRAMMAR / OF / THE ITALIAN LANGUAGE: / OR, / A PLAIN AND COMPENDIOUS INTRODUC-TION / TO / THE STUDY OF ITALIAN. /

By JAMES PAUL COBBETT

*1830, xvi, 392 pp. Printed for the author, and published at 183, Fleet Street, London. '6s. Boards.' [Bound with 12 pp. *List of Mr. Cobbett's Books*, c. 1832, at front.]

An Italian grammar by James Paul Cobbett published in May 1830 (see his *Journal of a Tour in Italy*, 1830 [178]). A second edition of the grammar was advertised in August 1835. In January 1834 he produced *Practical Exercises to Cobbett's French Grammar* (q.v.), and in March 1835 *A Latin Grammar for the use of English Boys*. He also translated from the French *A Sketch of the Life of General Lafayette*, 1830, and published *The Law of Pawns or Pledges*, 1841, 1849.

RURAL RIDES / IN THE COUNTIES OF / Surrey, Kent, Sussex, Hampshire, Wiltshire, Glou- / cestershire, Here-fordshire, Worcestershire, So- / mersetshire, Oxfordshire, Berk-shire, Essex, Suf- / folk, Norfolk, and Hertfordshire: / WITH / Economical and Political Observations relative to / matters applic-able to, and illustrated by the State / of those Counties respectively. /

By WILLIAM COBBETT

Contents of first edition (1830) first published intermittently in *Political Register*, 1821–6; contents of later editions first published in *Political Register*, 1821–34.

[167]

COBBETT'S / TOUR IN SCOTLAND; / AND IN THE FOUR / NORTHERN COUNTIES OF ENGLAND: / IN THE AUTUMN OF THE YEAR / 1832. /

By WILLIAM COBBETT

First published in *Political Register*, 29 September, 24 November 1832.

1830, [ii], 45–124* pp.; 1–668 pp. Printed by B. Bensley, Andover; published by William Cobbett, 183, Fleet Street, London, 12mo. [This copy is bound with 12 pp. *The Cobbett Library*, c. 1835, at end.]

*1833, '. . . Tour in Scotland; and in the four Northern Counties of England, in the Autumn of the year 1832'. ix, 11–264 pp. Published at 11, Bolt Court, London. 'Price 2s. 6d.' 12mo.

*1853 . . . SURREY, KENT, SUSSEX, HANTS, BERKS, OXFORD, BUCKS, / WILTS, SOMERSET, GLOUCESTER ,HEREFORD, SALOP, WORCESTER, / STAFFORD, LEICESTER, HERTFORD, ESSEX, SUFFOLK, NORFOLK, / CAMBRIDGE, HUNTINGDON, NOTTINGHAM, LINCOLN, YORK, LAN- / CASTER, DURHAM AND NORTHUMBERLAND, IN THE YEARS / 1821, 1822, 1823, 1825, 1826, 1829, 1830 AND 1832: / . . . . / A New Edition with Notes, / BY JAMES PAUL COBBETT . . . / [iv], [Portr., illus.], 684 pp. [incl. 'Addenda and Errata'] [+2 pp. publisher's advts.]. Published by A. Cobbett, 137, Strand, London, 12mo.

*1908, 2 vols., '. . . a new edition with notes by Pitt Cobbett, Vicar of Crofton, Hants.' [Portr.] xliii, 406, 408 pp. [incl. Index]. Published by Reeves and Turner, London, 8vo.

*1908, 'Selected and edited by J. H. Lobban . . . ' xx, 231 pp. [incl. 'Notes']. Published by Cambridge University Press, 8vo. [In the *English Literature for Schools* series.]

*[1910], vol. 2 only, 253 pp. [+2 pp. publisher's advts.]. Published by Robert Culley, 25–35 City Road, London. 8vo. [In the *Finsbury Library* series.] [Vol. 1 missing.]

*[1912], [reissue of J. P. Cobbett's 1853 edition], 2 vols. 'with an introduction by Edward Thomas,' xi [+1 p. Bibliog.], [i], 320 pp.; vii, 335 pp. + 'Notes' and Index. 8vo. Published by J. M. Dent & Sons, Ltd., London. [In *Everyman's Library*.]

*[1914], iii, 4–570 pp. [4 pp. publisher's advts.], [illus.]. Published by T. Nelson & Sons, London. 8vo. [In *Nelson's Classics* series.]

*1930, RURAL RIDES / IN THE SOUTHERN, WESTERN AND EASTERN COUNTIES / OF ENGLAND. TOGETHER WITH / TOURS IN SCOTLAND / AND IN THE NORTHERN AND MIDLAND COUNTIES OF / ENGLAND, AND / LETTERS FROM IRELAND / . . . / THE WHOLE, INCLUDING MANY RIDES AND TOURS / NEVER BEFORE REPRINTED, EDITED WITH AN INTRO- / DUCTION, NOTES, A BIBLIOGRAPHICAL RECORD OF UPWARDS / OF NINE HUNDRED PERSONS MENTIONED, AN INDEX OF / PLACES, AND A BIBLIO- GRAPHICAL NOTE / BY / G. D. H. AND MARGARET COLE, / WITH NUMEROUS VIGNETTES BY JOHN NASH, AND / A MAP OF COBBETT'S COUNTRY BY A. E. TAYLOR. / 3 vols., xi, 1064 pp. Published by Peter Davies, London. 8vo.

*1932, '. . . Selections . . . edited, with an introduction by Guy Boas', xiii, 152 pp. [illus.]. Published by Macmillan and Co., London. 8vo. [In *English Literature* series, No. 22.]

The *Rural Rides*, probably the most familiar and lasting of Cobbett's works, were originally a series of letters which began in the *Political Register* from the autumn of 1821. The first edition, announced at the end of 1829, seems to have been held up for some time, and was finally sold for 5s., half the original advertised price (*Political Register*, 19 December 1829, 30 October 1830). This delay explains, perhaps, the odd pagination of the book, rarely found in a work by Cobbett (see a valuable article, *Bibliographical Notes and Queries*, vol. ii, No. 12, May 1939, by A. Muirhead, for details of variant issues). *Rural Rides*, widely held to be a masterpiece of description and political journalism, has often been reprinted, most notably in 1930, in G. D. H. and Margaret Cole's edition—see above—where much material from the *Register* was included for the first time, together with comprehensive bibliographical, historical, and biographical notes (see also Cole, *Life . . .*, ch. xxi; for *Cobbett's Tour in Scotland*, 1832, and the *Letters of William Cobbett to Charles Marshall*, 1834, both included in the Coles' edition, see under their titles, [193] and [211], respectively).

[168]   1830

COBBETT'S EXPOSURE OF THE PRACTICE OF THE PRETENDED FRIENDS OF THE BLACKS.

By WILLIAM COBBETT

[1830, London (L. of C.).]

Reprinted from the *Political Register*, 26 June 1830.

Attacks on the opponents of negro slavery (for Cobbett's attitude, see *American Slave Trade*, 1822 [118], and Clarke's *Letter to Mr. Cobbett*, 1806 [65]).

[169]   1830

FRENCH REVOLUTION: AN ADDRESS TO THE PEOPLE OF PARIS AGREED TO AT THE LONDON TAVERN . . . AT A DINNER OF RADICAL REFORMERS, AUGUST 16, 1830 . . . .

By WILLIAM COBBETT

[1830, Birmingham (Goldsmiths' Libr., London).]

Reprinted from the *Political Register*, 21 August 1830.

A Birmingham reprint of the 'Address to the Brave People of Paris' read by Cobbett at a great dinner held in London in August 1830 to commemorate the French Revolution of the previous month (see the note to *Eleven Lectures on the French and Belgian Revolutions, 1830 [172]).

1830

[170]

TABLEAU DE L'ANGLETERRE EN 1830, PAR WILLIAM COBBETT. NUMEROS I, II, III.

By WILLIAM COBBETT

[1830, Paris (Bibliothèque Nationale, Paris).]

Translated from the *Political Register, 14, 21 August 1830.

These three articles from the *Register* (14, 21 August 1830) on the 'State of England' were published by Laran in Paris in a French translation. The series continued at home until seven articles had appeared, the last four in English and French.

1830

[171]

ADVICE TO YOUNG MEN / AND (INCIDENTALLY) TO / YOUNG WOMEN, / IN THE / Middle and Higher Ranks of Life. / IN A SERIES OF LETTERS, ADDRESSED TO / A YOUTH, A BACHELOR, A LOVER, A HUSBAND, A FATHER, / A CITIZEN, OR A SUBJECT. /

By WILLIAM COBBETT

['1829', London, Andover printed (B.M.); *1829, London; 1831, New York (Library Company, Philadelphia); 1833, New York (Historical Society of Pennsylvania); 1837, London (B.M.); &c.; 1851, 1881, Philadelphia; 1842, 1889, Paris; 1861–1937, London, numerous eds. (B.M.).]

[First issued in fourteen monthly parts June 1829–September 1830.]

*'1829', [actually 1830], [pp. unnumb.], 355 paras. Printed by Mills, Jowett and Mills; published by the author, 11, Bolt Court, Fleet Street, London. 12mo.

*1868, 'new edition', [portr.], x [+1 p. publisher's advts.]. 335 pp. Published by Charles Griffin and Company, Stationers' Hall Court, London. 8vo.

*1887, 'With an introduction by Henry Morley', 286 pp. [+9 p. publisher's advts.]. Published by George Routledge and Sons, Broadway, Ludgate Hill, London. 8vo. [In *Morley's Universal Library*, No. 48.]

*1906, 'from the edition of 1829,' 303 pp. [+4 pp. publisher's advts.]. Published by Henry Frowde, London and Oxford University Press, Humphrey Milford, London. 8vo. [Reprint dated 1923.]

*1926, 'With a preface by the Rt. Hon. Philip Snowden', xv, 335 pp. Published by Peter Davies, London. 8vo.

*1930, 'With illustrations after Gillray. Edited with a Preface by Earl E. Fisk', [pp. unnumb., illustrated]. Alfred A. Knopf, London, New York. 4to.

The *Advice to Young Men . . .*, in some ways, one of Cobbett's greatest works, contains less directly political matter than most of his writings at this time, although Cobbett, announcing its appearance in sixpenny monthly parts, seemed to be as pointed as ever. 'I shall begin with the Youth,' he wrote, 'go to the Young Man or the Bachelor, talk the matter over with him as a Lover, then consider him in the character of Husband; then as Father; then as Citizen or Subject, though if he will be ruled by me, he will, if he can, contrive to exist in the former of those two capacities' (*Political Register*, 25 April 1829). The first number 'covered by a [printed] wrapper made of the corn paper', duly appeared on 1 June 1829, and it was followed by thirteen other numbers, each, except for two delays (November 1829, February 1830) issued once a month (some of Cobbett's original manuscripts for these are to be found in the Cole Collection, see [280]). The fourteen numbers (not twelve, as had originally been announced) were thus completed in September 1830, and in November, after odd numbers (and labels for binding) had been nearly cleared, Cobbett announced that the work would be sold for 5s. bound in boards (*Political Register*, 20 November 1830). Meanwhile it was proving fairly popular. By April 1830, Nos. 2 and 3 were being reprinted and by the following October there was news of a French edition, published (not by Cobbett) in Paris (*Political Register*, 20 April, 9 October 1830; another French edition of 1889 is in the B.M.). The *Advice to Young Men*, although one of the most frequently republished, was not, however, the most widely circulated of Cobbett's works. This, perhaps, because, as its title indicates, it was one of his few writings not primarily intended for a working-class public, and not mainly concerned with politics. The *Advice* is chiefly a restatement of Cobbett's outlook on life, in which he tries to show, with an egotism that never offends, how others could follow the road he had hewn for himself. Happiness could be won only by work and by a spirit of independence: to illuminate his text Cobbett set forth some of the facts of his own life. Yet with all this, there is not a whisper of the priggish, pompous 'good book' that at this time and later preached a superficially similar sermon, nor of the morbid censure that usually went with such a theme. (For a more thorough appraisal, see Cole, *Life . . .*, ch. xx.) *Advice to Young Men*, despite the backward-looking character of some of its ideas, thus remains an essentially modern book, retaining its popularity in the twentieth century in at least six editions since 1900, the latest (an extract) as recently as 1937, and another reproducing anti-Cobbett cartoons by Gillray, published in 1930 (see above).

1830

[172]

ELEVEN / LECTURES / ON THE / FRENCH AND BELGIAN / REVOLUTIONS, / AND / ENGLISH BOROUGHMONGERING: / DELIVERED IN THE / THEATRE OF THE ROTUNDA, BLACKFRIARS BRIDGE, / BY / WILLIAM COBBETT. / WITH A PORTRAIT. /

By *WILLIAM COBBETT*

First published in eleven parts, September 1830–October 1830.

*1830, [11 parts:] 8 pp.; 16 pp. [second edition]; 16 pp.; 12 pp.; 12 pp.; 12 pp.; 16 pp.; 16 pp.; 16 pp.; 16 pp.; 12 pp.; [+2 pp. title-page and contents] [portr. missing.] Published by W. Strange, 21, Paternoster Row, London. 8vo. [First *Lecture*, price 2*d.*, others 3*d.*; the 11 parts are bound with works by Cobbett and others in a volume entitled 'Cobbett's Register & Lectures' on the spine.]

At the end of July 1830, when Reform agitation was mounting in England, the news of the successful Revolution in France, followed by that in Belgium, electrified middle- and working-class Reformers alike. The limited nature of these *coups* was not yet clear—all that was noticed was the upsurge of working class Paris, Brussels, and then Warsaw—against despotic government. This Cobbett warmly supported, seeing it as a precedent for action at home, although he remained firmly opposed to a violent English revolution or, indeed, to an English Republic. On 16 August he presided at a great dinner in honour of the French people (*Political Register*, 7 August 1830); between 9 September and 7 October he began this series of eleven popular lectures at the Rotunda, Blackfriars Road, and meanwhile he vigorously collected funds for the widows and orphans of the fallen (more than £50 was collected from his mainly working-class audiences at the Rotunda; see *Ninth Lecture* . . ., 30 September, op. cit.) The lectures, sometimes two in a week, were immediately published by the Radical bookseller W. Strange, apparently as they were taken down by a reporter. Even in print they give some idea of Cobbett's remarkable histrionic power (cf. *Tait's Edinburgh Magazine*, November 1832; and S. T. Hall, *Sketches of Remarkable People*, 1873). In this series he delighted his audience with his many tricks of voice and gesture, switching for instance from bitter indignation at one moment to comic parody at another (see, for example, his dialogue between a Malthusian lawyer and a farmer—*Third Lecture*, 9 September, op. cit.). Once he read the whole of a petition to the King, making suitable asides (see *Fourth Lecture* . . ., 13 September, op. cit., also *A Letter to the King*, 1830); on another occasion, with a masterly sense of stagecraft, he had a young Frenchman up on the platform to sing the *Marseillaise* (*Second Lecture* . . ., 6 September, op. cit.). The lectures seem to have been as popular in pamphlet form as they had been at the Rotunda, and they were sold together with a title-page and a portrait of Cobbett (missing from above copy) for 3s. Soon they were supplemented by his advanced *Plan of Parliamentary Reform* (*Political Register*, 30 October 1830, reprinted November, see [177]), which with his lecture tours placed Cobbett in the forefront of the battle for the franchise.

[173]   1830
A LETTER TO THE KING. /

                                                By WILLIAM COBBETT

Taken from Cobbett's *Petition to the King*, 15 September 1830.

*[1830], [portr.], 8 pp. Printed and published by W. P. Chubb, 18, Holywell Street, Strand, London. 8vo.

An adaptation from Cobbett's petition to the King in favour of

Parliamentary Reform and against the sinecure system, presented to and acclaimed by an audience numbering '1,348 persons at the least' (*Political Register*, 18 September 1830) at the fourth (13 September 1830) of Cobbett's popular lectures on the continental revolutions (see his *Eleven Lectures on the French and Belgian Revolution*, 1830 [172]). The editor, probably W. P. Chubb, gives no indication that this *Letter* was originally a petition. It is prefaced by an unusual portrait of Cobbett (by Pickering) and it closes with some details of pensions, headed 'Nice Pickings', which appear to be taken from a broadside of that title (Goldsmiths' Libr., London) published by Hetherington of Kingsgate Street, Holborn (referred to in the *Eleventh Lecture*, op. cit.). There was also an anti-Cobbett pamphlet called '*Nice Pickings*', published by Rivington.

[174]   1830

HISTORY / OF THE / REGENCY AND REIGN / OF / *King George the Fourth.* /

By WILLIAM COBBETT

First published in monthly parts from September 1830; partially and intermittently reprinted in the *Political Register*, 8 January 1831–28 January 1832.

> *1830, vol. i, [vi], [pp. unnumb.], 220 paras. Printed by Mills, Jowett and Mills, Bolt Court; published by William Cobbett, 183, Fleet Street, London. 12mo. [This copy is bound with *List of Mr. Cobbett's Books*, 12 pp., c. 1832, at end.]

> *1834, vol. ii, [pp. unnumb.], paras. 221–511 [+17 pp. 'Chron. Table' + 16 pp. Index]. 'Price 10s. 6d. the two volumes.' 12mo. [This copy is bound with *Books published by Mr. Cobbett*, 2 pp. at end.]

Cobbett published this *History* . . . in monthly parts (No. 1, September 1830), the first two numbers being priced at 8d. and then at 6d. It was not completed till 1834, when the intermittently produced numbers were collected in two volumes—see above (No. 1, vol. I, is to be found in manuscript in the Cole Collection; see [280]). Cobbett seems to have wearied of his task, or given his attention to other matters, for the work is for the most part a dull chronicle without the strength and sparkle shown in his journals and pamphlets. Perhaps, for similar reasons, he failed to fulfil his earlier ambition, promised at the launching of this work, to publish 'a complete History of England'.

1830

Á TALLEYRAND PERIGORD.

By WILLIAM COBBETT

Reprinted from the *Political Register*, 16 October 1830.

A French translation of Cobbett's 'First Letter to Talleyrand.'

[176] 1830

AUX BRAVES OUVRIERS DE PARIS.

By WILLIAM COBBETT

Reprinted from the *Political Register*, 30 October 1830.

An Address first published in English in the previous week.

[177] 1830

COBBETT'S PLAN / OF / PARLIAMENTARY REFORM; / ADDRESSED TO / THE YOUNG MEN OF ENGLAND. /

By WILLIAM COBBETT

First published in the *Political Register*, 30 October 1830.

*[1830], 14 pp. [+2 pp. publisher's advts.]. Published by W. Strange, Paternoster-Row, London. 'Price Two-pence.' 8vo.

Cobbett addressed this appeal to the young men of England because, he says, unlike 'us, their fathers', the young are still unbroken in spirit. The *Plan* . . ., published at first in the *Political Register*, 30 October 1830 (reprinted and widely distributed as a pamphlet, November; see above) was the programme of the most advanced section of the Parliamentary Reformers. It called for Annual Parliaments, one vote for all men over eighteen years of age, no exclusion of pauper, soldier, or sailor voters, an adult, residential non-property qualification for members, and the introduction of the ballot. Cobbett in his *Plan* . . . went even farther than the 'Father of Reform', Major John Cartwright (1740–1824), had done, and he criticizes the latter's 'fanciful notion that the members ought to be apportioned to the landed property'. Cobbett supplemented his *Plan* . . . by a new intense round of lecturing and writing, and then escaped from a trumped-up charge (see **A Full and Accurate Report of the Trial*, 1831 [182]), to emerge as one of the most redoubtable leaders of the Reform agitation.

[178]   1830

JOURNAL / OF / A TOUR IN ITALY, / AND ALSO IN PART OF / *France and Switzerland*; / . . . FROM OCTO-BER, 1828, TO SEPTEMBER, 1829 / . . . .

By *JAMES PAUL COBBETT*

*1830, 392 pp. Published at 11, Bolt Court, Fleet Street, London. [This copy is bound with 12 pp. *List of Mr. Cobbett's Books* at the end and 1 p. publisher's advts. at the front.]

This was the second tour on the Continent by James Paul Cobbett (see **A Ride of Eight Hundred Miles*, 1824 [129]), and these impressions of his travels, chiefly in Italy, were published in November 1830, six months after his **Grammar of the Italian Language* ([165]).

[179]   1831

A / SHORT ACCOUNT / OF THE / *Life & Death* / OF / SWING, THE RICK-BURNER; / WRITTEN BY ONE WELL ACQUAINTED WITH HIM. / TOGETHER WITH THE/CONFESSION OF THOMAS GOODMAN,/ NOW UNDER SENTENCE OF DEATH, IN HORSHAM JAIL, / FOR RICK-BURNING. /

By *G.W.S-E.* [*possibly by H. N. COLERIDGE*]

*[1831], 26 pp., [illus.]. Printed by R. Clay, Bread-street, Hill; published by Effingham Wilson, 88, Royal Exchange, London. 'Price Two-pence or 1s. 6d. per Dozen.' 12mo. [This copy is bound with other items in a volume entitled 'Machine Breaking &c.' on the spine, this item being the sixth in the volume.]

In July 1831, more than six months after the 'Last labourers' revolt' had been suppressed, Cobbett had crushingly defeated the latest attempt to implicate him in the 'rising' (see **A Full and Accurate Report of the Trial*, 1831 [182]). One of the most infamous of the earlier efforts to involve him in the rioting was the obtaining of a bogus 'confession' from an unfortunate youth of eighteen, Thomas Goodman (see *Imposture Unmasked*, 1831), who, lying under sentence of death, was visited by the local gentry and clergy and induced to write a statement blaming Cobbett's 'lactures' [*sic*] for the fires and riots. Soon two more 'confessions' followed, each of which improved on its predecessor, and Goodman was quickly pardoned, although others at least as young and as culpable were being hanged or transported (see *Political Register*, 1 January, 8 January, 19 February 1831). This pamphlet, bitterly anti-Cobbett in tone, reprints at the end the whole of the final version of Goodman's 'confession', which it illustrates in lurid fashion on the front page. The pamphlet begins with a pretended life of 'Swing', the mysterious organizer of the fires, who is said to be a gin-sodden small farmer, partly of Irish descent. The author, possibly, Henry Nelson Coleridge (1798–1843; see J. W. Wood's *Selections from the Letters of Robert Southey*, 1856, iv. 222) showed no less imagination than those peers in the House of Lords who thought the riots were the work of foreigners. There were also other pretended lives of 'Swing' appearing at this time, among them one published by Carlile, and another reviewed by Perronet Thompson in the *Westminster Review*. 'Swing' (derived according to Cobbett, from an old term for part of a flail, then being displaced by machinery) was the signature adopted by individuals, or bodies of farm-labourers and craftsmen, from all over the southern and western counties, and even farther north, without any other plan than the threat of arson if their demands were not met (see *Political Register*, 13 November 1830, where 'Swing' appears in Kent; 11 December, in Yorkshire, and 25 December, in Suffolk where he is 'apprehended'; see also Hammonds' *The Village Labourer*, 1911).

[180]   1831

SURPLUS POPULATION: / AND POOR-LAW BILL. / A COMEDY, / IN THREE ACTS. /

By WILLIAM COBBETT

First published in the *Political Register*, 28 May 1831, and in *Cobbett's Twopenny Trash*, vol. i, No. xii, June 1831.

*[In *Cobbett's Twopenny Trash*, vol. i, No. xii, June 1831, pp. 265–92.]

*[1835?], [no title-page], 24 pp. Printed by William Cobbett, Johnson's Court, London. 12mo. [This copy is bound with other works by Cobbett in a volume entitled 'Cobbett Tracts' on the spine.]

Cobbett sometimes wrote parts of his political articles, and delivered parts of his speeches, in the form of effective dramatic dialogues. Almost a year before this play was first printed in the *Register* (28 May 1831) he described himself as the author of three dramatic works (*Political Register*, 19 June 1830), and presumably *Surplus Population* was one of these. The others, *Big O and Sir Glory*, 1825 (see [141]), and *Mexico, or the Patriot Bondholders* (1830), seem to have been most unsuitable for stage presentation. The earlier piece is full of heavy satire directed against Daniel O'Connell and Sir Francis Burdett, whilst *Mexico* is even less actable (one scene has twenty-six place-names being solemnly pointed out on a map). *Surplus Population* was much brighter stuff with its Malthusian economist, Peter Thimble (a not too unfriendly hit at Francis Place), its wicked seducer, the Baronet, Sir Gripe Grindum (another blow at Burdett), and its pair of triumphant, young village lovers eager to marry and have their 'quiver-full' of children. It reappeared in *Twopenny Trash* in June 1831, and was later revised in a new edition sold at sixpence and first advertised in the *Political Register* in 1835 (11 April 1835). Cobbett now included topical matter relating to the Poor Law Bill and stated that the play had already been performed in the villages around his farm in Normandy in Surrey, and would shortly go on tour in Hampshire, Sussex, and Kent. Alas for these hopes, in Tonbridge permission to perform it was refused by the authorities after the playbills had been printed— a ban which Cobbett condemned with great force only a fortnight before his death (*Political Register*, 6 June 1835). It would appear from one of his last articles that Cobbett had yet another play almost ready for publication before he died. This was to be a comedy called 'Bastards in High Life' (*Political Register*, 23 May 1835).

[181]   1831
LECTURES / TO / THE LABOURING CLASSES / AND / THEIR EMPLOYERS / IN THE COUNTY OF SUSSEX, / AND ELSEWHERE. / NOT / BY A FOLLOWER OF / WILLIAM COBBETT. /

LECTURE I. / ADDRESSED TO THE LABOURERS. /

By *A COUNTRY GENTLEMAN*

*1831, 24 pp. Printed by Ibotson and Palmer, Savoy Street, Strand; published by J. Hatchard and Son, 187, Piccadilly, London. 'Price 4*d*. or 3*s*. 6*d*. the dozen.' 12mo.

*Another issue, 2nd edition with 2 pp. frontisp.

The writer, who styled himself a 'Country Gentleman', claimed to have paid during the past ten years sums of over £5,000 in wages and £1,200 in parish rates, whilst making no profit on his land. This served as an introduction to a homily for the agricultural labourers to marry later in life, to be content with their lot, and to resist the blandishments of the 'threepenny lectures' and the 'incendiaries', then active in the country-side. The pamphlet, one of the sort often given away to the labourers, was priced at 4d., and was followed by another by the same author, *Lecture II, addressed to the Landowners and Gentlemen*, sold for 6d.

[182]   1831

A FULL AND ACCURATE REPORT / OF / THE TRIAL / OF / WILLIAM COBBETT, ESQ. / (BEFORE LORD TENTERDEN AND A SPECIAL JURY), / *On Thursday, July 7*, 1831, / IN THE / COURT OF KING'S BENCH, GUILDHALL. /

Edited anonymously

[1831, London, numerous editions; 1831, New York (Historical Society of Pennsylvania).]

*1831, 1st edition [1], 45 [+3 pp.]. Published by W. Strange, 21, Paternoster Row, London. 8vo. [Bound with other items by Cobbett in a volume entitled 'Cobbett's Trial, Normandy Farm &c.' on the spine—this being the first work in the volume.]

The autumn and winter of 1830 had seen the bloodless riots of hungry farm-labourers in the southern and western counties, crushed by the Whig Government almost as savagely as if the movement had been an armed uprising. Cobbett, whilst deploring the violence and arson associated with the labourers' protests, feelingly recorded their struggle, and reminded his readers how often he had said that hunger and desperation would lead to such a blind revolt. Worse, however, was to follow from the point of view of both Whig and Tory, for Cobbett in his *Register* welcomed the gains won by riotous farm-labourers and now from many sides serious attempts were made to silence him. Reform and anti-reform newspapers attacked him violently; in the House of Commons (23 December 1830) Arthur Hill Trevor, a Tory, moved a motion for his prosecution; bogus confessions implicating Cobbett were obtained from a young farm-labourer (see *A Short Account of the Life and Death of Swing . . . with the Confession of Thomas Goodman*, 1831), and finally, after some delay, he was brought to trial (7 July 1831) charged with publishing a libel in the *Political Register* of 11 December 1830, calculated to incite the labourers to acts of violence. Cobbett rose to the occasion magnificently. In his 68th year, he brilliantly conducted his own defence and thoroughly discomfited the Government by bringing Lords Grey, Melbourne, Durham, Palmerston, Goderich, and Brougham to the court on *subpœna*. The last, the Whig Lord Chancellor, admitted that as President of the Society for the Diffusion of Useful Knowledge he had written to Cobbett, a few days after the publication of the alleged libel, asking for permission to republish his 1816 warning in the *Political Register* against machine-breaking, the 'Letter to the Luddites'.[1] After this there was little chance of a conviction, and although the judge's summing-up was unfavourable, the jury, after an all-night retirement, was divided, and Cobbett was free. This pamphlet report of the trial,[2] promptly published by W. Strange, a friendly Radical bookseller, at a shilling, enjoyed a wide sale—a third edition was called for in four weeks, a fifth, reduced to sixpence, appeared in December 1831, and an American edition was issued. Cobbett meanwhile advertised the pamphlet, announcing that it was not his habit to 'rob other people of the fruit of their labour', and contenting himself with a long article in the *Register* commenting on the trial, and the publication of a large full-length portrait of himself, 'represented in the dress' which he wore at the trial and suitably inscribed with a facsimile of his own handwriting (*Political Register*, 9, 16, 23 July, 20 August, 10 December 1831; a copy of this portrait is in Oldham Corporation Art Gallery).

---

[1] In the event, the Society decided not to republish Cobbett's 'Letter to the Luddites', instead it issued *An Address to the Labourers on the Subject of Destroying Machinery*, 1830, and Charles Knight's *The Results of Machinery*, 1831.

[2] See also *Reports of State Trials*, N.S., ii, 789–904, 1889.

1831

COBBETT'S / TWO-PENNY TRASH; / OR, / POLITICS
FOR THE POOR. /

By WILLIAM CORBETT

Original articles (vol. i, Nos. 1 to 6; vol. ii, Nos. 4 and 10), together with extracts
from the *Political Register*, published in 24 monthly parts, July 1830–July
1832; in 2 volumes, 1831, 1832.

> *1831, vol. i, 12 nos., 292 pp. [No. 12 wrongly placed at front.] Printed by
> the Author and sold at No. 11, Bolt Court, Fleet Street. 12mo. [Bound
> with:]
>
> *[1832, title-page missing], vol. ii, 11 nos. [Nos. 1–7, 9–12—No. 8 miss-
> ing.] 288 pp. Printed and published by the Author. 12mo.

Twopenny Trash consisted, for the most part, of extracts from the
Political Register, republished in twenty-four monthly parts between
July 1830 and July 1832 (no number for March 1832) and in two
small volumes each sold for 2*s*. 6*s*. (3*s*. for the two in 1834). Eight
articles (vol. i, Nos. 1–6, vol. ii, Nos. 4, 10) were originally written
for the series and did not appear in the *Register*. Its title was derived
from the nickname abusively bestowed on Cobbett's tremendously
popular, cheap *Register* of 1816–20 by William Gifford and other
Tory journalists of the time, whilst its format, monthly appearance,
and its content were dictated by the Act of 1819–20 (the last of
the 'Six Acts'). Even its price was governed by this Act to some
extent, for no unstamped periodical of a certain size could be sold
for less than sixpence unless it was published not more than once a
month. Cobbett, in 1830, writing for an enthusiastic working-class
public, was not slow to take advantage of this opportunity, already
triumphantly tested by the *Sermons* (published between 1821 and
1822). To the rage of his enemies, the series succeeded brilliantly;
and spurious issues followed.[1] Little profit appears to have been

---
1

1831

COBBETT'S PENNY TRASH / For the Month of [February, March, April,]
1831./

Edited anonymously

> Published in three parts—February, March, April 1831; No. 1 also issued as
> *Cobbett's Genuine Twopenny Trash.*

Wrongly attributed to Cobbett with extracts from his writings selected to discredit
him.

made on the *Twopenny Trash*, however; at one of his lectures Cobbett offered a copy to all who entered, and he later claimed that the price was 'hardly paying for the paper and the print' (*Political Register*, 6 November 1830, 1 January 1831). Its political character was made plain from the start. No. I, which appeared on 1 July 1830, was announced as the herald of 'that really Radical Reform now at no great distance' and Cobbett assured his readers that his publication wanted 'no pushing about'. In contrast to the 'half given away' 'tracts' and 'humbug' of Brougham's 'Useful Knowledge' Society (advertised, incidentally, in the *Register*), the *Trash* would 'contain a spring, in its inside, to . . . keep it in motion'. The bombast was pardonable. Cobbett reprinted some of his best articles in the series and reached out to a mighty audience. Plain, forceful, and intensely human, *Twopenny Trash* did much to arouse the great movement that pushed forward to achieve the first Reform Act, and later expressed its disillusionment with the Whigs (see in this connexion the numbers for November 1830, April 1831, June, July 1832, on the Reform Bill; January 1831, on Tithes— an article which provoked angry replies,[2] and was promptly trans-

---

*[1831] No. II, 'For the Month of March 1831, NOTES OF MY LIFE / BY W. C.' 24 pp. Printed by T. C. Hansard; published by Roake and Varty, 31 Strand, London. 12mo.

*[1831] No. III, 2nd edition, 'For the Month of April 1831, NOTES OF MY LIFE CONTINUED / BY / W. C.' 22 pp. [+4 pp. publisher's advts.]. Printed by T. C. Hansard; published by Roake and Varty, 31, Strand, London. 12mo.

These were hostile pamphlets occasioned by the success of Cobbett's *Twopenny Trash*. They consisted in the main, as did so many like publications, of compilations from Cobbett's earlier writings, contrasted with his current radicalism, and similarly, their titles were calculated to appeal to his readers. No. I of this series (B.M.), also issued as *Cobbett's Genuine Twopenny Trash*, was 'addressed to the Labourers of England', and other pamphlets issued by the same publishers bore similar titles (see list of 'Publications in support of Social Order and the Constitution' attached at end of No. III above).

[2]   1831

[185]
IMPOSTURE UNMASKED; / IN A LETTER / TO THE / LABOURERS & WORKING PEOPLE / OF ENGLAND, / ON THE / SCHEMES OF THE CHURCH ROBBERS & REVOLUTIONISTS / WITH REGARD TO THE CHURCH. / BY A TRUE ENGLISHMAN. /

                                   By *A TRUE ENGLISHMAN*

*[1831], 24 pp. [illus.]. Printed by R. Clay, Bread-Street Hill; published by Roake & Varty, 31, Strand, London. [This copy is bound with other items in a volume

lated into Welsh, according to Cobbett, *Political Register*, 29 January 1831; June 1831, a reprint of *Surplus Population*, q.v.; and March, July 1831, May 1832, on Emigration—see *Emigrant's Guide*). Some of the original manuscripts of these parts of *Twopenny Trash* are in the Cole Collection (see [280]).

[186]   1831

A / SPELLING BOOK, / WITH / APPROPRIATE LESSONS IN READING, / AND WITH / A STEPPING-STONE TO ENGLISH GRAMMAR. /

By WILLIAM COBBETT

[1831, London, 1st edition (B.M.); 1831, 2nd edition; *1832, 3rd edition; 1834, 4th edition (B.M.); 1845, 9th edition (Arnold Muirhead Collection).]

*1832, 'third edition' [illus.]. 192 pp. Published at 11, Bolt Court, Fleet Street, London. 12mo.]

Cobbett, in a preface dated 'Kensington, August 22nd, 1831,' says this work was written by him 'before six o'clock in the morning', and previous to the day's ordinary business. It is recommended for children, for whose benefit it is, unlike 'all the other spelling-books', without religious instruction or arithmetic. The former, he says, needs to be 'implanted in the heart', not 'learned by rote', whilst the latter, together with geography and astronomy, only tends to 'load, confuse and bewilder' the mind of the young child not yet able to read. Cobbett concluded his book with a section designed to introduce the reader to his famous *Grammar of the English Language* (see [96]).

---

entitled 'Machine Breaking, Etc.' on the spine—this being the first item in the volume.]

*[1831], another edition, COBBETT'S IMPOSTURE UNMASKED: / 24 pp. Printed by R. Clay, Bread-Street Hill; published by Roake & Varty, 31, Strand, London. 'Price Three-halfpence.' 12mo.

A pamphlet attacking Cobbett at the time of the 'last labourers' revolt'. It is written in defence of the Church and of tithe-paying, and is intended to counteract the effect of No. 7 of *Twopenny Trash*, which is said to have brought a sentence of death on 'poor Goodman' (see note to *A Short Account of the Life & Death of Swing*, 1831 [179]).

COBBETT'S LETTER ON THE ABOLITION OF TITHES AND TAXS [sic] FROM THE DUBLIN EVENING POST.

By WILLIAM COBBETT

[1831 ? Dublin (Bodl.).]

Reprinted from the *Political Register*, 10 September 1831.

Cobbett's election address containing his thirteen pledges 'to the electors of Manchester', reprinted in a shortened version as a broadsheet in Dublin. Like *Mr. Cobbett's Propositions* . . . 1831, Manchester (Goldsmiths' Libr.), it had first appeared in the *Political Register* (10 September 1831).

COBBETT'S / MANCHESTER LECTURES, / IN SUPPORT OF HIS / FOURTEEN REFORM PROPOSITIONS; / Which Lectures were delivered in the Minor Theatre in that town, / on the six last days of the year 1831. / TO WHICH IS SUBJOINED / A Letter to Mr. O'Connell, on his Speech, made in Dublin, on the / 4th of January, 1832, against the Proposition for the establishing of / Poor-Laws in Ireland. /

BY WILLIAM COBBETT

*1832, xii, 179 pp. Published [by the author] at No. 11, Bolt Court, Fleet Street, London, sold by Mr. Lewis, Market Street, Manchester; Mr. T. Smith, Liverpool; Mr. Wilcoxon, Preston . . . . 12mo.

These six lectures were delivered by Cobbett in the Minor Theatre in Manchester (26–31 December 1831). He was then a prospective parliamentary candidate for the seat, having been adopted in August, and was shortly to agree (July 1832) to stand at Oldham as well. Cobbett was now in the midst of his second Northern Tour (the first was in 1829), and these lectures were part of his intense political activity at the time. They are described as being 'speeches' delivered from a half-sheet of quarto paper and they contain Cobbett's 'fourteen reform propositions', a programme further advanced than anything he had yet proposed, for it not only repeated his earliest attacks on the sinecure system, the standing army, the tithes, and the Irish Church, but went on to demand the wiping out of the National Debt by the sale of ecclesiastical estates, Crown lands, and the 'misapplied property of corporate bodies'. Interest payments on the debt would end after two years, only a greatly reduced and cheaply collected land-tax charged on real property would remain, and restitution would be made for the 'arbitrary charges made by . . . the late parliaments . . . in the value of . . . money'. These 'propositions' made a redoubtable political platform when taken together with his *Plan of Parliamentary Reform* (see *Political Register*, 30 October 1830, reprinted, November), and Cobbett addressed enthusiastic meetings in its favour all over the country in 1832. These Manchester lectures were published by Cobbett with a preface (dated Manchester, 3 January 1832) and a *Letter to Mr. O'Connell* in which he takes the Irish politician to task for his opposition to a Poor Law for Ireland. A second series of Manchester Lectures took place in the autumn of 1832, just before Cobbett's election at Oldham to the first reformed Parliament (he had withdrawn from Manchester on the first day of the poll).

[189]   1832

A / GEOGRAPHICAL DICTIONARY / OF / ENGLAND AND WALES; / CONTAINING / The names, in Alphabetical Order, of all the Counties, with their several Subdi- / visions into Hundreds, Lathes, Rapes, Wapentakes, Wards, or Divisions; and / an Account of the Distribution of the Counties into Circuits, Dioceses, and Par- / liamentary Divisions. / ALSO, / The Names (under that of each County respectively) in Alphabetical Order, of all / the Cities, Boroughs, Market Towns, Villages, Hamlets, and Tithings, with the / Distance of each from London, or from the nearest Market Town, and with the / Population, and other interesting particulars relative to each; besides which there are / MAPS; / First, one of the whole country, showing the local situation of the Counties relatively / to each other; and, then, each County is also preceded by a Map, showing, in the / same manner, the local situations of the Cities, Boroughs and Market towns. / FOUR TABLES / Are added; first, a Statistical Table of all the Counties, and then three Tables, showing / the new Divisions and Distributions enacted by the Reform-Law of 4 June 1832. /

By *WILLIAM COBBETT*

* 1832, lxxxiv, 546 pp. [+2 pp.], [maps]. Published by William Cobbett, 11, Bolt Court, Fleet Street, London. Price 12s. 8vo.

This work was proudly, but perhaps mistakenly, claimed by Cobbett as having been written in the 'very room' once occupied by Dr. Johnson. He included many political hints in the work (cf. *Grammar . . . see [96]), and in a preface (dated 11, Bolt Court, 28 June 1832) he explained that he had inserted a special table showing the effects of the Reform Act of June 4. Cobbett comments on the enormous labour involved, which had at last taught him 'that there is something that can fatigue', and he pointedly refers to the low price of the book (cf. the *Political Register*, 30 June 1832, where he says this is due to his desire to 'bring it within the compass of book-clubs of the working people'; see also *Political Register*, 22 September 1832). When Cobbett was defending himself against a charge that his children had 'written all his books', he explained that although 'the conception . . . the plan and arrangement' of the *Geographical Dictionary* were his own, he had been greatly assisted by his secretary, C. M. Riley, his son, John Morgan Cobbett (assigned the copyright), who had written the 'histories of the counties and cities', and one of his daughters, who had compiled the 'copious index' (cf. Cobbett MSS., Cole Collection [285]).

[190]   1832

COBBETT'S / TEN / CARDINAL VIRTUES /

Edited anonymously

Extracts selected to discredit Cobbett.

*1832, 'Third Edition', 34 pp., sold by Charles Ambery, 91, Market Street, Manchester. 8vo.

This anti-Cobbett pamphlet is another version of the widely distributed *Cobbett's Gridiron*, 1822 (see [119]). It was published in Manchester with suitable emendations when Cobbett contested that seat and Oldham in the elections for the first reformed Parliament. Ultimately he withdrew from Manchester and was elected for Oldham (see also *Cobbett's Manchester Lectures*, 1832 ([188]); for an account of both elections see *Political Register*, 22 December 1832 and for Oldham alone, see *Memory Sketches* . . . by Benjamin

Grime, Oldham, 1887). The publisher of *Ten Cardinal Virtues* advertises a similar anti-Cobbett compilation, *Cobbett's Reflections on Politics*. Earlier versions of this had already appeared in various places in 1820 (see note to *The Beauties of Cobbett*, 1820 [106]).

[191]   1832

THE / ADDRESS OF CHARLES WILKINS, ESQ., / To the PEOPLE OF MANCHESTER / ON THE INCOM-PETENCY OF MR. WM. COBBETT / TO REPRESENT THEM IN PARLIAMENT. /

By CHARLES WILKINS

*[1832] 24 pp. Printed by T. Forrest, Market Street, Manchester. 8vo.

The author, Charles Wilkins (1800?–57), constantly referred to by Cobbett as 'the mountebank' and the 'strolling-player', was a barrister who became a Sergeant-at-Law (1847), after a life of the most extraordinary vicissitudes. He spoke against Cobbett in the Manchester election of 1832, and in this pamphlet report of his three-hour speech he reiterates all the familiar charges of inconsistency, advises his audience to read *Cobbett's Ten Cardinal Virtues* ([190])—which he may have helped to prepare—and professes to be neither Whig nor Tory, but an Ultra-Radical. Cobbett as usual gave more than he received and alleged, on good grounds, that Wilkins was originally an Irish actor who had canvassed elsewhere for Whig candidates and was at that moment the secret guest of Thomas Potter (1773–1845, knighted 1839), the influential Whig draper of Manchester (see *Political Register*, 22 September 1832).

[192]   1832

MANSELL AND CO.'S / REPORT / OF THE / Important Discussion / HELD IN BIRMINGHAM, / AUGUST the 28TH and 29TH, 1832, / BETWEEN / WILLIAM COB-BETT, / THOMAS ATTWOOD, / AND / Charles Jones, Esqrs. / ON THE QUESTION / Whether it is best for the safety and welfare of the nation to attempt / to relieve the existing distress '*by an action on the Currency*,' or by an / '*Equitable Adjustment*' of *the Taxes, Rents, Debts, Contracts, and Obli- | gations, which now strangle the industry of the Country? |*

Edited Anonymously

[1832, Birmingham, 1st edition (B.M.).]

*[1832] '2nd edition', 32 pp. Printed by F. & J. Turner, Snow Hill, Birmingham, and published by Mansell and Co., Union Street, Birmingham . . . . 'Price sixpence.' 8vo.

*[Another copy bound with other items in a volume entitled 'Cobbett's Letters' on the spine.]

The celebrated debate here reported had taken place before about 1,400 people (about 1,500 according to the pamphlet), each of whom had paid one shilling entrance fee to Mr. Beardsworth's repository in Birmingham. Cobbett had challenged ('invited' he preferred to call it) Thomas Attwood (1783–1856), the Radical currency reform banker, and Charles Jones (*fl.* 1824–41), an active figure, like Attwood, in the Birmingham Political Union, 'to discuss with me this great question before the people of Birmingham'. Attwood and Jones—there were some minor differences between them—were advocates of a controlled inflationary policy and opponents of the gold standard. They wanted a managed monetary system to be 'employed for the purpose of increasing production, consumption and distribution'. The regulation of the supply of money was to be in the hands of either the National Debt Commissioners or a nationalized Bank of England, with powers to enlarge or diminish paper money by the buying or selling of government stock. Cobbett, on the other hand, although he shared their dislike of the 'murderous Peel Bill' (see *Paper against Gold*), was a bitter enemy of paper money and the fund-holders, and no friend either of the expanding industrial and commercial system, a point shrewdly made by Attwood in the debate. He wanted a return to cash payments and the gold standard, which would be operated in the interests of 'the industrious classes'. For this purpose he demanded his famous 'equitable adjustment'—a halving of the National Debt, a gradual extinction of the payment of the debt's interest, the abolition of all internal taxes, the disbandment of the standing army, and a fair adjustment of old contracts and debts. The debate went on for two days with astonishingly long speeches—Attwood spoke first for four and a half hours, supported by Jones for about an hour, then Cobbett spoke for two more, and Attwood finally took another two hours to reply. Cobbett, in reporting the debate (*Political Register*, 8 September 1832), warmly commended the audience on their patience, but not without a barb for their 'discipline'. The division at the end showed a majority for Attwood, but its size was doubtful. Cobbett claimed that the voting was nearly equal and that it was taken in the meagre light of one candle, but the newspapers claimed anything between a three-to-one and a ten-to-one majority (*Birmingham Journal*, 1 September 1832; *Political Register*, 8 September 1832; C. M. Wakefield's *Life of Thomas Attwood*, 1885, Cole Collection). To counter such reports, J. Russell of Birmingham published *Extracts from Cobbett's Register . . . being the Address of the Non-Electors, and Mr. Cobbett's Remarks on the late discussion at Birmingham* [1832] (Birmingham Reference Libr.). Indeed, the debate aroused some acrimony between Cobbett and Attwood; nevertheless, they were soon to collaborate in the first reformed Parliament as resolute opponents of the Whigs.

[193]   1832

COBBETT'S / TOUR IN SCOTLAND: / AND IN THE FOUR / NORTHERN COUNTIES OF ENGLAND: / IN THE AUTUMN OF THE YEAR / 1832. /

By WILLIAM COBBETT

[See *Rural Rides . . .*]

First published in the *Political Register*, 29 September–24 November 1832.

*1833, ix, 11 pp., 264 pp. Published at Bolt Court, Fleet Street, London. 'Price Two Shillings and Sixpence.' 12mo.

The *Tour in Scotland* first appeared in the *Political Register* between 29 September and 24 November 1832. It was reprinted and published as a half-a-crown book on 10 January 1833 with a hitherto unpublished conclusion on the *Highlands of Scotland* and a dedication and preface that had appeared during the previous week in the *Register*. Cobbett's son, James Paul Cobbett, included part of the *Tour of Scotland* in his 1853 edition of the *Rides*, and it was republished in full in the Coles' standard edition of 1930, which also includes, for the first time in book form, the *Letters from Ireland*, 1834 (see note to [211]), originally published in the *Political*

Register (27 September–29 November 1834), as well as many English Rides. The *Tour in Scotland* also contains *Cobbett's Advice to the Chopsticks . . . of the South of England*, two letters from Edinburgh and Glasgow, respectively, in sharp condemnation of the 'industrial' conditions of Scottish agriculture, which first appeared in the *Political Register* (20, 27 October 1832). Cobbett publicly directed his printer to reissue 10,000 of each (both broadsheets are in Yale University Libr.).

1832

[194]

MR. COBBETT'S ANSWER / TO / MR. STANLEY'S MANIFESTO. /

By WILLIAM COBBETT

First published in the *Political Register*, 29 December 1832.

*[1833], 16 pp. Printed by William Cobbett, Johnson's Court, Fleet Street, London. 'Price Threepence.' 8vo. [Bound with other works by Cobbett in volume entitled 'Cobbett's Letters' on the spine, this being the fifth item in that collection.]

Cobbett wrote this pamphlet, which first appeared in the *Register* (29 December 1832), a week after his election for Oldham to the first reformed Parliament. It was written in answer to a speech made by Edward George Geoffrey Stanley (1799–1869), then the Whig Secretary for Ireland (later Prime Minister and 14th Earl of Derby), in which his former opponent at the Preston election of 1826 (see *Cobbett's Poor Man's Friend*, 1826) had declared finally against any further parliamentary reform. Cobbett, writing with great force, attacked as unconstitutional, impudent, and arrogant the notion that the House of Commons should not legislate for shortening the duration of Parliament or for the introduction of the ballot. The article, 'as much print as is usually contained in a shilling pamphlet', was first republished (10 January 1833), for threepence, in about three to four thousand copies, then reprinted in the *Register* once more, and finally issued in yet another cheap edition (*Political Register*, 19 January 1833).

1833

COBBETT'S / POOR MAN'S FRIEND / OR, / A
DEFENCE OF THE RIGHTS OF THOSE WHO DO THE
WORK / AND FIGHT THE BATTLES. / ADDRESSED
TO THE / WORKING MEN OF SCOTLAND. /

By WILLIAM COBBETT

First published in the *Political Register*, 5 January 1833.

*[1833], 14 pp., 48 paras. Printed by William Cobbett, Johnson's Court,
Fleet Street, London. 'Price Threepence.' 8vo.

A shortened and revised version of an earlier *Poor Man's Friend*
first issued in five numbers 1826–7 ([144]). It was published by
Cobbett in January 1833 in accordance with a pledge he had made
in the previous October, when, amidst the excitement preceding
his election to the reformed Parliament, he had toured Scotland
(see *Cobbett's Tour in Scotland*, 1833 [193]) and, as a mark of his
'gratitude' for their kindness, had promised the 'working people
of Glasgow and its environs' a free gift of 5,000 copies of the *Poor
Man's Friend*. For this purpose he adopted the earlier pamphlet,
first publishing the new version in the *Political Register* (5 January
1833) and then reprinting it as a threepenny pamphlet. The revision
gives an indication of Cobbett's growing disillusionment with the
poor-law reformers. Thus in the earlier versions of the pamphlet
(1st edition, Letter III, para. 86; new edition, Letter II, para. 50),
in describing the 'tyranny' of vagrancy laws unrelieved by a just
poor law, he had admitted that 'generally speaking the poor laws are,
as yet, fairly executed and efficient'. It is significant that in this new
version (para. 47) Cobbett omits this limited praise and closes his
pamphlet with a stirring appeal for the 'overthrow of the tyrant, or
tyrants' who would attempt to deny the rights of relief to 'every
necessitous creature'.

1833

THE SPEECHES OF W. COBBETT, M.P. FOR OLDHAM

By WILLIAM COBBETT

[1833, London (Goldsmiths' Libr., London).]

Cobbett's speeches in the House of Commons (7, 11, 18 February

1833) reprinted from the reports in the *True Sun*, 'corrected by W. Cobbett'. They were published by James Watson in the form of two penny pamphlets 'uniform in size with the *Working Man's Friend*', another of Watson's current publications (see WATSON, Cole Collection).

[197]   1833

THE FLASH IN THE PAN; OR PEEL IN A PASSION.

By WILLIAM COBBETT

[1833, London (New York Public Libr.).]

Reprinted from the *Political Register*, 18, 25 May 1833.

Speeches in the House of Commons on 16 May 1833, when Cobbett moved his motion to dismiss Peel.

[198]   1833

COBBETT'S MAGAZINE: / A / MONTHLY REVIEW / OF / POLITICS, HISTORY, SCIENCE, LITERATURE, AND RURAL / AND DOMESTIC PURSUITS. /

Edited by JOHN MORGAN COBBETT and JAMES PAUL COBBETT

[Monthly periodical; 1833–4, known as *The Shilling Magazine* from April 1834. London.]

*1833, vol. i, Nos. 1–6, February–July 1833, iv, 592 pp.; vol. ii, Nos. 7–12, August 1833–January 1834, 420 pp., 64 pp. [pp. 65–72 missing at end]. Published at 11, Bolt Court, and Effingham Wilson's, Royal Exchange, London. 8vo.

*[Additional copies Nos. 1 and 2 of vol. i are bound with other items at the end of a volume entitled 'Cobbett's Trial. Normandy Farm &c.' on the spine.]

A monthly two-shilling magazine, fairly Radical in politics, started and edited by two of Cobbett's sons, John Morgan and James Paul, in February 1833. Cobbett himself wrote only a few articles for it, but it was published from the *Register* office and was generally assumed to be under his inspiration. This led to difficulties, and in March 1834 he announced that his sons were no longer connected with the journal. Moreover, although it was still said to be Radical, Cobbett plainly dissociated himself from it. In the following month, at Cobbett's request, the title was changed to the *Shilling Magazine*, although he now gave it his political blessing (*Political Register*, 8 March, 26 April 1834).

[199]   1833

DISGRACEFUL SQUANDERING OF THE PUBLIC MONEY, THE GREAT CAUSE OF OPPRESSIVE TAXATION. NO. 1 THE NAVY JOB!!!

By WILLIAM COBBETT

[1833, Glasgow (Harvard Libr.)]

Reprinted from the **Political Register*, 15 June 1833.

A Glasgow reprint by McPhun of an article by Cobbett attacking 'The cost and management of the Navy'. This was in part a reference to a parliamentary squabble which had arisen when Cobbett presented a petition from two naval officers dismissed from the service.

[200]   1833

THE RIGHTS OF THE POOR AND THE POOR LAWS

By JOHN MORGAN COBBETT

[1833, London (Arnold Muirhead Collection).]

A reprint (revised) of an article in **Cobbett's Magazine*, July 1833.

A sharp attack by John Morgan Cobbett on the *Extracts from the Information* . . . issued in February 1833 by the Poor Law Commissioners before their official *Report* was published. J. M. Cobbett's condemnation of the *Extracts* and the Commissioners first appeared as an article in **Cobbett's Magazine* (July 1833). In the same month it was reprinted in a revised form as a threepenny pamphlet and published by William Cobbett.

[201]   1833

THE CURSE / OF / PAPER-MONEY AND BANKING; / OR / A SHORT HISTORY OF BANKING / IN THE /

UNITED STATES OF AMERICA, / WITH AN
ACCOUNT OF ITS RUINOUS EFFECTS ON LAND-
OWNERS, FARMERS, / TRADERS, AND ON ALL THE
INDUSTRIOUS CLASSES OF / THE COMMUNITY, /
BY Wm. M. GOUGE ... / TO WHICH IS PREFIXED /
AN INTRODUCTION. / BY WILLIAM COBBETT,
M.P. FOR OLDHAM. /

> By *WILLIAM M. GOUGE; edited with an introduction by*
> *WILLIAM COBBETT*

Preface and introduction published in the *Political Register*, 20 July 1833; the
rest taken from Gouge's *A Short History of Banking . . .*, 1833. Philadelphia.

> *1833, xxii, [+i] 200 pp. [+4 pp. publisher's advts.]. Published at 11,
> Bolt Court, Fleet Street, London. 'July 1833.' Price 4s. 12mo. [Bound in
> covers with 'Cobbett on Banking' on the spine.]

This work was taken by Cobbett from chapters 5–24 of *A Short
History of Banking in the United States . . .* (Philadelphia, 1833) by
William M. Gouge (1796–1863), an erratic American opponent
of the banking system, whom he describes as a 'dull', 'awkward',
and 'confused' writer, valuable only for the facts he has assembled.
Cobbett published it on 17 July 1833 in the thick of the controversy
associated with the Bank Charter Act over legal tender, adding a
preface and introduction which he reprinted in the *Register* during
the same week (20 July 1833).

[202]   1833

A NEW / FRENCH AND ENGLISH / DICTIONARY. /
IN TWO PARTS / PART I. FRENCH AND ENGLISH. /
PART II. ENGLISH AND FRENCH. /

> By *WILLIAM COBBETT*

> 1833, xiv, 418 pp., 428 pp. Published [by the Author] at 11, Bolt Court,
> Fleet Street, London. 8vo.

Published on 24 July 1833, this *Dictionary* was proudly announced
by Cobbett as 'the best book of the kind that ever was in print, and
perhaps that ever will be'. Like his *French Grammar* ([130]) it was
to be a 'useful' book, not an 'amusing' one, and with both, the
language could be learned in six months. Cobbett repeated his belief

that he was publishing it from 'perhaps the very room', in Bolt Court, out of which Dr. Johnson had issued his famous *Dictionary*, but he admitted, more modestly, that although he had himself superintended the work, he had relied on 'a very clever Frenchman by the name of Aliva'[1] for the compilation. Cobbett was busy in the first reformed Parliament at this time, and shortly after the publication of the *Dictionary* he announced that the advertised price of 10s. 6d. would have to be raised to 12s., since 'being more engaged *in Parliamenting*' than in his own affairs he had miscalculated the cost (*Political Register*, 22 June, 27 July, 7 September, 5 October, 28 December 1833).

[203]   1833

POPAY, THE POLICE SPY.

By *WILLIAM COBBETT*

[1833, London (University College London Libr.).]

Reprinted from the **Political Register*, 17 August 1833.

A report of the evidence laid before the House of Commons by a Select Committee on the use of policemen as political spies. It was printed in the *Register* (17 August 1833) and republished for Cobbett by John Cleave (31 August 1833) as a threepenny pamphlet. The Select Committee, of which Cobbett was a member, had been appointed largely at his suit, when members of the National Union of the Working Classes complained, in a petition, that William Stewart Popay had entered their Union as a police spy (see *Cole's *Life*, 403–5). Cobbett presented about 250 petitions in the same session—some others dealt with similar cases—but they also covered a great variety of subjects.

[204]   1833

FOUR LETTERS / TO THE / HON. JOHN STUART WORTLEY; / IN ANSWER TO HIS / 'BRIEF INQUIRY INTO THE TRUE AWARD OF AN EQUITABLE

---

[1] The Bodleian Library (S.C. 25440, f. 95) has a letter (November? 1830) from Cobbett to R. Alliva [*sic*] asking the latter to translate a 'letter to the French king'.

ADJUST- / MENT BETWEEN THE NATION AND ITS
CREATORS'. /

By *WILLIAM COBBETT*

First published in the *Political Register*, 31 August–19 October 1833.

*1834, iv, 86 pp. [+2 pp. publishers' advts.]. Published at 11, Bolt Court, Fleet Street, London. 8vo. [Bound with other works by Cobbett in a volume entitled 'Cobbett's Letters' on the spine, this being the first item in that collection.]

*[Another copy bound in a volume entitled 'Cobbett's Register & Lectures' on the spine.]

These four letters first appeared in the *Political Register* (31 August, 7, 28 September, and 19 October, 1833) and were published as a pamphlet in January 1834 for 2s. They are written in an angry, urgent style, and the preface to the first edition (see above) addressed 'to the members of the two Houses of Parliament', is dated 1 January 1834, eighteen months before Cobbett's death. The letters were a reply to a pamphlet (*A Brief Inquiry into the True Award of an Equitable Adjustment . . .*, 1833) by John Stuart Wortley (1801–55, later the second Lord Wharncliffe), who, basing his argument mainly on the changes in the value of money, had attacked the 'unflinching impudence' of those who sought to reduce the interest on the National Debt. Nothing could more surely provoke Cobbett to fury than a member of the 'landed estates' defending the hated fundholders or the 'funding system' which mortgaged 'the labour of the child unborn'. Cobbett was convinced that a blind and corrupt aristocracy, by 'fighting . . . the labourers who are your natural friends' (pp. 81–82), would first lose their lands to the 'stock-jobbers', and then precipitate a revolution of the working people. In the circumstances he dealt fairly lightly with Stuart Wortley, calling him a 'generous youth of the crack-skull county of York' and reminding him that twenty-two years before (in *Paper against Gold*, [81]), and then not for the first time, he had warned the country of the dangers of paper money and the funding system (see also *Cobbett's Manchester Lectures*, 1832 [188], for his proposals on the debt).

1833

RIGHTS OF INDUSTRY.

By WILLIAM COBBETT and JOHN FIELDEN

[1833, London (Goldsmiths' Libr., London).]

Reprinted from the *Political Register*, 14 December 1833.

These letters between Cobbett and John Fielden (1784–1849) Cobbett's fellow-member for Oldham and a large employer in the cotton industry, were in favour of an eight-hour day without wage reductions to be achieved by a refusal to work more than eight hours. Based in part on dissatisfaction with the 1833 Factory Act but influenced also by the Owenites and the idea of a general strike, the movement, led by Fielden, made rapid progress. Cobbett, Robert Owen (1771–1858), John Doherty (1797–9?–1854), and other prominent leaders supported it; a Society for Promoting National Regeneration was formed; central offices were opened in Manchester; a journal *The Herald of the Rights of Industry* was issued, and numerous branches were established in Lancashire and Yorkshire despite the opposition of Oastler and Bull, the leaders of the Ten Hours' Agitation. By the summer of 1834 however, the National Regeneration Society, as it was sometimes called, had collapsed, its demise hastened by the employers' offensive and by the strikes and lockouts that marked the decline of the Owenite movement.

1834

MR. COBBETT'S SPEECH AND THE OTHER SPEECHES ON HIS MOTION FOR AN ABOLITION OF THE MALT TAX.

By WILLIAM COBBETT

[1834, London (Birmingham Reference Libr.).]

Reprinted from the *Political Register*, 22 March 1834.

A debate (17 March 1834) initiated by Cobbett in the House of Commons on the abolition of the Malt Tax. Cobbett's motion was defeated (142 votes to 59), but he considered the subject of 'such vast importance' that he departed from his usual practice and printed a report of the whole proceedings, including a list of the Minority, in the *Register* (22 March 1834). A few days later this was re-published as a fourpenny pamphlet (see also note to *The Malt Tax kept upon the Backs of the People*, 1835 [213]).

[207]   1834

LIFE / OF / ANDREW JACKSON, / PRESIDENT / OF / THE UNITED STATES OF AMERICA. / ABRIDGED AND COMPILED / BY WILLIAM COBBETT, M.P. FOR OLDHAM. / WITH AN INTERESTING FRONTIS-PIECE, INCLUDING A / PORTRAIT. /

Edited by *WILLIAM COBBETT* from the '*Life*' by *JOHN HENRY EATON*

[*1834, London; 1834 (Harper) New York (B.M.); 1834 (Richards) New York; 1834, Baltimore; 1834, n.p.; (L. of C.).]

*1834, x, 142 pp. [portr., illus., 1 p.]. Published at 11, Bolt Court, Fleet Street, London. 12mo. [This copy is bound with 12 pp. *List of Mr. Cobbett's Books*, c. 1833–4, at end.]

For the most part an abridged version of *The Life of Andrew Jackson* (Philadelphia, 1824) by John Henry Eaton (1790–1856), an American politician. Cobbett was drawn to Andrew Jackson (1767–1845), then the very popular re-elected President of the United States, partly because of the latter's Irish parentage and also by reason of the successful struggle the President had waged against the Bank of the United States. The work has a 'dedication to the working people of Ireland', a similar preface (both dated London, 27 March 1834), and an 'interesting frontispiece' somewhat crudely executed by Cobbett's eldest son, William. Several American editions followed in the same year.

[208]   1834

GET GOLD! GET GOLD!

By *WILLIAM COBBETT*

[1834 (Leeds Public Libr.).]

Reprinted, in part, from the *Political Register*, 16 August 1834.

An enthusiastic article in praise of President Jackson's financial policy, originally written for the *Political Register* (16 August 1834) and reprinted in a slightly shortened version in Leeds by Mrs. Alice Mann, the Radical bookseller. Cobbett expected paper money to become worthless and he urged his readers to convert their notes into gold.

[209] 1834

LETTERS TO THE EARL OF RADNOR.

By WILLIAM COBBETT

[1834, London (Birmingham Reference Libr.).]

Reprinted from the *Political Register*, 9, 23 August, 20 September, 18, 25 October 1834.

Five friendly letters admonishing the Earl for his support of the Poor Law Bill; each was republished separately as a twopenny pamphlet.

[210] 1834

THREE LECTURES / ON THE / *Political State of Ireland*, / DELIVERED IN / FISHAMBLE-STREET THEATRE, DUBLIN, / BY WM. COBBETT, ESQ., M.P. / FAITH-FULLY REPORTED / With an Analysis and some Notes Appended, / BY T. HUGHES, ESQ. /

By WILLIAM COBBETT; reported with notes by T. HUGHES

*1834, 48 pp., iv, 5–48 pp. Published by P. Byrne, 37, Anglesey Street, Dublin. 12mo. [Bound with other works by Cobbett in a volume entitled 'Cobbett' on the spine—this being the first item.]

Cobbett, now very active in the Irish cause in Parliament, arrived in Dublin on 15 September 1834 to begin his Tour of Ireland (see *Letters to Marshall* in *Political Register*, 27 September–29 November 1834, and *Rural Rides*, 1930 edition). O'Connell, his ally again, greeted him as 'one of the greatest benefactors of literature, liberty and religion' (*Political Register*, 27 September 1834), and Cobbett was treated to a great public welcome throughout the country. In Dublin he gave three lectures (24, 25, 26 September) at the Fishamble Street Theatre, and these were promptly published in this Irish edition. (The first lecture only appeared in a slightly

different version in the *Political Register*, 4 October 1834.)
Cobbett's speeches here are a powerful condemnation of the terrible
distress he saw in the midst of a magnificently fertile country, and
an eloquent plea for the introduction into Ireland of pre-Reformation laws for the relief of the poor.

[211]   1834
LETTERS OF WILLIAM COBBETT TO CHARLES
MARSHALL, 1834. [Typescript.]

By WILLIAM COBBETT

First published in the *Political Register*, 27 September–29 November 1834.

  *65 pp. typescript.

  *1930, reprinted in Coles' 1930 ed. of *Rural Rides*.

These ten letters from Ireland were sent by Cobbett to Charles
Marshall, one of his farm-labourers at the Normandy farm, and
were first printed in the *Political Register* (27 September–29
November 1834). They described, in a simple, yet moving style,
the sad state of the Irish peasantry. Before the series was over Cobbett
publicly instructed his printer to reprint 500 of each number as a
pamphlet (*Political Register*, 4 October 1834), but there is no
evidence that this was ever done. The *Letters* were first reprinted in
book form in the Coles' 1930 edition of *Rural Rides* (q.v.).

[212]   1835
COBBETT'S / LEGACY TO LABOURERS; / OR, /
What is the Right which the Lords, Baronets, and / Squires have to
the Lands of England? / IN SIX LETTERS, / ADDRESSED
TO THE WORKING PEOPLE OF ENGLAND. / WITH
A / DEDICATION TO SIR ROBERT PEEL, BART. /

By WILLIAM COBBETT

  ['1834', actually 1835, 1st edition (B.M.); 1872, another edition (B.M.).]

  *1835, 'Third edition', [ii], 141 pp. [+2 pp. publisher's advts.]. Pub-
lished [by William Cobbett] at 11, Bolt Court, Fleet Street, London. 12mo.

Cobbett announced the forthcoming publication of this work in one
of his letters from Ireland (*Political Register*, 22 November 1834).

193

Provoked by the passing of the Poor Law Bill, he determined to carry on the fight against the Act by appealing once again to the labourers, and in this simply written series (there were two others, the *Legacy to Parsons and the posthumously republished *Legacy to Peel [223]) he provided much ammunition for working-class opposition to the Whigs and Tories. The *Legacy to Labourers* in particular, with its ironical dedication to Peel (separately published as *A Letter to Sir Robert Peel*, 1836 [224]), was to become almost a handbook for the opponents of the new Poor Law. Sold for 1s. 4d., strangely like a prayer book in appearance, bound in leather to last, and of 'waistcoat pocket' size to suit Cobbett's working-men readers, it called for a return to the 'institutions and fundamental laws of England' and gave powerful expression to the common feeling that these were being filched away from the people by the 'Reformed Parliament'. The publication of the *Legacy to Labourers*, despite its preface of 9 December 1834, and the advertised date of 31 December, was delayed by the bookbinders until late in January 1835, when Cobbett explained the matter in the *Register* (31 January 1835), adding that 2,000 bespoken copies of the 5,000 printed had not yet been delivered. In 1872 the book was republished by the younger William Cobbett with a lengthy preface. Nine years earlier, in 1863, he had also published *Legacy to Lords* (q.v.), a compilation of his father's miscellaneous writings, intended, he said, to form yet another of the series. This eldest son met some misfortunes immediately after Cobbett's death, and on 1 January 1836, in his *'History of Normandy Farm' (q.v.), he complained that he had been deprived of the profits on the *Legacy to Labourers*, the *Legacy to Parsons*, and *Surplus Population*, which he claimed had trebled their circulation to a combined total of 45,000 copies by 1 December.

[213]   1835

THE MALT TAX KEPT UPON THE BACKS OF THE PEOPLE BY THE WHIGS.

By WILLIAM COBBETT

[1835, London (Harvard Libr.).]

Reprinted from the *Political Register*, 21 March 1835

Cobbett's bitter attack on the 'Whigs' for joining with Peel in

194

defeating by 350 votes to 192 a motion (10 March 1835) to repeal the Malt Tax (see also *Mr. Cobbett's Speech . . . on . . . the Malt Tax*, 1834 [206]).

[214]   1835

COBBETT'S / LEGACY TO PARSONS; / OR, / Have the Clergy of the Established Church an equi- / table right to the Tithes, or to any other thing called / Church Property, greater than the Dissenters have / to the same? And ought there, or ought there not, to / be a separation of the Church from the State? / IN SIX LETTERS, / Addressed to the Church-Parsons in general, including / the Cathedral and College Clergy and the Bishops. / WITH A / DEDICATION TO BLOMFIELD, BISHOP OF / LONDON. /

By *WILLIAM COBBETT*

*1835, 192 pp. Published at 11, Bolt Court, Fleet Street, London. 'Price 1s. 6d., handsomely bound in leather.' 12mo.

This *Legacy*, the last book published by Cobbett, appeared on 18 April 1835, two months before his death, and was intended as a supplement to the series begun with the similarly bound *Legacy to Labourers* ([212]). It began with an ironical dedication to James Blomfield (1786–1857, then Bishop of London), which Cobbett also used occasionally as an advertisement in the *Register*. The bishop was attacked on three grounds—for having been 'a poor-law commissioner', for zealously defending 'the Dead-Body Bill', and also for being a 'Church-reform commissioner' who had appointed another Blomfield to rich plural livings. Cobbett was at his most effective when he thought he saw a nepotist bishop consigning the living to the Malthusians and the dead to 'unchristian burial'. He began, as he had done in the *History of the Protestant Reformation* (q.v.), with the abuses said to have been brought in with the Establishment, passed on to deal sympathetically with the Dissenters, and lastly to express his final view of the necessity for a separation of Church and State. The *Legacy to Parsons* was probably the most popular of all the *Legacy* series. Six editions as well as a translation into Welsh were issued before the end of the year. The first edition (of 5,000) was said to have been sold out in nine days, and a second (of 10,000) was called for about three weeks later (*Political Register*, 23 May 1835). The work aroused some hostile replies, as did so many of Cobbett's successes, but it has outlived its critics long enough to be republished in 1869 with a preface written by Cobbett's eldest son, William; in 1876 as the privately printed *There being no Gospel for Tithes* . . . with an introduction by George Pitt (B.M.); and in 1947 with a foreword by Ernest Thurtle, M.P.

PART II

SELECTIONS, EXTRACTS,
AND OTHER WRITINGS,
BY, OR RELATING TO,
WILLIAM COBBETT
PUBLISHED AFTER HIS
DEATH

Caledonian Mercury

[Newspaper cutting from the *Caledonian Mercury*, 22 June 1835.]

> *[1835], 1½ cols., *Caledonian Mercury*, Monday, 22 June 1835. [Bound with works by Cobbett and others in a volume entitled 'Cobbett's Register & Lectures' on the spine, this being the last item in the volume.]

A cutting of 1½ cols. from the *Caledonian Mercury* (the title-page is cut but has been identified) of Monday, 22 June 1835, giving obituary notices of Cobbett, taken from the *Morning Chronicle*, *The Times*, the *Morning Post*, the *True Sun*, and the *Sun*.

[216]

THE LIFE OF / WILLIAM COBBETT, ESQ., / LATE M.P. FOR OLDHAM. / INCLUDING / ALL THE MEMORABLE EVENTS / OF HIS / EXTRAORDINARY LIFE, / FROM THE EARLIEST PERIOD TO THAT OF HIS DECEASE; / WITH AN / IMPARTIAL CRITIQUE ON HIS PUBLIC / CHARACTER, / AND A FULL EXPOSITION OF THE VARIOUS IMPORTANT / SUBJECTS THAT ENGAGED HIS ATTENTION; THE WHOLE / BEING COMPILED FROM / AUTHENTIC SOURCES, / ACCESSIBLE ONLY TO THE EDITOR OF THE PRESENT WORK. / Embellished with Portraits. /

Edited anonymously

> *1835, [portr.], 216 pp. [Printed and] published by John Duncombe & Co., 10, Middle Row, Holborn, London. 12mo.

A sympathetic biography which, unlike the eulogistic *Memoirs* published by Mrs. Alice Mann of Leeds (q.v.), permits itself to utter a small, if still friendly note of criticism on Cobbett. In parts, however, the two biographies (this, and that of Leeds) are word for word the same. This one (published also in Manchester with a different title-page) was probably the first, and bears internal evidence of having been written in August 1835.

[217]

THE LIFE OF / WILLIAM COBBETT, / DEDICATED TO HIS SONS. /

ANONYMOUS

*1835, [illus. portr.], xvi, 422 pp. [Printed by J. Leighton, Johnson's Court, Fleet Street, London; published by] F. J. Mason, 444, West Strand, London. 8vo.

A fairly sympathetic biography drawn mainly from Cobbett's own writings. It reprinted also Hazlitt's essay on him, 'Character of Cobbett' from *Table Talk* (see note to [219]); a number of newspaper articles, and Ebenezer Elliott's poem 'William Cobbett'.

[218]

MEMOIRS / OF / WM. COBBETT, ESQ., M.P., / FOR OLDHAM; / AND / THE CELEBRATED AUTHOR OF THE / 'POLITICAL REGISTER'. /

ANONYMOUS

*1835, [facs.], 184 pp. Printed and published by A. Mann, Leeds. 12mo.

A highly eulogistic biography of Cobbett drawn mainly from his writings and published by Mrs. Alice Mann, the widow of a Leeds bookseller, James Mann (d. 1832?), who with his son Alfred and his wife were extreme Yorkshire Radicals, active in the struggle for a free press, and friends of both Cobbett and Henry Hunt. The text of these *Memoirs* is exactly similar in parts to another *Life* . . . (q.v.), published also in 1835 by Duncombe of London.

[219]

THE CHARACTER OF W. COBBETT, M.P. BY WILLIAM HAZLITT TO WHICH IS ADDED, SEVERAL INTERESTING PARTICULARS OF MR. COBBETT'S LIFE AND WRITINGS.

By WILLIAM HAZLITT and others

[First published in Hazlitt's *Table Talk*, vol. i, 1821 as 'Character of Cobbett'; afterwards in *The Spirit of the Age*, 2nd edition, 1825.]

*1835, 16 pp. Published by J. Watson, 18, Commercial Place, City Road, London. 8vo. [Bound with other pamphlets in a volume entitled 'R. D. Owen, etc.' on the spine.]

Soon after Cobbett's death James Watson (1799–1874), the Radical publisher, reprinted Hazlitt's essay on him (first published in *Table Talk*, 1821) and added an obituary notice from *The Athenaeum* (27 June 1835) and his own short tribute.

THE / ENGLISH HOUSEKEEPER: / OR, / MANUAL OF DOMESTIC MANAGEMENT: / CONTAINING / ADVICE ON THE CONDUCT OF HOUSEHOLD AFFAIRS, IN A SEPARATE / TREATISE ON EACH PARTICULAR DEPARTMENT, AND / PRACTICAL INSTRUCTIONS / . . . .

By *ANNE COBBETT*

*[1835?] xxiii, 481 pp.+xii pp. Index. Published by Anne Cobbett, 10, Red Lion Court, Fleet Street, London. 'Price 6s., boards.'

Anne (1795–1877), Cobbett's eldest daughter, kept on her father's bookselling business for many years after his death (although not the one at Bolt Court, which passed out of the family). In 1835 she published this housekeeper's manual, a popular work which reached a sixth edition in 1842. Anne's accounts of the family are to be found in the Cole Collection in MS. (see [283] and [284]; also M. L. Pearl in *The Countryman*, 1951, vol. xliii, No. 2; vol. xliv, Nos. 1, 2).

[221]

MEMOIRS / OF THE LATE / WILLIAM COBBETT ESQR., / *M.P. for Oldham.* / From / Private and Confidential Sources. /

By *ROBERT HUISH*

*1836, 2 vols., [portrs., illus.], x, 496 pp., 474 pp. Published (for the Proprietors) by John Saunders, 25, Newgate Street, London. 8vo.

A hostile biography, marred by many inaccuracies, but useful for the many critical notices it contains. Robert Huish (1777–1850) was a prolific writer, of Radical sympathies, who wrote numerous biographies, among them one of Henry Hunt. (See Hunt, Cole Collection.)

[222]

BEAUTIES OF COBBETT. / (Being Extracts from the 12 vols. of the Porcupine, the earliest work of the / late Mr. Cobbett, M.P., including a period of seventeen years from / 1783 to 1800.) /

By *WILLIAM COBBETT*; [*edited by JESSE OLDFIELD*]

[Published in twenty-eight monthly parts—vol. i—all published.]

*1836, vi, [incl. Index], 442 pp. [portr.]. Published [by J. Oldfield] at Cobbett's Register Office, 11, Bolt Court, Fleet Street, London. 8vo.

This selection from *Porcupine's Works* (q.v.) was published in twenty-eight monthly parts by J. Oldfield, who, to the dismay of the Cobbett family, had proved that shortly before Cobbett's death he had acquired a large number of his copyrights. Unlike an earlier publication similarly named, it was not a hostile compilation, despite its selection from Cobbett's earlier Tory writings. Oldfield (d. 1853) was active in trying to promote the Cobbett Monument Committee in 1836 and 1838 (see *Cobbett and Burdett*, 1836— B.M.—and *Faithfull MSS. [289]) but he never healed the breach between himself and the Cobbett family (see *Cobbett's Will . . . 1837*, Arnold Muirhead Collection; and *English [Law] Reports*, vol. 156, 1916).

[223]

COBBETT'S / LEGACY TO PEEL; / OR, / An inquiry with respect to what the Right Honourable / Baronet will now do with the House of Commons, / with Ireland, with the English Church and the Dis- / senters, with the swarms of pensioners, &c., with / the Crown Lands and the Army, with the Currency / and the Debt. / IN SIX LETTERS. /

By WILLIAM COBBETT

First published in the *Political Register*, 24 January–18 April 1835.

*1836, vi, 7–192 pp. Published at Cobbett's 'Register' Office, 11, Bolt Court, Fleet Street. 'Price 1s. 6d., handsomely bound in leather.' 12mo.

Exactly similar in format to *Cobbett's Legacy to Labourers* and the *Legacy to Parsons* (q.v.), although republished in 1836 after his death when the Cobbett family no longer possessed the old business or occupied the famous shop, this work consisted of seven (not 'six') letters to Sir Robert Peel (1788–1850), first printed in the *Register* between 24 January and 18 April 1835. Peel was still Prime Minister when they were begun, and Cobbett, hating 'Peel's Bill' of 1819 and his 'Bourbon-like police' more than he did the man, had written these able articles as a statement of his policy offered for adoption by the new Tory Government. Like the preface to the *Legacy to Labourers*, they have much less of the personal bitterness expressed in some previous polemics against Peel (cf. Cobbett's *The Flash in the Pan, or, Peel in a Passion*, 1833, reprinted from *Political Register*, 18, 25 May 1833, see note to [197]). The last letter written on the fall of the Government offers a 'hearty welcome' to Peel's still unknown successor.

[224]

A LETTER / TO / SIR ROBERT PEEL, BART. /

By WILLIAM COBBETT

[At top: MR. COBBETT / AND THE / NEW POOR LAW ACT. /]

Taken from *Cobbett's Legacy to Labourers*.

> *[1836], 24 pp. [incl. 1 p. publisher's advts.]. Published by J. Oldfield] at 11, Bolt Court, Fleet Street, London. 'Price Threepence.' 12mo. [Bound with other items in a volume entitled 'Cobbett Tracts' on the spine.]

The dedication to Sir Robert Peel from *Cobbett's Legacy to Labourers* (see [212]), republished as a threepenny pamphlet.

[225]

DOOM / OF / THE TITHES. /

Introduction by WILLIAM COBBETT to a translation from the Spanish with an 'Advertisement' by the Publisher. [J. OLDFIELD.]

First published intermittently in the *Political Register*, 3 March–5 May 1832.

> *1836, iv, 114 pp. Published by J. Oldfield, Register Office, 11, Bolt Court, Fleet Street, London. 'Price 1s. 6d. stitched.' 12mo. [Bound in a volume entitled 'Cobbett Tracts' on the spine, containing other works by Cobbett, this being the first.]

Cobbett, in the midst of the agitation for the Reform Bill, never forgot the struggle against tithes, and when, in 1831, a friendly correspondent in Madrid sent him the *Historia y origen de las rentas Iglesia . . .*, a Catholic defence of Church property as a gift held in trust for the poor, he promptly had the book translated into English. It had originally been published in 1793 against the French Revolutionary Government's confiscation of Church property and had been republished in 1828 to justify the restoration of that property. Cobbett finally decided not to issue it as a separate work, but to print it in the *Register* (3 March–5 May 1832) together with a long introductory essay in which he roamed over many fields, applying the moral of his *History of the Protestant Reformation* (q.v.), finding time for a side-kick at Brougham for plagiarism, but constantly returning to his theme—'after the Reform Bill this [the Tithes] is the most important of all the subjects that can engage public attention'. Early in 1836, a short time after Cobbett's death, J. Oldfield, who had acquired his business and premises, republished these articles for the first time in book form, entitling the volume *Doom of the Tithes*.

[226]

SELECTIONS / FROM / COBBETT'S POLITICAL WORKS: / BEING / A COMPLETE ABRIDGEMENT OF THE 100 VOLUMES WHICH COMPRISE THE / WRITINGS OF 'PORCUPINE' AND THE 'WEEKLY POLITICAL REGISTER' / WITH NOTES, / HISTORICAL AND EXPLANATORY. /

> By *WILLIAM COBBETT*; edited by *JOHN MORGAN COBBETT* and *JAMES PAUL COBBETT*

[Published in weekly parts, 1835-7, and in six volumes.]

*[1835-7], 6 vols., xiv, 16-544 pp., iv, 508 pp., iv, 524 pp., iv, 528 pp., iv, 508 pp., iv, 812 pp.+Index xxxviii pp. [Vols. i-v published by Anne Cobbett, 10, Red Lion Court, London; vol. vi published by Anne Cobbett, 137, Strand, London.] 8vo.

These wide selections from Cobbett's political writings were taken from *Porcupine's Works* and the *Political Register* (q.v.) by Cobbett's two sons, John Morgan and James Paul, and were published by Cobbett's daughter Anne in weekly parts between November 1835 and October 1837. These parts made up six volumes, which together with numerous notes by the editors provide a valuable repository of Cobbett's political views.

[227]

A / POLITICAL TRACT / BY THE / COBBETT CLUB OF LONDON. / No. 1. / ADDRESSED TO THE PEOPLE OF THE UNITED KINGDOM. /

> By the *Cobbett Club of London*

*1839, 56 pp. Published by J. Cleave, 1, Shoe Lane, Fleet Street, London. 'Price Six-pence.' 12mo.

The Cobbett Club was formed in London in 1838, five years after Cobbett's death, by a group of his old friends and admirers. It met monthly at the Dr. Johnson Tavern, Bolt Court, Fleet Street, with B. Tilly,[1] a draughtsman who had fallen foul of the Cobbett family (see Carlyle, *William Cobbett . . .*, 1904), as its Honorary Secretary. It proclaimed its programme and its test of admission to be annual parliaments, universal suffrage, the ballot, the right to relief, and the 'Equitable Adjustment of the National Debt'. This pamphlet, the first of a number of intended 'occasional publications' (no more appear to have been issued), supports various aspects of the extreme Radical programme, including a condemnation of 'moral force' Chartism, and it explains the Club's failure to revive Cobbett's *Register* by the fact that its members are working men without the time or power to fight the 'Gagging Acts . . . passed by the *reformed* parliament'. In 1841 the Club was mildly criticized by John Cleave, the moderate Chartist (1792?–1847?), who had published this pamphlet, for submitting a petition to the House of Commons which called for only three of the points of the Charter. This Cleave found more remarkable since George Rogers, the Club's treasurer, had also been the treasurer of the 1839 Chartist Convention. In fact Rogers, who was a London tobacconist, had seceded from the Convention early in May of that year, following Cobbett's son, J. P. Cobbett, and others who had resigned earlier; the Club, however, sent a message of support to Vincent, the Chartist candidate at Banbury (1841 Election Papers, Banbury Public Libr.; see also Cleave's weekly periodical, *The English Chartist Circular*, vol. i, No. 42, 1841, and *Gammage's History of the Chartist Movement*, 1854). According to an anonymous *Life*

---

[1] Benjamin Tilly is described as a foreman tailor in the hostile *Cobbett's Will . . .* 1837, by W. Cobbett, junior, who falsely accused him of forging the deed by which Cobbett had transferred his copyrights to Oldfield (see B.M. Add. MSS. 31125). In fact, Tilly was a man of many parts devoted to the interests of the elder Cobbett. He acted as one of his secretaries, campaigned for the 'lodger franchise' in 1835, and even tried his hand at setting to music a song in one of Cobbett's plays. Later he took part in the Cobbett Monument Committee and when this failed he became secretary of the Cobbett Club set up in its place. He was also the secretary of a John Frost Committee in 1840 (see *Northern Star*, 4 January 1840). Tilly carefully preserved all the relics of his association with Cobbett including the bones of Tom Paine (see *Notes and Queries*, 1909, 10th series, xii. 197–8 which suggests that Tilly died about 1878 and that Paine's remains came into the hands of George Reynolds, a Baptist minister in East London; see also Moncure Conway's *Life*; some Cobbett relics preserved by Tilly are in the Goldsmiths' Library; MSS. are in the B.M. and the Arnold Muirhead Collection).

of William Cobbett, Dedicated to his Sons, 1835 (q.v.), Cleave published a 'Memoir' of Cobbett, in which he acknowledged his gratitude for the latter's standing security for him when he had been sent to jail for issuing an unstamped periodical.

[228]
SECOND GALLERY OF LITERARY PORTRAITS.

By GEORGE GILFILLAN

*1852, 2nd edition, 330 pp. Published by James Hogg, Edinburgh. ['William Cobbett', pp. 204–14.]

A collection of short and, for the most part, slight estimates of famous writers, by George Gilfillan (1813–78). That on Cobbett includes a brief personal impression of him as a public speaker in Edinburgh in 1832.

[229]
THE LAST OF THE SAXONS: LIGHT AND FIRE FROM THE WRITINGS OF WILLIAM COBBETT.

Edited by EDWIN PAXTON HOOD

[1854, London (B.M.).]

Selections and extracts.

A sympathetic compilation by Edwin Paxton Hood (1820-85), a Congregational minister, of extracts from Cobbett's autobiographical writings.

[230]
COBBETT'S REASONS / FOR / WAR AGAINST RUSSIA IN DEFENCE OF TURKEY. / WITH A REPRINT OF / THE EMPEROR NICHOLAS'S CATECHISM OF LOYALTY, AS / TAUGHT IN THE RUSSIAN SCHOOLS. / Extracted from Cobbett's Weekly Register. /

By WILLIAM COBBETT; edited anonymously.

[From the **Political Register*, 1822, 1828, 1829, 1833, 1834.]

*1854, 15 pp. [+1 p. publisher's advts.]. Published by A. Cobbett, 137, Strand, London. 'May 1854 . . . Price Sixpence.' 8vo.

Cobbett took the view, common among Radicals in particular, that the power of Russia must be curbed and that of Turkey upheld. Shortly after the outbreak of the Crimean War in 1854 his eldest daughter, Anne (1795–1877), who had kept on a bookselling business, published this sixpenny pamphlet composed of extracts from her father's bellicose writings on the subject in the *Register* between 1822 and 1834.

[231]
WILLIAM COBBETT

ANONYMOUS

*[1853–4] 32 pp., [portr.]. 'No. 66' [of *Chambers's Repository of Instructive and Amusing Tracts*, Nos. 1–96, Edinburgh, 1852–4.]

A short and enthusiastic account of Cobbett's life published in a series of weekly penny sheets by W. and R. Chambers.

[232]
MR. COBBETT'S REMARKS / ON OUR / INDIAN EMPIRE / AND / COMPANY OF TRADING SOVE-REIGNS. / (Reprinted from the *Register* of 1804 to 1822) / MR. JOHN FIELDEN / ON / 'COTTON SUPPLY.' / (Quotations from his *Pamphlet* of 1836.) /

By WILLIAM COBBETT and JOHN FIELDEN; edited anonymously

*1857, 23 pp. [+1 p. publisher's advts.]. Published by Simpkin, Marshall and Co., Stationers'-Hall-Court, London; and by John Heywood, Manchester. 'Price Sixpence, London, Sept. 1857.' 8vo.

An anonymously edited selection of Cobbett's writings on India extracted from the *Political Register* of 1804 to 1822 and republished during the Mutiny. Cobbett had always condemned the policy of the East India Company, and the editor, taking an unpopular view, added his own comments deploring the current spirit of revenge and repression which had made a Roman Catholic member of Parliament call for the ploughing over of 'the ground on which Delhi stands' and which had led even John Bright to support the 'measures . . . deemed necessary to suppress the existing disorder'. The editor also condemns other colonial wars then proceeding, including the war in China, and closes with a commentary on some quotations from Cobbett's old parliamentary colleague, the Radical manufacturer, John Fielden (1784–1849), who in his *Curse of the Factory System*, 1836 (q.v.), had urged spinners to work less time and produce less goods as a means of overcoming the high price of cotton. This old advice, the editor claims, is applicable to the contemporary scarcity of the commodity and its relatively high price. John Morgan Cobbett (1800–77), Cobbett's second son, then an Independent M.P. (Oldham, 1852–67), later a Conservative (Oldham, 1872–7), may have had something to do with the publication. He had married Fielden's daughter in 1851.

[233]
COBBETT'S / LEGACY TO LORDS: / BEING / SIX LECTURES ON THE HISTORY / OF / *Taxation and Debt in England.* / TO WHICH IS SUBJOINED / A SCHEME OF SUBSTITUTION FOR TAXES. / DEDICATED TO THE TAX-PAYERS OF ENGLAND, / SCOTLAND AND IRELAND. /

By *WILLIAM COBBETT; edited with an additional chapter and an introduction by WILLIAM COBBETT, junior*

*1863, xxxiii, 162 pp. [incl. Index]. Published by H. J. Tresidder, 17, Ave Maria Lane, London. 'Price Three Shillings.' 8vo.

Cobbett intended to produce a *Legacy to Lords*, a climax to his other *Legacies* ... (q. v.), which would show 'how the aristocracy have treated the people in the last three hundred years' (*Political Register*, 18 April 1835). He never lived to fulfil this ambition, and in 1863 his eldest son, William, published these six 'Lectures' by the elder Cobbett, together with his own *Scheme of Substitution for Taxes*. He entitled it *Cobbett's Legacy to Lords*, but it is not at all clear that this was the work Cobbett had intended.

[234]
HISTORICAL GLEANINGS ....

By *JAMES E. THOROLD ROGERS*

*1869, 185 pp. .... Published by Macmillan and Co., London. ['William Cobbett', pp. 141–85.]

A short sympathetic biography. The author, J. E. Thorold Rogers,

(1823–90), the political economist and historian, thought that 'the condition of the peasant is now [1869] lower than it was even in Cobbett's time'.

[235]
BIOGRAPHIES OF JOHN WILKES AND WILLIAM COBBETT.

By Rev. JOHN SELBY WATSON

*1870, 407 pp. [portrs]. Published by William Blackwood and Sons, Edinburgh. ['William Cobbett', pp. 115–407.]

Somewhat better than the author's 'John Wilkes', which it accompanies (see WILKES, Cole Collection), but still a poor piece of work. The author was the notorious Reverend John Selby Watson (1801–84), who was sentenced to penal servitude for the murder of his wife.

[236]
ESSAYS CRITICAL AND NARRATIVE.

By WILLIAM FORSYTH

*1874, 462 pp. Published by Longmans, Green and Co., London. ['William Cobbett', pp. 409–37.]

A collection of articles and lectures by William Forsyth (1812–99) the barrister, M.P., and man of letters. He edited the *Annual Register* for twenty-six years

[237]
WILLIAM COBBETT: A BIOGRAPHY.

By EDWARD SMITH

*1878, 2 vols., xi, 328 pp., viii, 330 pp. [incl. Bibl., Index] [portr.]+32 pp. publisher's advts.]. Published by Sampson Low, Marston, Searle, & Rivington, Crown Buildings, 188, Fleet Street, London.

This two-volume work was the first sound, full-length biography of Cobbett and is still useful despite a marked tendency towards uncritical hero-worship. It has much information on anti-Cobbett publications and also a valuable, if incomplete, bibliography of his works. Smith compiled a scrapbook of Cobbettiana which is now in the New York Public Library.

[238]
BIOGRAPHICAL LECTURES.

By GEORGE DAWSON

*1886, 553 pp. [+46 pp. publisher's advts.]. Published by Kegan Paul, Trench & Co., London. 'William Cobbett', pp. 516–22.]

A collection, taken mostly from newspaper reports, of extremely popular lectures by the well-known preacher and lecturer, George Dawson (1821–76). That on Cobbett is laudatory in the extreme.

[239]
HISTORICAL CHARACTERS...

By SIR HENRY LYTTON BULWER

*1900 [reprinted from 4th edition], 591 pp. Published by Macmillan and Co. Ltd., London. ['Cobbett, The Contentious Man', pp. 307–58.]

A collection of portraits by Sir Henry Lytton Bulwer (1801–72), later Baron Dalling and Bulwer, first published in 1867. Cobbett is here pictured as a 'contentious man' who fought rather for the 'pleasure of fighting' than for devotion to any cause.

[240]
SOME SOCIAL AND POLITICAL PIONEERS OF THE NINETEENTH CENTURY.

By RAMSDEN BALMFORTH

*1902, 2nd edition, 232 pp. Published by Swan Sonnenschein and Co. Ltd., London. ['William Cobbett and the struggle for reform, 1762–1835', pp. 8–24.]

A collection of articles most of which were first published in the *Co-operative News*. The short chapter on Cobbett attempts to connect his life with an historical narrative of his time.

[241]

WILLIAM COBBETT, A STUDY OF HIS LIFE AS SHOWN IN HIS WRITINGS.

By E. I. CARLYLE

*1904, xii, 318 pp. [incl. Index] [illus.]. Printed in Edinburgh; published by Archibald Constable and Co. Ltd., London.

A valuable biography based on a wide knowledge of Cobbett's writings. It has very full references to books dealing with Cobbett and his period. Other useful material includes a list of manuscripts, sources of Cobbett's portraits, a correction of the previously accepted date of Cobbett's birth, and reproductions of a number of cartoons by Gillray and Doyle.

[242]

THE LIFE AND LETTERS OF WILLIAM COBBETT IN ENGLAND & AMERICA BASED UPON HITHERTO UNPUBLISHED FAMILY PAPERS.

By LEWIS MELVILLE [ps. of LEWIS BENJAMIN]

*1913, 2 vols. [portrs., illus.], xv, 330 pp., ix, 335 pp. [incl. Bibl., Index] [+16 pp. publisher's advts.]. Published by John Lane, The Bodley Head, London.

A two-volume biography, superficial in manner, but chiefly valuable for its long quotations from the Cobbett Papers in the possession of the family. The work has numerous illustrations and a useful, if slightly inaccurate and incomplete, bibliography of his writings.

[243]

MEMORIALS OF THE COBBETT FAMILY COLLECTED BY WILLIAM V. H. COBBETT. WITH REMINISCENCES OF SOME OF THE LATER MEMBERS AND APPENDICES.

By WILLIAM VINES HOLT COBBETT

*1915, 146 pp. [portrs., illus.]. Privately printed.

The author, W. V. H. Cobbett (1851–1942), was informed by Sir William Cobbett, of Manchester, a grandson of William Cobbett, that no relationship could be traced between the two families. A Pitt Cobbett is mentioned in a genealogy in these *Memorials*. This was also the unusual name of a Hampshire clergyman who edited the *Rural Rides* in 1885.

[244]

A HISTORY OF THE LAST HUNDRED DAYS OF ENGLISH FREEDOM BY WILLIAM COBBETT, WITH AN INTRODUCTION, 'MAIN EVENTS OF COBBETT'S LIFE', AND A BIOGRAPHICAL INDEX BY J. L. HAMMOND.

By WILLIAM COBBETT; edited with an introduction, etc. by J. L. HAMMOND

First published intermittently in *Cobbett's Weekly Political Pamphlet (The Political Register)*, 26 July–18 October 1817.

*1921, [iii], 114 pp. Published by the Labour Publishing Company, Ltd., 6 Tavistock Square, and George Allen and Unwin, Ltd., London. (In *Labour Classics*, No. 2.)

See note to *A History of the Last Hundred Days of English Freedom* [92].

[245]

REMEMBRANCES OF LIFE AND CUSTOMS IN GILBERT WHITE'S, COBBETT'S, & CHARLES KINGSLEY'S COUNTRY.

By J. ALFRED EGGAR

*[1923 ?] vi, 199 pp. [illus.]. Published by Simpkin, Marshall, Hamilton, Kent & Co., Ltd., London.

Includes some rambling personal memories of Farnham, Cobbett's birthplace.

[246]

COBBETT SELECTIONS WITH HAZLITT'S ESSAY AND OTHER CRITICAL ESTIMATES WITH AN INTRODUCTION AND NOTES BY A. M. D. HUGHES.

By WILLIAM COBBETT and others; edited by A. M. D. HUGHES

*1923, xv, 176 pp. [portr.] [+3 pp. publisher's advts.]. Published by Humphrey Milford, Oxford University Press, Oxford.

Mainly composed of short selections from Cobbett's works. The remainder includes Elliott's *Elegy* and various essays by Hazlitt, Carlyle, Lytton Bulwer, Thorold Rogers, Gilfillan, and Miss Mitford.

[247]
THE LIFE OF WILLIAM COBBETT WITH A CHAPTER ON *RURAL RIDES* BY THE LATE F. E. GREEN.

By G. D. H. COLE

*1924, x, 458 pp. [incl. Bibl., Index] [portr.]. Printed in Glasgow, and published by W. Collins, Sons & Co. Ltd., London.

*1947, 3rd edition, revised, xii, 455 pp. [incl. Bibl., Index]. Published by Home & Van Thal, London.

This invaluable work by Professor G. D. H. Cole has long been recognized as the standard *Life*, but it is also a vivid history of Cobbett's time. An edition of 1927 corrected some minor misprints, and another of 1947 added a preface with some details of a family quarrel in Cobbett's last years. A brief bibliography is included which corrects and goes some way towards completing the lists compiled by earlier writers.

[248]
WILLIAM COBBETT.

By G. D. H. COLE

[1925, No. 215 in *Fabian Tract Series*, No. 9 *Biographical Series*.]

A brief outline of Cobbett's life issued by the Fabian Society.

[249]
WILLIAM COBBETT.

By G. K. CHESTERTON

*[1926], 277 pp. Published by Hodder and Stoughton, Ltd., London.

A sympathetic outline of Cobbett's career by the noted writer, G. K. Chesterton (1874–1936).

LIFE AND ADVENTURES OF PETER PORCUPINE WITH OTHER RECORDS OF HIS EARLY CAREER IN ENGLAND & AMERICA VIZ: LIFE & ADVENTURES, THE SCARECROW, REMARKS OF THE PAMPHLETS, TALLEYRAND: A SPY, FAREWELL TO AMERICA, A COURT-MARTIAL, A RETROSPECT.

By WILLIAM COBBETT; introduction and notes by G. D. H. COLE

*1927, 164 pp. [illus.]. Printed by T. A. Constable, Edinburgh; published by the Nonesuch Press, London.
See **Life and Adventures of Peter Porcupine*, 1796.

This selection of Cobbett's earliest writings, with an Introduction and Notes by Professor G. D. H. Cole, forms 'a sort of autobiography of William Cobbett up to the time of his return from America in 1800'. It has a coloured reproduction of a Gillray cartoon as a frontispiece.

INDEX OF PERSONS COMPILED BY G. D. H. AND MARGARET COLE FOR THEIR EDITION OF COBBETT'S *RURAL RIDES*.

By G. D. H. and MARGARET COLE

*1930. Privately printed, pp. 939–1052.

A reprint of the valuable *Index of Persons* appended to the Coles' edition of *Rural Rides, 1930 (q.v.), containing nearly a thousand short biographies of persons mentioned in the *Rides*.

COBBETT AND CURRENCY.

By W. H. WALLER

*1930. 4 pp. [No printer or publisher.] Manchester.

A leaflet issued in Manchester and dated 18 August 1930. It quotes from Cobbett's writings in an appeal against the 'financial class'.

THE PROGRESS OF A PLOUGH-BOY TO A SEAT IN PARLIAMENT AS EXEMPLIFIED IN THE HISTORY OF THE LIFE OF WILLIAM COBBETT, MEMBER FOR OLDHAM.

By WILLIAM COBBETT; edited by WILLIAM REITZEL

*1933, vii, 332 pp. [incl. Index] [portr.]. Printed at the University Press, Cambridge; published by Faber and Faber, 24 Russell Square, London.

The editor, William Reitzel, used the autobiographical parts of Cobbett's writings to form a valuable *Life*. Editorial insertions linking the work, and the sources of all the material used, including the Cobbett Papers in Manchester, are clearly indicated. There are also some useful Notes.

[254]

PETER PORCUPINE, A STUDY OF WILLIAM COBBETT, 1762–1835.

By MARJORIE BOWEN [ps. of MARGARET GABRIELLE LONG]

*1935, xii, 312 pp. [incl. Bibl., Index] [portr.]. Printed in Bristol; published by Longman, Green and Co. Ltd., 39 Paternoster Row, London, E.C. 4.

The author claims that her work is no more than a portrait of Cobbett against a not too heavily detailed background. It is marred, however, by some careless misprints and inaccuracies.

[255]

LETTERS FROM WILLIAM COBBETT TO EDWARD THORNTON WRITTEN IN THE YEARS 1797 TO 1800. EDITED WITH / AN INTRODUCTION AND NOTES BY G. D. H. COLE.

By WILLIAM COBBETT; edited by G. D. H. COLE

*1937, xlvi, 127 pp. [incl. Index]. Published by Humphrey Milford, Oxford University Press, London.

See note to *Letters from William Cobbett to Edward Thornton* [30].

PERSONS AND PERIODS.

By G. D. H. COLE

*1938, vii, 333 pp. [+2 pp. publisher's advts.]. Printed in Edinburgh; published by Macmillan and Co. Ltd., St. Martin's Street, London.

A collection of essays by Professor G. D. H. Cole, which includes one on Cobbett himself (also published in *Great Democrats*) and another on the *Rural Rides*. The latter is taken from the three-volume edition of the *Rural Rides*, 1930, edited by M. and G. D. H. Cole (q.v.). *Persons and Periods* was republished in the *Pelican* series in 1945.

[257]
AN INTRODUCTION TO A BIBLIOGRAPHY OF WILLIAM COBBETT.

By ARNOLD M. MUIRHEAD

[Reprinted from the *Library*, June 1939.]

*1939, *The Library*, 4th series, vol. xx, No. 1, June 1939, 40 pp. Published by the Bibliographical Society, London.

A valuable paper read before the Bibliographical Society on 16 January 1939.

[258]
PETER PORCUPINE IN AMERICA: THE CAREER OF WILLIAM COBBETT, 1792–1800. A DISSERTATION . . . .

By MARY ELIZABETH CLARK

*1939, v, 193 pp., [with Bibl.]. University of Pennsylvania, Philadelphia.

A scholarly work, published in America, throwing new light on Cobbett's activities in the United States between 1792 and 1800. It includes a valuable bibliography of Cobbett and anti-Cobbett literature published in the same period.

[259]
THE OPINIONS OF WILLIAM COBBETT.

By *WILLIAM COBBET; edited by G. D. H. and MARGARET COLE*

Selections from the *Political Register*.

*1944, 340 pp. Published by the Cobbett Publishing Co., Ltd., London.

A well-arranged selection of extracts from Cobbett's writings in the *Political Register* (q.v.) for the whole of its existence from 1802 to 1835, with a valuable introduction and notes.

[260]
WILLIAM COBBETT.

By *W. BARING PEMBERTON*

*1949, 192 pp. Published by Penguin Books, Harmondsworth, Middlesex.

A lively new biography.

[261]
THE COUNTRYMAN.

[Quarterly periodical, 1927—in progress.]

*Cuttings from *The Countryman*, with whole numbers: January 1931; October 1932; January 1935; April 1935; July 1935 (2); October 1935, vol. xii, No. 2 (whole number); January 1936; Summer 1951, vol. xliii, No. 2 (whole number); Autumn 1951, vol. xliv, No. 1 (whole number); Winter 1951, vol. xliv, No. 2 (whole number).

These press cuttings consist mainly of previously unpublished Cobbett letters and other manuscripts. One (October 1932), of dubious authorship, however, is valuable for its mention of the obscure family quarrel in the last years of Cobbett's life (cf. Cole's *Life . . .*, 1947 ed., preface). See also, vol. xliii, No. 2, and vol. xliv, Nos. 1 and 2 (1951), for an account by the present writer of other Cobbett manuscripts now in the Cole Collection.

[262]
Journal of the Royal Society of Arts

*1930, 14 November 1930, vol. lxxix, No. 4069. [illus.]

Full-page reproduction of a portrait of Cobbett, painted by J. R. Smith, and engraved by William Ward in 1812. [See p. 246].

[263]
The Listener

*1935, 19 June 1935, pp. 1031-3. [illus.]

'Cobbett after a Hundred Years', a broadcast talk by Professor J. A. Scott, commemorating the centenary of Cobbett's death.

[264]
Southern Daily Echo

*1938, 18 August 1938. [illus.]

'Cobbett's Life at Botley', a newspaper article by 'G. H. S.' illustrated by views of Botley, and intended to stimulate interest in a proposed memorial at Botley.
'Cobbett Memorial for Botley.' Reprint of an article.

*1945, 16 July 1945.

'In Memory of William Cobbett.' Progress of the Memorial Fund.

*1945, 28 August 1945.

'Botley Memorial . . .' Botley Parish Council.

[265]
Portsmouth Evening News

*1938, 19 August 1938. [illus.]

'William Cobbett . . .' by Iconoclast; newspaper article with picture of Botley Town Hall.

[266]
The Times

*1938, 8 October 1938. [illus.]

'A Memorial to Cobbett'; an editorial article.

*'Proposed Memorial to Cobbett: Hampshire Links.' Two pictures of Botley and one of Twyford.

*1938, 9 October 1938.
'Cobbett Memorial'; a reader's letter.

*1938, 12 October 1938.
'Cobbett's Lane'; a reader's letter.

[267]
The Times Literary Supplement
*15 July 1939. Reprint with additions.
'Private Libraries, xix, Mr. Arnold Muirhead.' Account of Mr. Arnold Muirhead's Library, including a large Cobbett collection.

[268]
Farnham Herald
*17 August 1951.
Typescript copy, 'William Cobbett was born here. Plaque unveiled at the Jolly Farmer.' Account of the ceremony, on 15 August 1951.

PART III
MANUSCRIPTS AND PORTRAITS

COBBETT MSS. COLE COLLECTION

[269]

I. *The Cobbett–Thornton Correspondence* [edited by Professor G. D. H. Cole in his *Letters from William Cobbett to Edward Thornton in the years 1797 to 1800*. Oxford University Press, 1937].

A collection of letters from Cobbett to Edward Thornton (1766–1852), the Secretary to the British Embassy in the United States, written between 1797 and 1800, and containing vivid descriptions of events and personalities in America.

1. Philadelphia, 29 September 1797.
2. Bustleton, 27 August 1798.
3. Philadelphia, 13 June 1799.
4. New York, ? 16 November 1799.
5. Bustleton, 18 November 1799.
6. New York, 25 December 1799.
7. New York, 20 January 1800.
8. New York, 2 February 1800.
9. New York, 19 February 1800.
10. New York, 6 March 1800.
11. New York, 10 March 1800.
12. New York, 14 March 1800.
13. New York, 17 April 1800.
14. New York, 23 April 1800.
15. New York, 25 April 1800.
16. New York, 29 April 1800.
17. New York, 15 May 1800.
18. New York, 27 May 1800.
19. Off Sandy Hook, 2 June 1800.
20. Halifax, Nova Scotia ['New York' in error], 11 June 1800.
21. London, 18 July 1800.
22. London ['St. James's Street'], 4 September 1800.
23. London, 1 October 1800.
24. Extract from a Pamphlet addressed to the Electors of Pennsylvania.

[270]

II. *Letter from William Cobbett, Pall Mall, to Rev. Richard Polewhele, Manacan, Helston, Cornwall, 10 October 1800.*

> Leaves numbered 886, 887, 888; Endorsed: 'Answ'd Oct. 17. C. I. Re London mob.'

The letter, which contains some deletions, refers to Cobbett's 'Prospectus' [of the *Porcupine*, but this reference is deleted]; Polewhele's desire to 'contribute . . . towards the preservation of the country'; Gifford's office [as magistrate]; and a riot in which the 'London mob' having 'got drunk . . . very naturally clamoured for bread'.

[271]

III. *Letter from William Cobbett, Barn Elm, to Mr. [J.Y.] Akerman, 183, Fleet Street, 4 June 1829.*

Invitation to Akerman [his secretary] to dine with him and to bring proof of an article. Reference to the currency situation. Cobbett predicts a run on the Bank 'as there was in 1797. Precisely the same causes are now at work.'

[272]

IV. *The Cobbett–Sapsford Correspondence.*

> [A typescript Calendar and Index, compiled by Professor G. D. H. Cole, is at Nuffield College].

> A collection of letters from Cobbett, members of his family, and others, to S. Sapsford, a London master-baker who was a close friend of Cobbett's and gave him financial help. The letters bear closely on Cobbett's affairs, especially family affairs, and, with one exception, were written between 1822 and 1837.

1. *Kensington, 13 January 1822.*

    W. C. [William Cobbett] to S. Sapsford, 20 Queen Anne Street, Cavendish Square.
2. *Kensington, 4 June 1823.*
    W. C. to S. Sapsford.
3. *Barn Elm, 13 December 1824.*
    W. C. to S. Sapsford.
4. *Kensington, 18 March 1825.*
    W. C. to S. Sapsford.

224

5. *Kensington, 13 May 1825.*
   W. C. to S. Sapsford.

6. *Kensington, 21 June 1825.*
   W. C. to S. Sapsford.

7. *Kensington, 4 August 1825.*
   W. C. to S. Sapsford.

8. *Kensington, 13 September 1825.*
   W. C. to S. Sapsford.

9. *Kensington, 4 October 1825.*
   W. C. to S. Sapsford.

10. *Reigate, 5 January 1826.*
    W. C. to S. Sapsford.

11. *Kensington, 1 February 1826.*
    W. C. to S. Sapsford.

12. *Kensington, 26 February 1827.*
    W. C. to S. Sapsford.

13. *Kensington, 5 March 1827.*
    W. C. to S. Sapsford.

14. *Kensington, 13 July 1827.*
    W. C. to S. Sapsford.

15. *Barn Elm Farm, 27 October 1827.*
    W. C. to S. Sapsford.

16. *Liverpool, 28 December 1827.*
    W. C. to S. Sapsford.

17. *Barn Elm, 21 March 1828.*
    W. C. to S. Sapsford.

18. *Kensington, 6 May 1828.*
    W. C. to S. Sapsford.

19. *Burghclere, 8 August 1828.*
    W. C. to S. Sapsford.

20. *Andover, 10 August 1828.*
    W. C. to S. Sapsford.

21. *Barn Elm, 18 August 1828.*
    W. C. to S. Sapsford.

22. *Barn Elm, 9 September 1828.*
    W. C. to S. Sapsford.

23. *Barn Elm, 21 September 1828.*
    W. C. to S. Sapsford.

24. *Barn Elm Farm, 1 October 1828.*
    W. C. to S. Sapsford.
25. *Barn Elm Farm, 31 October 1828.*
    W. C. to S. Sapsford.
26. *Barn Elm Farm, 4 November 1828.*
    W. C. to S. Sapsford.
27. *Barn Elm Farm, 18 November 1828.*
    W. C. to S. Sapsford.
28. *Kensington, 25 November 1828.*
    W. C. to S. Sapsford.
29. *Barn Elm, 28 November 1828.*
    W. C. to S. Sapsford.
30. *Chilworth, Guildford, 5 January 1829.*
    W. C. to S. Sapsford.
31. *Barn Elm, [10 January], 1829.*
    W. C. to S. Sapsford.
32. *Barn Elm, 24 January 1829.*
    W. C. to S. Sapsford.
33. *Barn Elm, 28 January 1829.*
    W. C. to S. Sapsford.
34. *Barn Elm, 30 January 1829.*
    W. C. to S. Sapsford.
35. *Barn Elm, 19 February 1829.*
    W. C. to S. Sapsford.
36. *[No place], 27 February 1829.*
    W. C. to S. Sapsford.
37. *Barn Elm, 7 March 1829.*
    W. C. to S. Sapsford.
38. *Chilworth Mills, 13 April 1829.*
    W. C. to S. Sapsford.
39. *Kensington, 9 May 1829.*
    W. C. to S. Sapsford.
40. *Kensington, 16 May 1829.*
    W. C. to S. Sapsford.
41. *Kensington, 8 June 1829.*
    W. C. to S. Sapsford.
42. *Kensington, 22 June 1829.*
    W. C. to S. Sapsford.

43. *Kensington, 15 August 1829.*
J. M. C. [John Morgan Cobbett] to S. Sapsford.

44. *[No place], ? August 1829.*
J. M. C. to S. Sapsford.

45. *Kensington, 27 August 1829.*
J. M. C. to S. Sapsford.

46. *Barn Elm, 3 November 1829.*
W. C. to S. Sapsford.

47. *Derby, 24 December 1829.*
W. C. to S. Sapsford.

48. *Kensington, 1 February 1830.*
R. B. B. C. [Richard Baverstock Brown Cobbett) to S. Sapsford.

49. *St. Ives, 30 March 1830.*
W. C. to S. Sapsford.

50. *Bollitree, Ross., 4 June 1830.*
W. C. to S. Sapsford.

51. *Barn Elm, 8 July 1830.*
W. C. to S. Sapsford.

52. *Kensington, 10 August 1830.*
J. P. C. [James Paul Cobbett] to S. Sapsford.

53. *Bolt Court, 23 September 1830.*
W. C. to S. Sapsford.

54. *Bolt Court, 26 November 1830.*
W. C. to S. Sapsford.

55. *Paris, 10 December 1830.*
W. C. Jr. [William Cobbett, Junior], to S. Sapsford.

56. *Bolt Court, [2 February 1831].*
W. C. to S. Sapsford.

57. *Kensington, 30 April 1831.*
W. C. to S. Sapsford.

58. *Kensington, 10 June 1831.*
W. C. to S. Sapsford.

59. *Bolt Court, 17 June 1831.*
W. C. to S. Sapsford.

60. *London, [10 August] 1831.*
J. M. C. to S. Sapsford.

61. *Farnham, 11 August 1831.*
W. C. to S. Sapsford.

62. *Alresford, 12 August 1831.*
    W. C. to S. Sapsford.

63. *Bolt Court, ? August 1831.*
    W. C. to S. Sapsford.

64. *Kensington, 18 August 1831.*
    W. C. to S. Sapsford.

65. *Kensington, 8 October 1831.*
    W. C. to S. Sapsford.

66. *Kensington, 22 October ? 1831.*
    W. C. to S. Sapsford.

67. [No place] *1 November 1831.*
    W. C. to S. Sapsford.

68. *Kensington, 19 November 1831.*
    W. C. to S. Sapsford.

69. *Bolt Court, Sunday, n.d., 1831.*
    W. C. to S. Sapsford.

70. *Manchester, 22 December 1831.*
    W. C. to S. Sapsford.

71. *Bolt Court, 24 December 1831.*
    J. M. C. to S. Sapsford.

72. *Manchester, 3 January 1832.*
    W. C. to S. Sapsford.

73. *Stockport, 27 January 1832.*
    W. C. to S. Sapsford.

74. *Manchester, 28 January 1832.*
    W. C. to S. Sapsford.

75. *Kensington, 11 April 1832.*
    W. C. to S. Sapsford.

76. *Kensington, ? April 1832.*
    W. C. [in another hand] to S. Sapsford.

77. [No place] *21 April 1832.*
    W. C. to S. Sapsford.

78. *Kensington, 3 May 1832.*
    W. C. to S. Sapsford

79. *Bolt Court, 4 May 1832.*
    W. C. to S. Sapsford.

80. *Bolt Court, 9 June 1832.*
    W. C. to S. Sapsford.

81. *Kensington, 15 June 1832.*
    J. M. C. to S. Sapsford.
82. *Oldham, 13 December 1832.*
    W. C. to S. Sapsford.
83. *[No place] 2 February 1833.*
    J. M. C. to S. Sapsford.
84. *[No place] 16 February 1833.*
    J. M. C. to S. Sapsford.
85. *[No place] 23 March 1833.*
    J. M. C. to S. Sapsford.
86. *Bolt Court, 7 April 1833.*
    W. C. to S. Sapsford.
87. *Westminster, 10 May 1833.*
    J. M. C. to S. Sapsford.
88. *Westminster, 7 June 1833.*
    J. M. C. to S. Sapsford.
89. *Bolt Court, 24 November 1833.*
    W. C. to S. Sapsford.
90. *16, Cliffords Inn, 2 December 1833.*
    J. P. C. to S. Sapsford.
91. *Bolt Court, 8 December 1833.*
    W. C. to S. Sapsford.
92. *Bolt Court, 21 December 1833.*
    W. C. to S. Sapsford.
93. *[No place] ? 23 December 1833.*
    J. P. C. to S. Sapsford.
94. *16, Cliffords Inn, 23 December 1833.*
    From J. M. C. and J. P. C. in J. M. C.'s hand to S. Sapsford.
95. *[No place] 2 January 1834.*
    W. C. to S. Sapsford.
96. *Normandy Farm, 7 January 1834.*
    W. C. to S. Sapsford.
97. *Normandy Farm, 9 January 1834.*
    W. C. to S. Sapsford.
98. *Bolt Court, 21 January 1834.*
    W. C. to S. Sapsford.
99. *Bolt Court, 2 February 1834.*
    W. C. to S. Sapsford.

100. *Crown Street, 5 February 1834.*
     W. C. to S. Sapsford.
101. *Westminster, 28 February 1834.*
     W. C. to S. Sapsford.
102. [No place] *2 March 1834.*
     W. C. to S. Sapsford.
103. *Westminster, 18 March 1834.*
     W. C. to S. Sapsford.
104. *Westminster, 23 March 1834.*
     W. C. to S. Sapsford.
105. *Farnham, 11 May 1834.*
     W. C. to S. Sapsford.
106. *Normandy Farm, 15 July 1834.*
     W. C. to S. Sapsford.
107. *14, North Ann St., Dublin, 30 October 1834.*
     W. C. to S. Sapsford.
108. *Cliffords Inn, 24 March 1835.*
     J. M. C. to S. Sapsford.
109. *Normandy [Farm], 18 June 1835.*
     W. C. Jr. to S. Sapsford.
110. [No place] *21 January 1836.*
     J. P. C. to S. Sapsford.
111. [No place] *[7 May] 1836.*
     J. M. C. to S. Sapsford.
112. [No place] *? 15 November 1836.*
     J. P. C. to S. Sapsford.
113. *10, Red Lion Court, 7 April 1837.*
     R. B. B. C. to S. Sapsford.
114. *Fleet Street,* [undated].
     W. C. to S. Sapsford.
115. *Fleet Street,* [undated].
     W. C. to S. Sapsford.
116. *Kensington, ? January or February 1829.*
     W. C. to S. Sapsford.
117. *Barn Elm,* [undated].
     W. C. to S. Sapsford.
118. *Bolt Court,* [undated].
     W. C. to S. Sapsford.

119. *St. James Park, 24 June 1833 or 1834.*
      W. C. to S. Sapsford.
120. [No place], [undated].
      W. C. to S. Sapsford.
121. [*Probably Kensington*] [undated].
      W. C. to S. Sapsford.
122. [No place], [undated].
      W. C. to S. Sapsford.
123. *Kensington, 5 December ?*
      W. C. or W. C. Jr. to S. Sapsford.
124. *Paris,* [undated].
      W. C. Jr. to S. Sapsford.
125. [No place], [undated].
      J. M. C. to S. Sapsford.
126. [No place], *20 January ?*
      J. M. C. to S. Sapsford.
127. *Cliffords Inn, 25 June 1835 ?*
      J. M. C. to S. Sapsford.
128. *Kensington,* [undated].
      J. M. C. to S. Sapsford.
129. *Kensington,* [undated].
      J. M. C. to S. Sapsford.
130. *Kensington,* [undated].
      J. M. C. to S. Sapsford.
131. [No place], [undated].
      R. B. B. C. to S. Sapsford.
132. *Staple Inn,* [undated].
      R. B. B. C. to S. Sapsford.
133. *16, Cliffords Inn, ? 3 November ? 1835.*
      R. B. B. C. to S. Sapsford.
134. *Paris, ? April 1832.*
      P. P. Martin to S. Sapsford.
135. [No place] *28 August 1811.*
      Geo. Appleyard to S. Sapsford.
136. [No place], [undated].
      H. L. Wilson to S. Sapsford.
137. *Kensington, ? August 1828.*
      R. Ronayne to S. Sapsford.

[273]

V. *The Life of William Cobbett, Esqre., The Political Hercules of England by C. M. Riley, his secretary.*

[With 6 other papers: Riley–Sapsford Correspondence.]

1. 175 folios all written on one side of leaf.

    Numbered [in pencil 1–175] in ink by author. The author's enumeration shows gaps at ff. 162–3 (17 folios); 163–4 (87 folios); 166–7 (39 folios); 172–3 (9 folios). These gaps appear to be caused by the omission of long quotations from Cobbett's published works. The *Life* is unfinished and deals almost entirely with Cobbett's first sojourn in America up till 1800.

2. *Barn Elm Farm, 5 September 1828.*
   C. M. Riley to S. Sapsford.

    Wants to borrow £80. Encloses MS. of the '*Life* of the Political Hercules', which he offers as security. In addition will provide a promissory note.

3. *Putney, Monday Morng., 8 September 1828.*
   C. M. Riley to S. Sapsford.

    Impossible for him to see Sapsford and therefore sends promissory note.

4. *Promissory Note to Mr. Sapsford from C. M. Riley, London, 8 September 1828.*

    Payable in three months at 183 Fleet Street.

5. *Putney, Friday Morn. 4 o'clock. [no date—October ? 1828].*
   C. M. Riley to S. Sapsford.

    Unable to meet Sapsford. Starting for Farm, 'where I shall be engaged *all day* in writing a dedication to the Quakers of Mr. O'Callaghan's book'. [Dedication in *P.R.*, 11 October 1828.]

6. *Collins Row, Putney, 16 December 1828.*
   C. M. Riley to S. Sapsford.

    Desires to know when promissory note is due. The 'governor' in reply to Riley's request for money for '*a great emergency*' has replied that 'he will let me have some shortly'. Riley very anxious about note, 'the thought of dishonouring it absolutely frightens me'. Compliments Sapsford and his sister for 'praise-worthy' corn-flour experiments.

7. *Rye Institute, Westchester Coy., New York, 4 August 1835.*
   C. M. Riley to S. Sapsford.

'Melancholy intelligence of Mr. Cobbett's death' has 'almost bewildered Riley with astonishment and grief'. Has constantly had Sapsford in mind, 'at no time without deep regret at being incapacitated to pay you'. Now ready to return to England from America, where he is a teacher; clear himself of his obligation; and write the 'history of this great man', if Sapsford 'will say that I *ought*'. Hopes Sapsford averse to a republic in England; Riley's American experiences have 'taught me to despise a Republic'. Asks whether cedar walking-sticks can be sent duty-free to England, and gives some news about the wheat crop and the weather.

[274]

VI. *Articles written for the POLITICAL REGISTER.*

1. *P.R.,* 12 September 1818.
   Letter to the Rt. Hon. Geo. Tierney (see note to [93]).
2. *P.R.,* 2 January 1819.
   On the Trial of Miss Mary Toker; part of *Letter X to Henry Hunt*; part of an anti-Burdett letter not identified.
3. *P.R.,* 27 February 1819.
   Letter I to the Prince Regent.
4. *P.R.,* 13 March 1819.
   Letter II to the Prince Regent.
5. *P.R.,* 27 March 1819.
   To the Blanketeers.
6. *P.R.,* 25 September 1819.
   Letter II to Lord Folkestone.
7. *P.R.,* 17 July 1824.
   Mrs. Baring and Capt. Webster.
8. *P.R.,* 27 November 1824.
   Letter to Mr. O'Connell.
   Going! Going!
   Fauntleroy.
   Protestant Reformation.

9. *P.R.*, 12 March 1825.
   Part (about three-fifths) of *To the Electors of Westminster*.
10. *P.R.*, 19 March 1825.
    Freeholders of Ireland.
    Mr. Lawless' Letter.
    Letters from France and the Netherlands.
    Seeds.
    Gardening Book.
11. *P.R.*, 2 April 1825.
    Freeholders of Ireland.
12. *P.R.*, 19 July 1828.
    To the Duke of Wellington.
    Part of *Mr. O'Connell.*
    Part of *Budget Sinking Fund.*
    Errors in the last Register.
13. *P.R.*, 16 August 1828.
    To the Duke of Wellington.
    American Tariff (see note to [155]).
14. *P.R.*, 10 April 1830.
    Address to Political Friends.
    [Republished as *Mr. Cobbett's Address* . . . (see note to [163]).
15. *P.R.*, 15 May 1830.
    Part of *To Mr. Haywood.*
    Midland Tour.
    Swedish Turnip Seed.
    Minor unidentified items.
16. *P.R.*, 3 July 1830.
    To the Prince of Waterloo.
    Big O's Proclamation.
    To Daniel O'Connell.
    Tour in the West.
17. *P.R.*, 21 January 1832.
    To Mr. O'Connell.
    Church Reformer's Magazine.
    Reform Bill.
18. *P.R.*, 15 September 1832.
    To the Readers of the Register.
    American Veto.

[All the articles are in Cobbett's hand. In some cases (MSS. Nos. 12, 13, 16,

17) newspaper cuttings are attached to the MSS., and in one case (No. 12) two letters received by Cobbett are attached. One of these was from a Charles Forbes, whose name did not appear in the *Register*.]

[275]
VII. *Political doggerel.*

(1) s.sh., written on one side of leaf in Cobbett's hand.

[Six verses, numbered 1 to 6. The first line of verse runs: 'Come little children, lend an ear.' This piece of doggerel, accompanied by six similar verses, first appeared in the *Political Register*, 21 November 1818, in an article entitled 'A Letter to the Blanketeers'. Cobbett called the lines 'trash', and intended them to be a parody of the 'base and blasphemous stuff that the hirelings of the Borough-mongers prepare for the schools'. He reprinted part of the article with these verses in the *Political Register* of 9 May 1835. This undated MS. may be the original copy written for the first article. The paper carries a watermark (showing the figure of Britannia within a crowned shield) which also appears with the addition of the date '1806' on a wrapper used in 1831—see XI. 1.]

[276]
VIII. *Title and Contents pages for Political Register, volume LIX, from 2 April to 25 June 1825.*

Two leaves, written on three sides.

[In Susan Cobbett's hand.]

[277]
IX. *Miscellaneous papers.*

1. s.sh., written on one side.

[List of fourteen nicknames or epithets frequently used by Cobbett, e.g. 'Gaffer Gooch', 'Suck-Mugs', &c.: in Cobbett's hand.]

2. s.sh., written on one side.

[A child's writing exercise '. . . Your affectionate Niece, Edith Cobbett.']

[278]
X. *Warrant for the appointment of a Master Gunner from the Duke of Richmond to Serjeant Thomas Reid. 23 August 1792.*

[Sergeant Reid was Cobbett's father-in-law; this Warrant appointed him as Master Gunner at Stirling Castle from 1 September 1792.]

XI. *'Papers relating to Whig Trial . . 1831 . . .'*

1. Outer wrapper: 'Papers relating to Whig Trial of Wm. Cobbett 1831. Two letters of Brougham & one of Ld. Radnor.'

    [These letters are missing; the paper bears a watermark similar to VII. 1 with the addition of the date '1806'.]

2. Inner wrapper listing 'Documents used on the Trial'.

3. 'Easter ['Hilary' deleted] Term. Wm. 4, 1831, London. Office Copy of Indictment. Faithfull & Co.'

    [Three folios, all written on one side of leaf, except for short descriptive title on last folio.]

4. 'London, February Session, 1831. Copy of Indictment. Faithfull.'

    [Three folios, all written on one side of leaf, except for short descriptive title on last folio.]

5. 'Dates of Printed Documents.'

    [One large folio folded, written on one side of leaf, except for short titles; in Cobbett's hand.]

6. 'Hampshire Slaughter.'

    [s.sh., written on one side of leaf only, except for short title; in Cobbett's hand; brief notes of the heavy penalties imposed by the Special Commissioners after the 'rural war'; concludes: 'if so pressing—why not *try after Hilary Term?*']

7. Affidavit of David Lovell.

    [s.sh., written on one side of leaf only, except for one line of writing which is deleted; evidence relating to Baring and Cook sworn at Kensington, 6 July 1831.]

8. Battle declaration.

    [Two folios, written on both sides; a declaration relating to the agricultural riots of 1830–1 signed by residents of Battle in Sussex.]

XII. *MSS. of Books, Pamphlets, and POLITICAL REGISTER Articles by Cobbett.*

[Bound in two volumes entitled 'William Cobbett MSS. I, II' on the spine.]

Vol. I

1. *Letter VIII to Landlords.* [*P.R.*, 10 November 1821.]

    14 folios, all written on one side of leaf in Cobbett's hand.

2. *To the Money Hoarders, No. I.* [*P.R.*, ibid.]
   6 folios, as in 1.

3. *To Correspondents.* [*P.R.*, ibid.]
   1 folio, as in 1.

4. *Sir Robert Wilson.* [*P.R.*, ibid.]
   1 folio, as in 1.

5. *Journal.* [*P.R.*, ibid.]
   6 folios, as in 1.

6. *Mr. Canning at School. Letter I.* [*P.R.*, 26 October 1822.]
   9 folios, as in 1.

7. *Mr. Canning at School. Letter III.* [*P.R.*, 7 December 1822*].
   17 folios, as in 1.

8. *'Will there be War.'* [*P.R.*, ibid.]
   1 folio, as in 1.

9. *Mr. Canning at School. Letter IV.* [*P.R.*, 14 December 1822.]

10. *Mr. Canning at School, Letter VI.* [*P.R.*, 28 December 1822.]
    15 folios, as in 1.

11. *Feast of the Gridiron.* [*P.R.*, 21 December 1822.]

12. *History of the Regency and Reign of George the Fourth, No. 1,* 1830 (see note to [174]).
    20 folios, as in 1.

13. *Sermons, No. 13, Good Friday,* [1830] (see note to [164]).
    14 folios, as in 1.

14. *Sermons [No. 10], The Unnatural Mother,* [1822] (see note to [112]).
    13 folios, as in 1.

15. [A short unidentified item.]
    1 folio, as in 1.

Vol. II

16. Part of *Advice to Young Men,* 1829 (see note to [171]).
    18 folios, as in 1.

17. *No. IV. of Cobbett's Poor Man's Friend*, 1826 (see [144]).
15 folios, as in 1.

18. Part of *Advice to Young Men*, 1829 (see [171]).
'Copy of Advice, No. 9.'
21 folios, as in 1.

19. Part of *Advice to Young Men*, 1829 (see [171]).
'Copy of Advice, No. 12.'
14 folios, as in 1.

20. *Twopenny Trash, No. 1*, 1830 (see [185]).
17 folios, as in 1.

21. *Twopenny Trash, No. III.* 1830 (see [185]).
[Entitled 'No. 2' in error, in covering folio.]

22. *Twopenny Trash, No. 6*, 1830(see [185]).
9 folios, as in 1.

23. *Postscript to the Emigrants' Guide*, 1830(see [158]).
9 folios, as in 1.

[For the following, XIII, XIV, XV, XVI, XVII, and XVIII, see three articles by M. L. Pearl in *The Countryman*, vol. xliii, No. 2, Summer 1951; vol. xliv, No. 1, Autumn 1951; No. 2, Winter 1951; and a typescript calendar at Nuffield College compiled by M. L. Pearl.]

[281]

XIII. 1. *Farm Account Book of Expenditure at Botley between January 1808 and June 1819.*

[Approx. 5¼″ × 8″; bound in brown leather covers; begins at both ends; there is a 'cut-away' alphabetical index at one end leading to a section (pagination: a.1 to a.26) showing mainly the names of persons employed by Cobbett with sums paid to them at different dates (in addition, some accounts attached by wafers have been inserted); at the other end (pagination: b.1 to b.24) the section shows day-by-day expenditure chiefly on wages; the centre part of the *Farm Account Book* consisting of 22 pages has been torn out and is missing. Apart from minor exceptions the whole is in Cobbett's hand (a few insertions, attached by wafers, carry notes by Susan Cobbett, his daughter, and one account in another hand is similarly attached).]

2. *Account from Thomas Page to W. Cobbett, 20 April 1809.*

[Approx. 9″ × 4″; s.sh. torn across; written on both sides; a bill for £23. 8s. 6d. for an '18 Inch Roller Complete' and other goods.]

3. *Receipt from R. Woodman to W. Cobbett.* ['Mr. Carbott'—*sic*]. 24 September 1809.

[Approx. 8″ × 3½″; s.sh. torn across; written on one side; a receipt for £6. 16s. 6d. for tiles supplied; note by Susan Cobbett: 'for the cottages'.]

4. *Agreement.* 8 April 1810.

[s.sh. removed from the *Farm Account Book*; torn into four pieces; gives details of 'bargains' for woodcutting made between Cobbett and two separate parties; 'both bargains made in the presence of John Dean', the foreman labourer, who signed as a witness.]

[282]

XIV. *'A Memoir of William Cobbett* by James Paul Cobbett.'

[Approx. 8⅞″ × 11⅛″; 70 folios, all written on one side of leaf (bearing watermark: 'J. Whatman 1861') + 1 blank folio and 1 cover at front; the 'introductory' chapter is dated Manchester, 1 October 1862; the 'Memoir' is unfinished and deals mainly with the period up to 1794.]

[283]

XV. 1. *Account of the Family* by Anne Cobbett.

[Approx. 7½″ × 9″; dark blue covered exercise book; pages numbered 1–46 in ink, written on both sides of leaf; remaining half of book has been left blank; at end two cuttings from periodicals have been inserted; one from *The Ladies Companion and Monthly Magazine,* the other from *The Oldham Standard* (of 29 December 1860, according to a note). This *Account of the Family* is the work of Cobbett's eldest daughter, Anne, but there are also numerous annotations and corrections in the hand of her sister, Susan (one of these is dated 1887). In addition, a few insertions by Susan are attached by wafers (these are nearly all written on the backs of MSS. listing the names of parishes—cf. XVII. 2.) See also XVI and XVII, *Additional Notes* by Anne and Susan intended to supplement this *Account of the Family.*]

2. *Note* by R. C.

[s.sh. giving the title of (1): 'Anne Cobbett's Account of the Family from 1801 when they came from America. R. C.' R. C. is probably Richard Baverstock Brown Cobbett, the youngest son.]

[284]

XVI. 1. *Additional Notes* by Anne Cobbett.

[6 leaves, all written on both sides of leaf; intended as an addition to her

Account of the Family, it deals mainly with the period 1800–12; the top half of page 1 has been cut out and is missing.]

2. *Political Register* references by Anne Cobbett.

[4 leaves, all written on both sides of leaf; it gives *P.R.* references to a wide variety of subjects.]

3. *List of Books* by Anne Cobbett.

[s.sh., written on one side; short list of books by Cobbett published between 1818 and 1834.]

[285]
XVII. *Additional Notes* by Susan Cobbett.

1. [5 leaves, all written on one side of leaf; on other side, part of the manuscript in another hand of a French–English vocabulary. There are also short insertions attached by wafers. Like XV. 1 and the following 2, 3, 4, 5, and 6, these *Notes* were intended as an addition to Anne's *Account of the Family*. This section, and as the following 2, 3, and 6, begin with a page or a quotation reference to the passage they were intended to supplement.]
2. [4 leaves, all written on one side of leaf; on other side part of the MS., in another hand, of a gazetteer of English parishes arranged in counties.]
3. [5 leaves, all written on one side of leaf; on other side, as 2, there are six short insertions.]
4. [2 leaves, both written on one side of leaf; on other side as 2; one leaf numbered '6'.]
5. [s.sh. written on one side; on other side, as 2.]
6. [5 leaves, 3 written on one side of leaf, 2 on both sides; of the former, one is written on the back of a letter—writing unknown; of the latter, one leaf bears the watermark '1840'.]

[286]
XVIII. *Note of Land bought by Cobbett in Hampshire* by Susan Cobbett.

[s.sh., written on one side; list of places, acreage, and cost of land bought by Cobbett between 1804 and 1809.]

[287]
XIX. *William Cobbett's Diary.*

[Approx. $4\frac{1}{2}'' \times 7''$; bound in brown leather covers; entries begin at both ends (pagination: a.1 to a.32, b.1 to b.56). Centre section (43 leaves) blank; paper bears watermark 'Whatman, 1832'. The Diary was kept by Cobbett from 17 May 1834 until a few days before his death in 1835. From then until 1839 it was used as a memorandum book, perhaps by Cobbett's second son, John Morgan Cobbett, who, according to a note signed by N. W. Senior, testified to its authenticity. The section kept by the elder Cobbett contains a sketch-map of Normandy Farm; a note on 'the preceding volume' of his Diary, 'down to the end of March 1834', which seems to have reference to his family troubles—'On the 29 of that mo. [March] I set off, ill, to Normandy [Farm]—What took place there, from the 30 of March to the 14 of May, I wish to forget as soon as possible'; a deleted note in French apparently of the same character; many farming entries; and details of his illness and political activities. One of the last entries reads: 'June 6, 1835 .... Began the great and terrible heat.' The final entry is: 'June 12, 1835, Ploughing home field.' Cobbett died in the early morning of 18 June 1835].

[288]

XX. *Typescript copies of Cobbett—Palmer Correspondence.*

1. *William Cobbett to William Palmer (of Bollitree).* Kensington, 9 March 1822.
2. Do. Kensington, 24 January 1825.
3. Do. Kensington, 5 February 1825.
4. Do. Kensington, 12 February 1825.
5. Do. London, 11 March 1825.
6. Do. Kensington, 14 March 1825.
7. Do. Kensington, 2 April 1825.
8. Do. Kensington, 3 April 1825.
9. Do. Kensington, 6 June 1825.
10. Do. Kensington, 14 June 1825.
11. Do. Bristol, 18 June 1825.
12. Do. Kensington, 5 August 1825.
13. Do. Fleet Street, 9 September 1825.
14. Do. Kensington, 3 April 1826.
15. Do. Kensington, 6 May 1826.
16. *James P. Cobbett to William Palmer.* Kensington, 13 May 1826.
17. *William Cobbett, jr. to William Palmer.* Kensington, 17 May 1826.
18. [on other side of 17] *J. M. Cobbett to William Cobbett, jr.* Preston, 15 May 1825 [1826].
19. *William Cobbett to William Palmer.* Kensington, 26 May 1826.
20. Do. Kensington, 14 September 1825.
21. [on other side of 20:][?] *to J. M. Cobbett.* St. Omer, 6 September [1825.]

22. *William Cobbett to William Palmer*. Shanford, 28 September 1826.
23. Do.   Weston, near Southampton, 19 October 1826.
24. Do.   Kensington, 13 November 1826.

[289]

XXI. *Faithfull MSS.*

[Edward Chamberlain Faithfull and George Lockton Faithfull (1790–1863, Radical M.P. for Brighton, 1832) were Cobbett's attorneys. A close friendship sprang up between the two families and Cobbett sent his youngest son Richard to Faithfulls to be articled as a solicitor. The papers, which include many Cobbett holographs as well as legal documents, cover the period 1823 to 1838. They have been made available by the kindness of Messrs. Faithfull, Gardner, Stanier and Thomas of Winchester, Solicitors.]

1. Bundle of papers relating to the assignment of the copyright of *English Grammar* to Richard and John Hinxman in 1818 and to its repurchase by Cobbett in 1824. (13 documents.)

2. Bundle of papers relating to leasehold property, 183 Fleet Street, 1800 to 1824. (9 documents.)

3. Bundle of papers relating to copyrights of *Woodlands*, *Geographical Dictionary*, *Spelling Book*, 1828–47. (3 documents.)

4. Bundle of papers relating to mortgaged copyrights to Sir Thomas Beevor, Bt., as security for a loan of £3,000 and legal action, Beevor *v.* Cobbett, 1829–34. (6 documents.)

5. W. Cobbett, junior–M. Bertheaux–E. C. Faithfull correspondence, 1827–31. (5 documents.)

6. Bundle of papers relating to the action J. W. Parkins *v.* W. Cobbett, 1823–24—numerous legal papers and letters —some by W. Cobbett, junior. (40 documents.)

7. Bundle of papers relating to the prosecution of James Maxted, 1827. (9 documents.)

8. Bundle of papers relating to Barn Elm Farm, 1826–30. (49 documents.)

9. Bundle of papers relating to the trial Rex *v.* Cobbett, 1831. (51 documents.)

10. Bundle of papers relating to the action Cobbett *v.* Helme, 1823. (18 documents.)

11. Bundle of papers relating to the action Hunt *v.* Cobbett, 1826. (35 documents.)

12. Books and papers relating to the Cobbett Monument Committee, 1836–8. (2 account books, Committee Minutes, and 13 other documents.)

13. Several bundles of papers relating to the Boxall Estate and the actions Cobbett *v.* Clutton, 1826; and Boxall *v.* Cobbett and others, 1829–33; numerous legal papers and letters. (27 separate folio size briefs and other legal papers of varying lengths—one Bill, 523 folios, but some papers only 2 or 3 folios in length; in addition, about 150 other documents.)

14. Bundle of papers relating to leasehold property, 10 Crown Street, Westminster, 1833. (3 documents.)

15. Bundle of papers relating to leasehold property, 11 Bolt Court, Fleet Street, 1830. (7 documents.)

16. Printed form *Newspaper affidavit* concerning the proprietorship of *The Globe and Traveller*, 1824. (1 document.)

17. Bundle of papers relating to cases against Toll-collectors, 1829. (6 documents.)

18. *Process notice*, in action Cobbett *v.* Stewart and Mudford, 1825. (1 document.)

19. Bundle of papers relating to the action, Farlar *v.* Cobbett, 1826. (25 documents.)

20. Bundle of papers relating to the action, French *v.* W. Cobbett, Junior, J. M. and R. Cobbett, and the action Riley *v.* W. and Ann Cobbett, 1829–30. (50 documents.)

COBBETT MANUSCRIPTS: SOME OTHER COLLECTIONS

The following is intended as a brief indication of some of the main depositories outside the Cole Collection in Nuffield College, but nothing like a complete list has been attempted. Cobbett manuscripts are widely dispersed throughout Britain and America, and many are in private possession. E. I. Carlyle's *William Cobbett, a Study of His Life ...*, 1904, and E. M. Clark's *Peter Porcupine in America ...*, 1939, are useful for further information on the subject; Carlyle also gives a list of portraits.

I. *British Museum.*

Add. MSS. 22906; 22907; 31125; 31126; 18204, f. 73; 22169; 22976, f. 212; 27937, ff. 51, 117; 28104, f. 71; 33964, f. 243; 34079, f. 90; 34455, ff. 393-414; 35149, f. 114.

The Champion, 1838 (manuscript notes, &c., by Cobbett's sons).

II. *Bodleian Library, Oxford.*

MS. Finch, d. 15 (41415, ff. 92, 221); (31508); MS. Top. Sussex C. 2; S.C. 25440, f. 95; S.C. 29204, f. iii; MS. Montague, d. 17; *An Eulogium ...* (Godwin Pamph. 314); MS. Eng. Letters, c. 144 f. 44.

III. *University of London.*

A.1 12, 19, 29, 30, 31, 32 (*Catalogue of the Manuscripts ...*, 1921); MS. Index to a collection of tracts. (A collection of Cobbett relics originally assembled by Benjamin Tilly is in Goldsmiths' Library.)

IV. *Arnold Muirhead Collection.*
Hornby Art Library, Liverpool Reference Library.
Huddersfield Public Library.
John Rylands Library, Manchester.
National Library of Scotland, Edinburgh.
Lancashire Record Office, County Hall, Preston.
Tolson Memorial Museum, Ravensknowle, Huddersfield.

V. American collections.
   Harvard University Library.
   Historical Society of Pennsylvania.
   Huntington Library.
   J. Pierpont Morgan Library.
   New York Historical Society.
   New York Public Library.
   Ridgeway Branch of the Philadelphia Library Company.
   Rutgers University Library.
   Yale University Library.

COBBETT PORTRAITS: COLE COLLECTION

I. *Engraving*: $3'' \times 4\frac{1}{2}''$; print not bordered; no date; 'MR. COBBETT. Published by G. Smeeton, 17, St. Martin's Lane'; Cobbett shown half-length, wearing light cravat, two buttons of his top coat buttoned.

II. *Engraving*: $8'' \times 11''$; (print bordered $3\frac{11}{16}'' \times 5\frac{3}{16}''$ in oval $3\frac{1}{2}'' \times 4\frac{1}{2}''$); 'WILLIAM COBBETT. Edward Smith del et fc. Engraved after a portrait taken on board the IMPORTER on her departure from Liverpool to AMERICA, March 27, 1817. Proof. Published, April 1817 by E. Smith, Liverpool.' Cobbett shown half-length, wearing light cravat, five buttons of his light waistcoat buttoned, his top coat with two buttons open.

III. *Engraving*: $3\frac{3}{4}'' \times 5\frac{1}{4}''$; print not bordered; no date; 'WM. COBBETT, ESQRE., London. T. North, 162 Fleet Street'; Cobbett shown half-length, seated, wearing light cravat, hands in lap, waistcoat buttoned, top coat open with four buttons showing.

IV. *Engraving*: $4\frac{3}{4}'' \times 8\frac{1}{4}''$; print not bordered; no date; 'Wm. Cobbett' [facsimile of signature] AUTHOR OF 'THE POLITICAL REGISTER'. Published by James Fraser, 215, Regent Street, London.' Cobbett shown full length in his seat in the House of Commons, a hat on his head, his arms folded. [By Maclise; this engraving first appeared in *Fraser's Magazine*, October 1835.]

245

V. *Engraving*: $25\frac{3}{4}'' \times 18''$ (with inscription), $23\frac{1}{2}''$ (without inscription), 1812. 'Painted by I. R. Smith. Engraved by William Ward. . . . To the Friends of Liberty of the Press, This Portrait of William Cobbett, Esq., Taken while he was in Newgate in 1812 . . . is respectfully dedicated by their humble servant, J. L. Cartwright, London. Pubd., July 9, 1812, by James Daniel, 480, Strand.' Cobbett shown whole length, sitting in an arm-chair, his hands folded in his lap. A writing-table is shown, and also a portrait of John Hampden on the wall.

VI. *Engraving*: $13\frac{3}{4}'' \times 17\frac{1}{2}''$ (print bordered, $9\frac{1}{4}'' \times 12\frac{1}{2}''$); no date; at top 'Plate 3. Of Friends to a Constitutional Reform of Parliament'; at bottom: 'WILLIAM COBBETT, ESQ., Done from the Life and published by Adam Buck, 17 Bentinck St. Man. Sq. Price 2s.' Cobbett shown half-length, seated in chair, one hand on arm of chair, the other in his lap.

VII. *Metal Medallion*: oval, diameter $3\frac{7}{8}''$; bust of Cobbett in high relief. 'WILLIAM COBBETT. P. ROUW. MOD. J. BADDELEY. FEC.'; reverse: in low relief, a plough, a pen, and a scroll of paper bordered by a wreath of foliage composed of oak and acacia-like leaves.

INDEX OF TITLES

Brief History of the Protestant Reformation, A, 1825, [134].

Brief History of the Protestant Reformation, A, 1826, [135].

Brief Inquiry into . . . an Equitable Adjustment, 1833, 189.

Britain Independent of Commerce, 1807, 84.

British Museum General Catalogue of Printed Books, 1945, 107, 145, 159.

Brunswick Weekly Political Register, 1817, 97.

Bulletin of the Institute of Historical Research, 1932–3, 76.

Caledonian Mercury, 1835, [215].

Candide, 4.

Cannibal's Progress, The, 1798, [39], 57.

Catalogue of American Trees . . ., 1826, 1827, [146], 148.

Catalogue of the Manuscripts (London University), 1921, 244.

Catholic Appeal, The, 1825, [137].

Certificate of Civism for Joseph Priestley, Jun., A, 1798, see Remarks on the Explanation . . . by Dr. Priestley, 1798.

Chambers's Repository of Instructive and Amusing Tracts, 1852–4, 207.

Champion, The, 1838, 114, 244.

'Character of Cobbett', see Character of W. Cobbett, M.P.

Character of W. Cobbett, M.P., The, 1835, [219], 200.

Christianity contrasted with Deism, 1796, [18].

Cobbett and Burdett, 1836, 202.

Cobbett and Currency, 1930, [252].

'Cobbett–Akerman Correspondence', 1829 (MSS.), [271].

Cobbett at the King's Cottage, 1826, [143].

Cobbett Library, The, (c. 1830), 117, 128, 144, 153, 154; (c. 1832–4), 119, 127, 159; (c. 1835), 160.

'Cobbett–Palmer Correspondence', 1822–6 (typescript), [288].

'Cobbett–Polewhele Correspondence', 1800 (MSS.), [270].

'Cobbett–Sapsford Correspondence', 1811, 1822–37 (MSS.), [272].

Cobbett Selections, 1923, [246].

'Cobbett–Thornton Correspondence', 1797–1800 (MSS.), [269].

Cobbett's Address to the Americans, 1817, [90], 99.

Cobbett's Advice, 1800, [46], 53.

Cobbett's Advice to the Chopsticks. . ., 1832, 183.

Cobbett's American Political Register (1816), [83], 69, 99, 102, 141; (1832), 69.

Cobbett's Annual Register, see *Cobbett's Political Register*.

Cobbett's Book of the Roman Catholic Church, 1825, [133], 138 n.

Cobbett's Collective Commentaries, 1822, [124], 10, 126.

Cobbett's Complete Collection of State Trials, 1809, [67], 77, 79, 113.

Cobbett's Evening Post, 1820, [105], 10, 69, 112, 124.

Cobbett's Exposure of the Practice of the Pretended Friends of the Blacks, 1830, [168].

Cobbett's Genuine Twopenny Trash, 1831, see *Cobbett's Penny Trash*, 1831.

Cobbett's Gridiron, 1822, [119], 113 n., 179.

Cobbett's Imposture Unmasked, 1831, see Imposture Unmasked, 1831.

Cobbett's Legacy to Labourers, 1835, [212], 202, 203.

Cobbett's Legacy to Lords, 1863, [233], 12, 194.

Cobbett's Legacy to Parsons, 1835, [214], 194, 202.

Cobbett's Legacy to Peel, 1836, [223], 194.

Cobbett's Letter on the Abolition of Tithes . . ., 1831, [187].

Cobbett's Magazine, 1833, [198], 186.

Cobbett's Manchester Lectures, 1832, [188], 92, 179, 189.

Cobbett's Monthly Religious Tracts, see Cobbett's Sermons.

Cobbett's New Year's Gift to Old George Rose, 1817, [87].

Cobbett's Oppression, 1809, [70], 108.

Cobbett's Parliamentary Debates, 1804, [61], 2, 67, 77, 80, 113.

Cobbett's Parliamentary History, 1806, [62], 2, 80, 113.

Cobbett's Parliamentary Register, 1820, [107], 10.

Cobbett's Penny Trash, 1831, [184].

Cobbett's Plan of Parliamentary Reform, 1830, [177], 166, 178.

Cobbett's Political Register, 1802–36, [52], 2, 3, 8, 9, 73, 79, 81, 90, 97, 102, 110, 130, 137, 151, 159, 200, 233–4, 240; books or pamphlets reprinted in or from, 11, 12, 71, 72, 74, 75, 83, 85, 86, 87, 88, 89, 93, 96, 98, 100, 114, 116, 118, 121, 122, 125, 127, 128, 129, 136, 138, 139, 140, 142, 146, 149, 151, 152, 153, 154, 158, 160, 162, 163, 167, 168, 170, 174, 177, 182, 183, 184, 185, 186, 187, 188, 189, 190, 191, 192, 193, 194, 202, 203, 204, 206, 207, 217; quotations from, *passim*.

Cobbett's Poor Man's Friend . . . addressed to . . . Preston, 1826, [144], 11, 70, 116, 119, 183, 184, 238.

Cobbett's Poor Man's Friend . . . addressed to . . . Scotland, 1833, [195], 119, 145.

Cobbett's Reasons for War against Russia, 1854, [230].

Cobbett's Reflections on Politics, 1832, 180.

Cobbett's Reflections on Religion, *see* The Beauties of Cobbett, 1820.

Cobbett's Register, see *Cobbett's Political Register*.

Cobbett's Remarks on Sir Francis Burdett's Letter . . ., 1810, [72].

Cobbett's Review of the Life of Thomas Paine, 1796?, 34.

Cobbett's Sermons, 1821, [112], 10, 11, 101, 159, 174, 237.

Cobbett's Spirit of the Public Journals, 1805, [63].

Cobbett's Ten Cardinal Virtues, 1832, [190], 113 n., 124, 180.

Cobbett's Too Long Petition, 1818, [93].

Cobbett's Tour in Scotland, 1832, [167], [193], 12, 162, 184.

Cobbett's Two-Penny Trash, 1831, [183], 12, 69, 70, 95, 155, 170, 171, 238.

Cobbett's Warning to Norfolk Farmers, 1821, [117], 129.

Cobbett's Weekly Political Pamphlet, see *Cobbett's Political Register*.

Cobbett's Weekly Political Register, see *Cobbett's Political Register*.

Cobbett's Weekly Register, see *Cobbett's Political Register*.

Cobbett's Will . . ., 1837, 202, 205 n.

Collection of Addresses, Squibs, Songs . . ., A, 1826, 143 n.

Collection of Facts and Observation relative to the Peace . . ., A, 1801 [50], 52, 54, 60, 74.

Compendium of the Law of Nations, A, 1795–1829, [9], 6.

Complete Collection of State Trials, *see* Cobbett's Complete Collection. . . .

Concise . . . History of . . . Suworow's Campaign in Italy, 1799, 1800, 57, 57 n.

Co-operative News, 210.

Copies of Original Letters . . . to Dr. Priestley, 1798, [41], 54.

Correspondence between Mr. Cobbett, Mr. Tipper and Sir Francis Burdett, 1819, [100].

Cottage Economy, 1821, [115], 11.

Countryman, The, 1931–51, [261], 82, 140, 156, 201, 238.

Country Porcupine, The, 1798, see *Porcupine's Gazette*, 1797.

Critical Examination of Cobbett's Grammar, 1819, [97].

Critical Review, The, 1795, 23.

Curse of Paper Money, The, 1833, [201].

Curse of the Factory System, The, 1836, 208.

Day and New Times, The, 1817, 97.

Decline and Fall of the English System of Finance, 1796–1844, [82], 91 n.

Defence of Mr. Cobbett against . . . Burdett, 1819, 109.

Democratic Judge, The, 1798, [31], 7, 40, 44.

Democratic Principles Illustrated by Example, 1798, [38], 24, 30.
Detection of a Conspiracy, 1798, [34], 49, 57.
Detection of Bache, 1798, [37].
Deutsche Porcupein, Der, 1798, see *Porcupine's Gazette*, 1797.
'Diary' (MSS.); *see* 'William Cobbett's Diary', 1834–5, MSS.).
Dictionary of Books relating to America, A, 1871, 153.
Diplomatic Blunderbuss, *see* Gros Mousqueton, 1796.
'Directions for a Sergeant-Major, or an Orderly', ?1791, 4.
Disgraceful Squandering of the Public Money . . ., 1833, [199].
Doom of the Tithes, 1836, [225].
Dublin Political Register, see *Weekly Register*.

Edinburgh Magazine, see *Tait's Edinburgh Magazine*.
Edinburgh Review, 1823, 120.
'Elegy on William Cobbett', 200, 213.
Élémens de l'histoire Romaine, *see* Elements of the Roman History, 1828.
Elements of Reform, 1809, [68], 90.
Elements of the Roman History, 1828, [147].
Eleven Lectures on the French and Belgian Revolutions, 1830, [172], 163, 167.
Emigrant's Guide, The, 1829, [158], 176, 238.
Empire Germanique, L', 1803, 73.
Empire of Germany, The, 1803, [56].
English Chartist Circular, The, 1841, 205.
English Gardener, The, 1828, [150], 11, 118.
English Grammar, *see* Grammar of the English Language, 1818.
Englishmen, Hear Me, 1829, [157].
English Historical Review, 1950, 126.
English Housekeeper, The, 1835, [220].
English [Law], Reports, 1916, 202.
Epitome of Mr. Forsyth's Treatise, An, 1803, *see* A Treatise on the Culture and Management of Fruit Trees, 1802.

Essay on Sheep, An, 1811, [73].
Essay on the Supposed Advantages of a Sinking Fund, An, 1828, 149.
Essays Critical and Narrative, 1874, [236].
Eulogium Intended to Perpetuate the Memory of David Rittenhouse, An, 1796, 7 n., 40 n., 244.
Examiner, The, 1819, 109.
Extracts from Cobbett's Register . . ., 1832, 182.
Extracts from the Information . . . (Poor Law Commission), 1833, 186.
Extraordinary Red Book, The, 1817, 96.

Facts for the Men of Kent, 1828, [152].
'Faithfull Papers', 1800–38 (MSS.), [289].
'Farm Account Book and Papers', 1808–10 (MSS.), [281].
Farmer's Friend, The, 1821, [116], 11, 125.
Farmer's Wife's Friend, The, 1822, [120], 122, 125.
Farnham Herald, 1951, [268].
Five Letters to Lord Sheffield, 1815, [77].
Flash in the Pan, The, 1833, [197], 203.
Fortgang der Menschenfresser, Der, *see* The Cannibal's Progress, 1798.
Four Letters to the Chancellor of the Exchequer, 1803, [58].
Four Letters to . . . Wortley, 1833, [204], 92.
Fraser's Magazine (1835), 245; (1862), 147.
French and English Dictionary, *see* A New French and English . . ., 1833.
French Arrogance, 1798, [35].
French Grammar, A, 1824, [130], 187.
French Revolution: An Address, 1830, [169].
French Verbs and Exercises, 1862, 132.
French versus Cobbett, 1829, [159].
Full and Accurate Report of the Trial

of William Cobbett . . ., A, 1831, [182], 70, 169.
Full Report of the Proceedings of a Public Meeting, A, 1819, [104].

Gentleman's Magazine, 1796, 42.
Geographical Dictionary, A, 1832, [189].
Germanic Empire, The, 1803, 73.
Get Gold! . . ., 1834, [208].
Giardiniere Americano, Il, 1826, see The American Gardener, 1821.
Gil Blas, 7, 40 n.
Glasgow Chronicle, 1831, 137 n.1.
Globe and Traveller, The, 1824, 125.
Gold for Ever, 1825, [140].
Good Friday, 1830, [164], 117, 237.
Gorgon, The, 1818–19, 107.
Grammar of the English Language, A, 1818, [96], 9, 13, 103, 130, 176, 179.
Grammar of the Italian Language, 1830, [165], 169.
'Gridiron, The', 10, 112, 124.
Gros Mousqueton Diplomatique, The, 1796, [22], 7, 56.

Halifax Commercial Chronicle, 1830, 157, 158.
'Hampshire Farmers' Address', 1812, see Rejected Addresses, 1812.
Hansard, 2, 76.
Herald of The Rights of Industry, The, 1834, 190.
Histoire abrégée des Empereurs . . ., 1829, see Abridged History of the Emperors, 1829.
Histoire du Clergé, L', 30.
Historia y origen de las rentas Iglesia, 1793, see Doom of the Tithes, 1836.
Historical Characters, 1867, 1900, [239].
Historical Gleanings . . ., 1869, [234].
History and Bibliography of American Newspapers . . ., 1947, 41.
History of England, A, 1819–30, 134.
History of Jacobinism, The, 1796, [23].
History of the American Jacobins, A, 1796, see The History of Jacobinism, 1796.

History of the Chartist Movement, 1854, 205.
'History of the Kings and Queens of England, A', 1781?, 3.
History of the Last Hundred Days of English Freedom, A (1817), 1921, [92], [244], 95.
History of the Protestant Reformation, A, 1824–7, [132], 11, 135, 138, 144, 147, 151, 195, 204, 234.
History of the Regency and Reign of George the Fourth, 1830–4, [174], 12, 87, 106, 237.
Horse-Hoeing Husbandry, The, 1731, 1822–9, [122], 11, 148.
Huskisson's Speeches, 1831, 153.

Imitation of Celebrated Authors, 1844, see Rejected Articles, 1826.
Impeachment of Mr. Lafayette, 1793, [3].
Important Considerations, 1803, [59], 8.
Imposture Unmasked, 1831, [185], 170.
Index of Persons (Coles's), 1930, [251].
Instructive Essay, see The Bloody Buoy, 1796.
Introduction to a Bibliography, An, 1939, [257].
Introductory Address to the Gazetteers, see Observations on the Emigration of Dr. Priestley, 1794.
Invincible Standard . . ., 1803, 72.

John Clothier and Sylvanus Planter, 1796, 30.
Journal of a Tour in Italy, 1830, [178], 160.
Journal of the Royal Society of Arts, 1930, [262].

Kick for a Bite, A, 1795, [6], 5, 24, 27, 38, 55.

Ladies Companion and Monthly Magazine, The, 239.
Last of the Saxons, The . . ., 1854, [229], 4 n.3.
Latin Grammar for the Use of English Boys, A, 1835, 160.

'MSS. of Books . . . and articles . . .',
1818–32 (MSS.), [274], [280].

Narrative . . ., 1823, 126.
Narrative of the Taking of the Invincible Standard, 1802, [55].
New French and English Dictionary, A, 1833, [202], 2.
New Monthly Magazine, 145.
New Year's Gift to the Democrats, A, 1796, [12], 6, 38, 56.
Nice Pickings (Hetherington), 1830, 167.
Nice Pickings (Rivington), 1830, 167.
Noble Nonsense, 1828, [149].
Norfolk Yeoman's Gazette, The, 1823, [126], 10, 122, 125, 129.
Northern Star, The, 1840, 205.
Norwich Mercury, (1821), 122; (1823), 129.
'Note of Land bought . . . in Hampshire', 1804–9 (MSS.), [286].
Notes and Queries, 1909, 205 n.
Notes of My Life, 1831, *see Cobbett's Penny Trash*, 1831.

Observations on Cobbett's . . . Scheme for the Annihilation of the Bank of England . . ., 1818, [98].
Observations on Mr. Paine's Pamphlet, 1796, 91 n.
Observations on the 'Age of Reason', *see* The Beauties of Cobbett, 1820.
Observations on the Debates of the American Congress, 1797, [27].
Observations on the Dispute between the United States and France, [33].
Observations on the Emigration of Dr. Joseph Priestley, 1794, [4], 5, 27, 38, 55.
Oldham Standard, The, 1860, 239.
Opinions of William Cobbett, The, 1944, [259].
Our Anti-Neutral Conduct Reviewed, 1817, 93.

Paper Against Gold, 1815, [81], 9, 11, 35, 68, 76, 91 n., 101, 118, 149, 181, 189.
'Papers relating to the Whig trial', 1831 (MSS.), [279].

Parliamentary Debates, *see* Cobbett's Parliamentary Debates.
Parliamentary History, *see* Cobbett's Parliamentary History.
Parliamentary Reform, 1816, *see* Elements of Reform, 1809.
Parliamentary Register, see Cobbett's Parliamentary Register.
Passages in the Life of a Radical, 1840–4, 95.
Persons and Periods, 1938, [256].
Peter Porcupine, 1935, [254].
Peter Porcupine in America, 1939, [258], 21, 46, 244.
Philadelphia Gazette, 1797, 39.
Plan of Parliamentary Reform, *see* Cobbett's Plan of Parliamentary Reform.
Political Censor, The, 1796, [15], 6, 7, 29, 30, 34, 37, 38, 39, 56.
'Political doggerel' (MSS.), [275].
Political Mountebank, The, 1826, 143 n.
Political Progress of Britain, 1792, 23.
Political Proteus, The, 1804, [60].
Political Register, The, see Cobbett's Political Register.
Political Tract of the Cobbett Club, A, 1839, [227], 125.
Politics and the Press, 1780–1850, 1949, 95.
Politics for the People, 1820, *see* The Beauties of Cobbett, 1820.
'Poor Man's Bible', 12.
Poor Man's Friend, *see* Cobbett's Poor Man's Friend.
Poor Man's Friend, The (Stemman's), 1826, 145.
Popay the Police Spy, 1833, [203].
Porcupine, The, 1800, [48], 8, 24, 52, 53, 59, 67, 71, 201.
Porcupine's Gazette, 1797, [28], 6, 7, 8, 30, 31, 44, 46, 48, 49, 51, 56, 57.
Porcupine's Works, 1796–7, [26], 27.
Porcupine's Works, 1801, [49], 15, 20, 22, 24, 26, 29, 30, 31, 35, 37, 39, 40 n., 41, 44, 45, 46, 48, 50, 113, 202, 204.
Portraiture of Domestic Slavery, A, 1817, *see* American Slave Trade, 1822.
Portsmouth Evening News, 1938, [265].

INDEX OF PERSONS

Fairburn, John (London publisher), 107, 142, 155.
Faithfull & Co., 236, 242.
Faithfull, Edward Chamberlain, 242.
Faithfull, George Lockton (1790–1863), 242.
Farlar, William, 243.
Farquharson, George, 111.
Fayolle (Paris publisher), 25.
Fearon, Henry Bradshaw (*fl.* 1817–33), 103, 103 n.
Fielden, John (1784–1849), 190, 207, 208.
Fisk, Earl E., 164.
Fithian, M. (Philadelphia publisher), 133.
Folkestone, Lord, William Pleydell-Bouverie, third Earl of Radnor (1779–1869), 79, 101, 148, 192, 233, 236.
Folwell, Richard (Philadelphia publisher), 22, 38.
Forbes, Charles, 235.
Ford, Worthington C., 37.
Forrest, T. (Manchester printer), 180.
Forsyth, William (1737–1804), 71, 72.
Forsythe, William (1812–99), 209.
Fox, Charles James (1749–1806), 42, 59.
Fraser, James (London publisher; d. 1841), 245.
Freeman, John, 102.
French, Daniel Andrew, 155, 156, 243.
Frost, John (1784–1877), 205 n.

Galloway, Joseph (1730–1803), 57.
Gammage, Robert George (1815–88), 205.
Gardner, J. (Bolton publisher), 80.
Gasquet, Francis Aidan (1846–1929), 133, 137.
George IV (1762–1830), 12, 77, 78, 87, 100, 101, 114, 116, 142, 166, 233, 237.
Gifford, John, earlier John Richards Green (1758–1818), 23, 24, 54, 224.
Gifford, William (1756–1826), 174.
Gillet, T. (London publisher), 80, 82.
Gillfillan, George (1813–78), 206, 213.
Gillies, James (Glasgow publisher), 37.

Gillray, James (1757–1815), 33, 164, 165, 211.
Ginger, J. (London publisher), 61.
Gleave, J. (Manchester publisher), 80.
Glindon, W. (London publisher), 79.
'Glory, Sir' (Sir Francis Burdett, q.v.).
Goderich, Viscount, Frederick John Robinson, Earl of Ripon (1782–1859), 173.
Gold, Joyce (London publisher), 80, 81.
Goldsmid, Abraham (1756?–1810), 91.
Goodman, Thomas, 169, 170, 173, 176 n.
Gordon, Lord George (1751–93), 42.
Gouge, William M. (1796–1863), 187.
Gould (afterwards Morgan), Sir Charles (1726–1806), 81.
Green, F. E., 213.
Green, John Richards (earlier name of John Gifford, q.v.).
Grenville, Lord, William Wyndham (1759–1834), 53, 59, 148, 149.
Grey, Lord, Charles, second Earl (1764–1845), 95, 173.
Griffin, Charles (London publisher), 119, 131, 163.
Griffith, William (1766–1826), 50.
Grime, Benjamin, 180.
'Grindum, Sir Gripe' (Sir Francis Burdett, q.v.).
Gurney, Richard (1790–1843), 107, 108.
Gye, M. (Bath publisher), 85.

Hall, George Webb (1765–1824), 121, 122, 125.
Hall, Lieut. John, 81.
Hall, Spencer Timothy (1812–85), 166.
Hamilton, Dr. Robert (1743–1829), 149.
Hammond, J. L. (1873–1949), 100, 212.
Hammond, J. L. and Barbara, 170.
Hampden, John (1594–1643), 246.
Hansard, Thomas Curson (1776–1833), 61, 76, 79, 80, 111, 113, 115, 124, 135 n., 175 n.
Harbord, Edward, *see* Lord Suffield.

Onwhyn (London publisher), 109.
Orme (London publisher), see Longman . . ., &c.
Owen (London publisher), 30.
Owen, Robert (1771–1858), 138 n., 190.

Page, Thomas, 239.
Paine, Thomas (1737–1809), 7, 9, 34, 35 n., 36, 37, 42, 91 n., 103, 111, 113 n., 142, 205 n.
Palmer (London printer), see Ibotson & Palmer.
Palmer, William (1782–1851), 241–2.
Palmerston, Lord, Henry John Temple, third Viscount (1784–1865), 173.
Parker, Charles Stuart (1829–1910), 147.
Parker, John (Philadelphia publisher), 21.
Parkins, Joseph Wilfred, 242.
Patmore, Peter George (1786–1855), 85, 145.
Paull, James (1770–1808), 79.
Peel, Sir Robert, second baronet (1788–1850), 100, 101, 124, 147, 181, 185, 193, 194, 202, 203.
Peltier, Jean Gabriel (1760 ?–1825), 73.
Pemberton, W. Baring, 217.
Penn, John (1760–1834), 27.
Pickering, 167.
Pickering, Timothy (1745–1829), 35.
Pitt, George, 196.
Pitt, William (1759–1806), 8, 42, 52, 54, 91, 149.
Place, Francis (1771–1854), 107, 110, 141, 171.
Plassan (Paris printer), 131.
Playfair, William (1759–1823), 36.
Plummer & Brewis (London printers), 90.
Polewhele, Rev. Richard (1760–1838), 224.
Popay, William Stewart, 188.
Potter, Sir Thomas (1773–1845), 180.
Powell, Capt. Richard, 81.
Price, Dr. Richard (1723–91), 149.
Priestley, Dr. Joseph (1733–1804), 5, 21, 22, 23, 27, 48, 49, 50, 51, 55, 57.

Priestley, Joseph, junior (1768–1833), 48, 49.
'Protestant, A', 135 n.
Purday, T. (London publisher), 32, 83.

'Querist' (ps., of Benjamin Davies, q.v.).

Radnor, third Earl of Radnor, see Lord Folkestone.
Randolph, Edmund (1753–1813), 28, 29, 36, 56.
Rees (London publisher), see Longman . . ., &c.
Reeves, John (1752–1829), 58, 74.
Reid, Thomas, 235.
Reitzel, William, 215.
Reynolds, Rev. George, 205 n.
Reynolds, Dr. James (d. 1807), 45, 49.
Richards (New York publisher), 191.
Richardson (London publisher), 22.
Richmond, third Duke of (1735–1806), 235.
Riley, Charles Mulvey, 156, 179, 232, 243.
Rittenhouse, David (1732–96), 7, 40 n.
Rivingtons (London publishers), 167.
Roake & Varty (London publishers), 175 n., 176 n.
Rogers, George, 205.
Rogers, James Edwin Thorold (1823–90), 208, 213.
Ronayne, R., 231.
Rose, George (1744–1818), 96.
Rouw, Peter (1770–1852), 246.
Rowan, Archibald Hamilton (1751–1834), 47, 49.
Rowson, Mrs. Susannah Haswell (1762 ?–1824), 24, 25.
Rush, Dr. Benjamin (1745–1813), 7 n., 40 n., 41, 44, 50, 51.
Russell, Joseph (Birmingham publisher), 157, 182.

Sabin, Joseph (1821–81), 153.
Sapsford, Silvester, 224–33.
Sarjeant, Ezra (New York publisher), 61, 75.
Saunders, John (London publisher), 201.

Scott, J. A., 218.
Sears, W. J. (London printer), 143.
'S. — E., G. W.' (H. N. Coleridge ?), 169.
Senior, Nassau William (1790–1864), 241.
Seton, Lieut. Christopher, 81.
Shakespeare, William (1564–1616), 13, 103.
Sheffield, Lord, John Baker Holroyd, first Earl (1735–1821), 86.
Sheridan, Richard Brinsley (1751–1816), 75.
Sheridan, Thomas (1775–1817), 75.
Sherwin, W. T. (London publisher), 35 n., 108.
Sherwood, Neely & Jones (London publishers), 82, 102.
Sidmouth, first Viscount, see Addington, Henry.
Sievrac, J. H. (fl. 1815–40), 146, 147.
Simpkin, Marshall & Co. (London publishers), 135 n., 207, 212.
Smeeton, G. (London publisher), 245.
Smith, Edward, 67, 137, 209, 210.
Smith, Edward (Liverpool publisher), 245.
Smith, 'Horace', Horatio (1779–1849), 85, 145.
Smith, James (1775–1839), 85, 145.
Smith, J. R., 218, 246.
Smith, Samuel Harrison (1772–1845), 24, 25, 29.
Smith, Thomas (Liverpool publisher), 177.
Snowden, Philip, later Viscount (1864–1937), 164.
Southey, Robert (1774–1843), 170.
Spence, William (1783–1860), 85.
Spragg, J. (London publisher), 74.
Stanley, Edward Geoffrey Smith, later fourteenth Earl Derby (1799–1869), 143, 183.
Stemman, Henry (London publisher), 113, 115, 124, 135 n., 145.
Stephens (New York publisher), 33.
Stewart, William (London publisher), 243.
Stockdale, John (London publisher; 1749–1814), 21, 22, 35 n., 73.
Stoddart, Dr. (later Sir) John (1773–1856), 97.

Stone, John Hurford (1763–1818), 48, 49, 57.
Stone, William, 49.
Strange, W. (London publisher), 165, 166, 168, 172, 173.
'Subaltern, A', 19.
Suffield, Lord, Edward Harbord, third Baron (1781–1835), 129.
'Sulpicius' (ps. of Lord Grenville, q.v.).
Sutton & Son (Nottingham publishers), 96.
Suworow, Alexei Vasilievitch (1729–1800), 57, 57 n.
Swanwick, John (1760 ?–1798), 34.
Swift, Jonathan (1667–1745), 4, 13.
'Swing, Captain', 169, 170, 173, 176 n.

Talleyrand - Perigord, Charles Maurice de (1754–1838), 32, 46, 168.
Tanner, Thomas, Bishop of St. Asaph (1674–1735), 136.
Taylor, A. E., 161.
Tenderden, Lord, see Abbott, Charles, Lord Chief Justice.
Thelwall, John (1764–1834), 47, 109, 110.
'Thimble, Peter' (Francis Place, q.v.).
Thistlewood, Arthur (1770 ?–1820), 100.
Thomas, Edward, 161.
Thompson, Thomas Perronet (1783–1869), 170.
Thornton, Sir Edward (1760–1852), 33, 43, 45, 48, 58, 215, 223.
Thurtle, Ernest, 196.
Tierney, George (1761–1830), 100, 101, 233.
Tilly (or Tilley), Benjamin (d. 1878 ?), 205, 205 n., 244.
Tipper, Mr., 106, 108, 109.
Tipper & Richards (London publishers), 77.
Tocker, Henry, 108.
Tocker (or Toker), Mary Ann, 107, 108, 233.
Tooke, John Horne (1763–1812), 47.
Torrey, Jesse, junior (fl. 1787–1834), 123.
Travers, Martin, 102.
Tredwell, Mrs., 119.